───── PRAISE FOR ─────

TOOLS FOR TEAM LEADERSHIP

"An extremely useful book. The illustrations, straightforward language, and practical tools make it very accessible for anyone leading teams. Designed for the practitioner, it clearly hits the mark."

—Hal Stack, Director, Labor Studies Center,
Wayne State University

"Offers excellent, concrete, and specific advice managers can actually use to meet the daunting challenges of making sure their teams really work."

—J. Frank Yates, professor, University of Michigan Business School;
author, *Decision Management*

"Those who lead or work with teams will find many practical resources that can be put to use immediately. Huszczo reaches out to the reader in plain, easy-to-understand language and offers the wealth of his experience through stories, examples, tips, and exercises."

—Sandra Krebs Hirsh and Elizabeth Hirsh, consultants,
Hirsh Consulting; coauthors, *Introduction to Type®* and
Teams and the *MBTI® Teambuilding Program*

"Provides you with practical tools and strategies, and a logical understanding."

—Edgell W. Turnquist, StaffRd. AFSCME/Executive Director,
Michigan Labor-Management Association

TOOLS FOR TEAM LEADERSHIP

TOOLS FOR
TEAM LEADERSHIP

Delivering the X-Factor in
Team eXcellence

Gregory E. Huszczo

DAVIES-BLACK PUBLISHING
MOUNTAIN VIEW, CALIFORNIA

Published by Davies-Black Publishing, a division of CPP, Inc., 1055 Joaquin Road, 2nd Floor, Mountain View, CA 94043; 800-624-1765.

Special discounts on bulk quantities of Davies-Black books are available to corporations, professional associations, and other organizations. For details, contact the Director of Marketing and Sales at Davies-Black Publishing: 650-691-9123; fax 650-623-9271.

Visit the Davies-Black Publishing Web site at www.daviesblack.com.

Printed in the United States of America.
12 11 10 09 08 10 9 8 7 6 5 4 3 2

Library of Congress Cataloging-in-Publication Data
Huszczo, Gregory E.
  Tools for team leadership : delivering the X-factor in team excellence / Gregory E. Huszczo.— 1st ed.
    p. cm.
  Includes bibliographical references and index.
  ISBN 978-0-89106-201-1 (hardcover)
  1. Teams in the workplace. 2. Leadership. 3. Management. I. Title.
  HD66.H873 2004
  658.4′022—dc22
                                                                    2004015274
FIRST EDITION
First printing 2004

This book is dedicated to my family . . .
a loving, learning, growing group

CONTENTS

EXERCISES

ACKNOWLEDGMENTS

I owe a great deal to the men and women whom I have witnessed help-ing teams in organizations. It has been encouraging to see them care and make a difference, and I have learned from their efforts to provide leadership. They have trusted me as I have attempted to help them help others.

I also owe a great deal to my family and other loved ones. Without them my life would never be in balance. Kathy has made our lovely house a home. Her love and faith make me happy. Sam has grown and blossomed. I am so proud of him. He has become a wonderful man. My mother still wonders why I like to work hard, but she and my dad taught me long ago that learning and helping others is why we are on this earth. Family members Mike, Jan, Amy, Stacy, and Annie have all added joy to my life.

I am grateful to my colleagues. I am blessed to have worked with tal-ented and patient people both through my consulting practice and in our MSHROD Program at Eastern Michigan University. The challenge of trying to articulate what I am observing, researching, and teaching has resulted in insights I could not have achieved without them.

The comments and support from key organizations and individuals must also be recognized. I would like to thank Jim Lomac and Cindy Hayes of the Management Research Group in Portland, Maine, and Paul Davis of the Scanlon Leadership Network for making their resources available to me. I also want to thank the people who reviewed the manuscript and provided their insights: Sue Bird-Johnson, Jack Buettner, Scott Fenton, Peter Geyer, Sandra and Elizabeth Hirsh, Pat McDonnell, Lee Sanborn, Mike Schippani, Maureen Sheahan, Hal Stack, Ed Turnquist, Mary Vielhaber, and Frank Yates.

This book would have never been completed were it not for the wonderful team of people at Davies-Black Publishing and CPP, Inc.

Connie Kallback, Senior Acquisitions Editor, has been particularly help-ful to me. She encouraged, cajoled, put up with my sense of humor, and kept me going. Laura Simonds, Director of Marketing and Sales, was so helpful in promoting my previous book and has been kind enough to do the same on this one. Lee Langhammer Law, Publisher, encouraged me to stay with Davies-Black and has convinced me of this company's effective-ness. Mark Chambers provided much-needed help as copyeditor.

Finally, I want to thank the readers of *Tools for Team Excellence*, who have given me useful feedback, especially regarding material needed to help those who are taking on the responsibilities of providing leader-ship to teams in their organizations.

ABOUT THE AUTHOR

Gregory Huszczo received his doctoral degree in industrial/organizational psychology from Michigan State University in 1975. Since then, he has served as a successful organizational change and development consultant to more than 100 organizations while also holding full-time university appointments as a college professor. He has taught at Southern Illinois University, Michigan State University, The University of Southwestern Louisiana, and Eastern Michigan University, where he also served as director of a master's degree program in human resources and organization development.

Huszczo has consulted for client organizations in the manufacturing sector (Ford Motor Company, General Motors, Freightliner Trucks, Navistar, J. I. Case, Unisys, Woodbridge, La-Z-Boy, and many smaller companies); in the service sector (Australian Postal System, Credit Acceptance Corporation, plus several hospitals, city administrations, and school systems); for unions (UAW, SEIU, AFSCME, UA, USW, BAC); and for institutes (National Coalition for Community and Justice, Society of Manufacturing Engineers, Facility Management Institute, and several labor-management associations and universities).

Author of more than fifty articles and papers on topics associated with teams, personalities, leadership, change, and union-management relations, as well as two previous books, he lives in Ann Arbor, Michigan.

INTRODUCTION

•

Did you ever play "King of the Hill" as a kid? One
kid stands atop an elevated piece of ground, and
the rest of the kids try to throw him off the perch
so that someone else can become king of the hill,
who eventually meets the same fate. This continues until everyone gets tired and frustrated or
someone gets hurt. Your organization cannot
afford to play this game as a way to determine
team leadership. Don't spend all that energy on
determining who is the toughest or the smartest.
The major benefits of a team concept occur only
when all involved have a chance to exert their
skills, knowledge, and influence.

•

You probably picked up this book because your organization is
attempting to use some form of a team concept to guide the way it operates. I assume you want to—or have to—help a team in your organization. This book is designed to help you help team members help
themselves, not to take over. If you want to play "King of the Hill," you
should probably look for a different book. This book will provide
you with the tools to develop the behaviors needed to effectively work
together in a team environment. It will encourage you to develop
people and help manage situations in a way that is conducive to team
excellence. It will prepare you to provide leadership in a team-based
organization.

You may have also picked up this book because you read my previous book, *Tools for Team Excellence.* That book was based on my twenty-five years of research on the subject of teams. In it I describe the seven key components of excellent teams in organizations:

- Clear goals and sense of direction
- Identification of talent
- Clear roles and responsibilities
- Agreed-upon procedures
- Constructive interpersonal relations
- Active reinforcement of team-oriented behaviors
- Diplomatic external ties

I have furthered that research since the book was first published in 1996. I have reconfirmed those seven components but have recognized an additional important factor for success with teams: leadership. Company after company, team after team, expressed the importance of leadership in attaining excellence within a team concept. At first I resisted their comments and the data because I had seen too many teams that demonstrated an overreliance on leadership. Despite their declaration of a team concept on paper, in reality a person or two on each team carried the load. However, the evidence is overwhelming. Coaches of sports teams often speak about the importance of "X-factors" for success. These are intangibles such as experience, intensity, or the ability to make the most out of opportunities. The X-factor in whether a team concept succeeds is leadership. This does not mean an overreliance on one or two key people, but rather a willingness on the part of many people to take on the responsibility of influencing people and events and helping a group of individuals move forward together. Ironically, organizations need to be full of leaders even when promoting so-called leaderless teams. I want you to be one of those leaders who makes a difference in your organization.

How This Book Will Help You Help Teams Help Themselves

This book gives you the tools to analyze a team with confidence and to provide constructive feedback. It provides you with the tools to creatively generate options among team members and then gain a consensus of what to try. It gives you tools to help the team plan the actions it needs to help itself.

Covered are ways to help the team with its task and relationship difficulties while adding more tools to your toolbox beyond those offered in *Tools for Team Excellence*. It furthers efforts to address the seven key components that separate the excellent organizational teams from the mediocre ones. You will learn how to help a team diagnose its strengths and weaknesses, help establish a clear sense of direction, improve communications, ensure systematic problem solving and decision making, resolve dysfunctional conflicts, motivate and coach team players, build diplomatic ties in the organization, and help teams get unstuck.

In reading this book you will have the opportunity to learn a lot about yourself as well as others. There is a natural leader within you, and this book will help you find it. If you are willing to give up your desire for perfectionism and control while steadfastly adhering to a desire to make a difference, you will benefit from this book. I want you to take teams seriously and yourself lightly. Helping a team by being a leader does not mean putting all the responsibility on your shoulders. You are to work with the team, not take it over. You are not being asked to be a saint or a martyr. You are being asked to serve and to lead. You are being asked to identify the leadership talent within the team even if you are the assigned leader of that team.

The main theme of chapter 1—that team leaders must help others help themselves—is carried throughout all subsequent chapters. At the end of each chapter you will be asked to complete a review to identify what you have learned and how you will attempt to *use* what you learned. Leadership development requires active learning. Merely gaining insights by reading will not be enough. You will need to practice the skills required of you as team leader: teambuilding, goal setting, communicating, problem solving, decision making, motivating, coaching, practicing diplomacy, monitoring, reviving stuck teams, leading executive leadership teams, and so on.

Be the X-factor in your organization's effort to build excellent teams.

Note: This book was written for both the person attempting to provide leadership to a single team within an organization and the leader overseeing the development of multiple teams within a larger organization. While the text is generally addressed to the former, the lessons contained herein are equally applicable to the latter.

CHAPTER 1

THE NEED FOR TEAM LEADERS AT ALL LEVELS

Helping Teams Help Themselves

•

Perhaps the best team I was ever part of was an education staff of a large organization. Virtually every member stepped up to the task of providing leadership from time to time. People genuinely respected each other but cared even more about providing the best programs and services. Peers challenged each other constantly. Whenever anyone acted blasé about an issue raised at a staff meeting, that person would be confronted and reminded of his ability and expressed commitment to address the issue in a better way. Everyone was task oriented, relationship oriented, and customer oriented. Isn't that what you want from leaders? While the team had an official "director" who reported to a vice president, she didn't tell us what to do—she simply made clear our team goals and created a climate for getting things done well. We were a team full of leaders, not a team whose individual actions were coordinated by a single leader. The best teams are leaderful, not leaderless.

•

Over the last couple of decades, companies have been encouraging the development of self-directed work teams, problem-solving committees and task forces, and even executive leadership teams. Attempts to use teams are evident in nearly every major organization today. Are you now in a position where you have the opportunity to be a leader? Whether your position is that of team leader, supervisor, area manager, coordinator, professional resource specialist, general manager, executive, union leader, or president of the company, the benefit of a team approach is to be found in collective action, not in the actions of individual heroes.

Three Chief Requirements for Building Team Leadership

If you truly want to help your organization with your team-oriented leadership, you will have to fulfill three chief requirements: raising awareness, generating options, and planning for success.

Raising Awareness

Your first assignment, if you have the courage to undertake it, is to get the team to take an honest look at itself. You need to serve as a large mirror, one free from distortion. It may seem like magic when a team jells, but there is a structure to that magic. Your job is to help each team make an accurate assessment of its actions and structure. Why do things go well when it is succeeding, and what are its problems when it is struggling? You need to be able to help the team describe what was and is happening so that it can live its life consciously. You are acting as a key catalyst by raising awareness for the whole team. It is a basic premise of this book that a team is better off knowing what is going on than not knowing. The team may be a little too close to its day-to-day activities and routines to notice the patterns. If you have a keen sense of the obvious, you are likely to be helpful to teams in organizational settings.

Helping a team understand its strengths and its problems is the first step in its becoming more effective.

Generating Options

If you are looking for a single best way to help teams, you are reading the wrong book. There is no one best way to capitalize on strengths and minimize weaknesses—instead there are many pathways to the same result. The members of your team—like all of us—develop habits and set ways of doing things; you need them to consider other options. The wisdom of teams results from the diversity of views available. You need to free up their minds to brainstorm strategies and tactics that can make a difference. You can also help by adding options for the team to consider, but be careful about getting sucked into making decisions for the team. It is best to facilitate consensus decisions.

If you want a committed, not merely compliant, team, you need to get the members to choose from among its options while staying within the boundaries set by your organization. Leaders in a team environment provide guidance in a process that alternates between expanding the thinking of the team and then gaining a focus regarding what is to be done to resolve the issues.

Planning for Success

Too often, teams are so relieved they have come up with a solution that they fail to take the steps needed to ensure the strategy is put into practice. Teams dump this responsibility on management or the system and then get frustrated when action does not follow. The team concept is not designed to create a new complaint department or to facilitate members lower in the organization in pointing the finger of blame at other teams or members of management. If you are going to help your team, you need to push it to make the ideas it produces operational. What tactics and actions are needed for an idea to be realized? Who needs to do what with whom by when?

You cannot second-guess the team after decisions have been made. You need to help the team produce an action plan for whatever solution the team decided on in the previous stage. The action plan must rely on actions taken by team members themselves—if it primarily dictates what others in the organization should do to solve the problem, the likelihood of successful implementation is low. Freedom of speech is important, but the key to empowerment is team self-reliance.

Leadership in a Team Environment

What do you know about leadership? What do you know about teams? Who has influenced your thinking about how to be an effective leader and how to be a part of a successful team? Exercise 1 provides you with an opportunity to think out loud about the lessons you have learned from your experience. As a pairing exercise, it also enables you to simultaneously practice the core relationship building skills of sharing information, listening effectively, and providing constructive feedback.

Six Key Lessons for Leaders in a Team Environment

While there have been thousands of research studies on the topic of leadership over the last one hundred years, the findings have not been all that consistent. It appears that leadership is as much an art as it is a science. However, a few things seem clear. The essence of leadership in a team environment is influence, not control. The key is developing collaborative partnerships while helping others help themselves. A review of the literature establishes six key lessons for leaders in a team environment to learn.

EXERCISE 1

Lessons from Experience

Phase I: Sharing Experiences

Directions: *Pair up with another person. Decide who will share experiences (the "sharer") first and who will take on the role of being an effective listener (the "listener"). The listener will also take on the role of providing feedback. After completing the exercise, switch roles and repeat the exercise.*

ROLE OF THE SHARER

Share your perceptions of yourself as a leader by answering the questions below. You will be given the total, undivided attention of your partner (the listener) for five full minutes.

- If you could take a leader (from today or the past) to dinner, whom would you choose, and what questions would you ask?
- Who is the person who has most influenced you as a leader?
- What was the best or the worst team you were ever on? What did your experience on that team teach you about teams in general?
- What has experience taught you about creating change and helping others?
- How would you describe the characteristics of your leadership style?
- What are your strengths as a leader?
- How does your organization's situation affect your approach to leadership?
- How much credibility do you have as a leader?
- What behaviors do you need to work on in the upcoming year to become a more effective leader at your level?

ROLE OF THE LISTENER

- Give your total undivided attention to the sharer
- Just listen very well—don't direct the conversation
- Don't interrupt too much
- Help the sharer feel comfortable but keep the focus of attention on the sharer

Phase II: Providing Feedback

Directions: *In your role as listener, provide your partner (the sharer) with constructive feedback. Be sure to describe what you hear before you interpret it. Try not to judge whether what the sharer said about his or her experiences, or what he or she learned from those experiences, is good or bad, right or wrong. Try answering the following questions in this order as you provide feedback.*

- What did you hear or notice? (describe)

- What did it mean to you? (interpret)

- What did you learn? (summarize)

Phase III: Identifying Learning

Directions: *Together with your partner, identify what you learned about*

- Listening

- Sharing skills

- Providing feedback

- Characteristics of effective leadership

- Characteristics of teams

- Creating changes in people and systems

- Each other

1. **Leaders are made, not born.** Some individuals will be born into more opportunities for leadership than others, but they are not actually born with the skills needed to succeed as a leader. Despite the expression "He's a born leader," researchers have yet to discover any DNA patterns that determine leadership talent. Some people develop their skills and nurture their opportunities and some squander them. What have you done to discover your natural talents and put them to use? What have you done with your opportunities? To what extent have you truly learned from your experiences? Have you learned from, or merely survived, your experiences? If you want to be a leader in a team environment, you must be willing to apply and develop your talents. Some people start this process quite late in life and others much earlier, but it is very difficult for people to change their basic values or even habits.

2. **No set of traits predicts leadership success.** Many candidates for leadership positions have technical knowledge and skills but have undeveloped "people" skills. Some others have people skills but are not technically competent. Research has found that there is no one set of physical, mental, or personality traits that leaders require, though it helps to be about as smart as the team you are trying to lead—if you are a lot less smart or a lot smarter, you will likely experience difficulty. No one set of personality traits predicts leadership effectiveness. Some extroverts make good leaders, and some just don't seem to be able to focus enough. Some introverts make good leaders by listening and thinking through issues in depth, but others fail to convert this trait into the actions teams need to succeed.

3. **You need to be both task and people oriented.** The key is being fully devoted to getting the job done well and simultaneously showing full respect for the people you are working with. Effective team leaders clarify goals and set challenging standards. They let others

know that getting the job done well is very important to them. But if they are not as relationship oriented as they are task oriented, they are not likely to have long-term success. Team leaders seek input on how to get things done—they listen and encourage effort. They don't see being task versus relationship oriented as a trade-off. They simultaneously exhibit both orientations.

4. **Leadership style must correspond to the work that needs to be done and the people available to do it.** A good team leader is like a quarterback who reads the situation as he comes to the line of scrimmage. He has worked with the coaching staff and the players to select a good plan during team meetings and in the huddle but is flexible enough to adjust the play to gain successful execution. In general, a participative style of leadership is most conducive to a team environment. This style gains commitment rather than mere compliance. However, situations of crisis and chaos, including when members are new to the task and to each other, occasionally require a more directive style to address more short-term concerns. A directive "tell and educate" style may be needed for a while, but its overuse can destroy a team approach. It creates either resentment or overdependence. Team leaders need to be flexible but must lean more toward the participative style over the long haul.

5. **You need to establish and maintain credibility.** Kouzes and Posner (1993) studied over thirty thousand leaders and found significant evidence that a leader's most important quality is credibility. You cannot be a leader without followers, and followers must believe in you. In order to be credible you must be trustworthy. Trustworthiness is a function of reliability and dependability, not likeability. It is basically doing what you said you would do. If you want to be a leader in a team environment—at any level—your actions must be consistent with your words. Be careful about what you promise; keep your promises small but make very visible signs that you are following through on those promises.

Credibility also requires that you be perceived as competent. Teams won't expect you, or want you, to know it all—but they will expect you to know something about the tasks, the operations, the organization, and the people. You cannot bluff your way through; you must be willing to put out the effort to continually enhance your knowledge and skills to be competent.

Finally, credibility requires that you show genuine enthusiasm in what you do and say. If your team senses that you are saying things just because you have to say them, or you present ideas (even competent ones) too matter-of-factly, you won't generate sufficient energy for the team to cope with the inevitable changes in business.

6. **Improved leadership effectiveness comes from a focused approach.** Leaders have so much to do and so much to keep track of—they need to stay focused. This is true even when it comes to improving themselves as leaders. They need and must want feedback in order to become more aware of their style and its impact and to develop a conscious plan to capitalize on the strengths inherent in that style. Effective leaders have strong egos but are not narcissistic. They like themselves and believe they have something important to offer the teams they are trying to help, but they are also well aware of their weaknesses. But instead of claiming to try to improve on every weakness they have, effective leaders take a focused approach to development. They don't try to improve on more than a couple of weaknesses at a time. They model continuous improvement through their actions. They do not try to be all things to all people and they focus their efforts to become better leaders.

A Team Concept
Requires Leaders at Every Level

An ironic outcome of an organization's decision to establish a team concept is that there must be many individual leaders at all levels. Let's examine how members at each level can help.

Leaders at the Top: "General Managers"

General managers—those at the top of the organization including executives, plant managers, committee chairs, union officers, and so on—set
the strategic direction for the organization and how the use of teams
will help accomplish its mission. They need to be clear on how teams
are to be formed in the organization and the rules and boundaries associated with the power given to the teams to make decisions and solve
problems. They must see the use of teams as a sound business practice.
These key leaders must avoid isolating themselves. Sometimes leaders at
this level in a team-based organization may feel like the supervisor of a
graveyard: lots of people under them, but nobody listening. They need
direct contact with teams and must listen to their concerns; they must
understand any differences between the plan and the realities. Leaders
at the top of the organization may also need to form a team of their
own. This can be a powerful way of modeling their true belief in the
team approach and an effective way to gain the collective wisdom to
identify the innovative strategies needed to address complex problems.

Resource Leaders: "Coaches"

Organizations wanting teams to succeed must provide the needed
resources. In addition to information, materials, equipment, and a
budget, they must provide people who can act as coaches. Coaches such
as area managers, supervisors, staff experts, trainers, consultants, and
others are subject matter experts who can provide insights for the team
to consider. They are usually not permanent members of the teams they
serve, but rather are brought in when an issue calls for their help.

When a problem-solving team is investigating sources of supplies or
tools to address a quality issue in the production process, perhaps a staff
expert from Purchasing should be invited to a team meeting to help
members understand the company's contracts and policies with current
suppliers and steps that may need to be taken to change the current
practice. When a team is struggling to contain costs, perhaps the con-

troller should attend a team meeting to help the team understand budgeting and accounting practices relevant to the team's portion of the operations. Trainers should be made available to teams to help them learn quality-enhancing procedures such as statistical process control or Six Sigma techniques. They can serve as coaches in the soft skills arena as well, facilitating exercises to develop the skills to communicate more effectively, to resolve conflicts more constructively, and to honor and capitalize on the diversity present among team members.

Area managers can serve as coaches to help broaden the horizons of team members so that they can make decisions in a manner that enhances, not interferes, with the workings of other teams in that area. Team coordinators can attend team meetings and provide feedback on how to enhance team processes for working together effectively. The emphasis here is on a coaching style that enlightens, educates, and expands a team's thinking, not one that dictates and controls.

Peer Leaders: "Captains"

Then there are those special people who can serve as team leaders even among peers. You probably remember team captains from youth sports. They called the coin toss and listened to the instructions of the referees. They were brought in to hear the explanation regarding disputed plays. They met with the coaches to gain a more in-depth understanding of the strategy being utilized. They were expected to spread the word with their peers and were counted on to have that special rapport with the other team members to help the team stay united.

Work teams can benefit from having a captain, too. So-called self-directed work teams typically have a peer as the team leader. This person might be elected by her peers or may be selected by management. Some companies establish a set of qualifications (e.g., know all the jobs on the team, have a distinguished attendance record, pass a series of training courses, etc.) for election or selection to this position. Other companies make it a rotating position that every team member is expected to fulfill. It is important that the duties this person is to perform be clarified. She is not there to dictate and direct or function as a "straw boss." She cannot be expected to be management's lackey or spy. She is to be chosen because of her understanding of the team's operations and especially because she is considered credible (i.e., trustworthy, competent, and enthusiastic) by members of the team.

Team Leader Training

Any organization attempting to utilize a team concept must prepare and continually develop its team leaders, at every level. This book is designed to provide you with insights, exercises, and tools to enable you to succeed. Your organization may decide to provide some developmental opportunities too. All good training efforts start with a training needs assessment. Exercise 2 provides a series of focus group interview questions; exercise 3 is a survey that was used by one organization that recognized the need to provide more training to current leaders. Notice that the questions attempt to recognize what is going well in addition to identifying the problems that the training was intended to fix. Table 1 outlines the training modules the organization ended up offering its team leaders.

Training can only be a solution when the problem involves the need to enhance skills and knowledge. If the problem is motivation, the organization needs to reexamine the degree to which it has made role expectations clear and the manner in which it reinforces fulfillment of these expectations.

It is difficult to anticipate all the specific training modules and tools you will need in your unique situation. Your general managers and human resource coaches need to conduct an assessment and design the training elements or find people who can provide them. What tools should your leaders be able to use? Maybe you need to think metaphorically. Exercise 4 can help you to identify which tools you think your leaders should have in their toolbox.

EXERCISE 2

Focus Group Interview Questions

Directions: *Have the group respond to the following questions regarding teams and team leaders.*

1. First, a general question: What are your perceptions regarding how successful the use of teams has been so far at this organization?

2. How would you describe the roles and responsibilities that team leaders play here? How does a leader help a team become more successful and satisfying?

3. What knowledge, skills, and personal qualities does a team leader ideally possess to help teams succeed in this organization?

   • Knowledge:

   • Skills:

   • Personal qualities:

4. What motivates team leaders to successfully fulfill their roles and responsibilities?

5. What gets in the way of the success of some team leaders? What are the obstacles?

6. What advice do you have for the joint steering committee as it prepares training plans to enhance the development of team leaders in this organization?

EXERCISE 3

Survey of Team Leader Training Needs

Directions: *This organization cannot offer every training module imaginable as it tries to enhance the development of team leaders. Review the list of potential topics below. Rate the importance of offering training modules on these topics using the following scale:*

1 = **Extremely important**—this module should definitely be offered

2 = **Important**—it would be good to offer this module if time permits

3 = **Not very important**—maybe nice but probably not necessary

Be sure not to place too many items in the first category. We must be practical regarding how much time we can afford to have team leaders in training sessions.

_____ How to establish/clarify team goals

_____ How to develop talent

_____ How to clarify roles and responsibilities

_____ How to improve the effectiveness of team procedures

_____ How to facilitate team meetings

_____ How to improve team problem-solving skills

_____ How to facilitate team decision making

_____ Building more constructive interpersonal relationships

_____ Improving communication skills (sharing information, listening effectively, providing useful feedback)

_____ Improving your conflict resolution skills

_____ Reinforcing team-oriented behaviors and maintaining accountability

_____ Building diplomatic relationships with key players outside your team (e.g., supervisors/advisors/management, skilled trades and maintenance, union representatives, resource staff, etc.)

_____ Strategies to gain/maintain credibility as a leader

_____ Planning skills

_____ Organizing/coordinating skills

EXERCISE 3 CONT'D

_____ Strategies to motivate people

_____ How to assess team progress

_____ Building commitment vs. gaining compliance

_____ Understanding why teams get stuck and what to do about it

_____ Understanding and utilizing the personalities on your team including your own

_____ Providing strategies to communicate organizational change plans (e.g., who to include as communicators of change, how to make messages "sticky," how the context affects the message)

_____ Identifying causes of stress and determining how to reduce them

_____ Developing your personal leadership development plan

Below list any other training modules you think should be considered and rate the importance of each.

TABLE 1

Proposed Objectives and Components for the Nontechnical Training and Development of Team Leaders

1. **Examine what your experience and research tell you about effective leadership**

2. **Identify strategies to gain/maintain credibility as a leader**
   - Trustworthiness
   - Competency
   - Enthusiasm

3. **Assess/enhance your skills as a participative leader in a team environment**
   - Planning, organizing, motivating, monitoring
   - Building commitment vs. gaining compliance

4. **Examine your approach to the seven keys to effective teams**
   - How to establish a clear sense of direction and set goals
   - How to develop talent
   - How to clarify roles and responsibilities
   - How to establish effective team operating procedures (facilitating meetings, problem solving, decision making)
   - How to enhance and maintain constructive interpersonal relationships (communicating, sharing information, listening effectively, providing useful feedback)
   - How to reinforce team-oriented behaviors and maintain accountability
   - How to build diplomatic relationships with key players outside your team (e.g., supervisors/advisors/management, skilled trades and maintenance, resource staff, etc.)

5. **Understand and utilize personalities on the team**
   - Understanding your personality
   - Capitalizing on the strengths of your personality
   - Strategies to work with personalities different from your own
   - Personalities and change
   - Personalities and leadership styles

TABLE 1 CONT'D

6. Develop conflict resolution strategies
- Assess/enhance your abilities to utilize the five basic conflict resolution strategies:
  - The avoiding approach
  - The accommodating approach
  - The competing approach
  - The compromising approach
  - The collaborative ("win-win") approach
- See the advantages and disadvantages of conflict on a team
- Learn how to deal with particularly difficult people

7. Examine strategies to communicate organizational change plans
- Who to include as communicators of change—connectors, mavens, and salespersons (see pp. 220–222)
- How to make messages "sticky"
- How the context affects the message

8. Understand and deal with stress on the team
- What is stress?
- What causes stress?
- What are the consequences of stress?
- Examine three strategies to reduce stress:
  - Reducing stressors
  - Reframing perceptions about the situation
  - Activating your relaxation response

9. Develop a plan to make use of these training sessions
- What is the diagnosis of the team's current state?
- When has this team been stuck, and what should be done about this?
- What is your plan to develop yourself as a leader in this environment?

EXERCISE 4

A Dozen Tools for Team Leaders

Directions: *From the list below, pick a dozen tools for your team leader toolbox. Come up with creative ideas for how team leaders at your facility could use each tool metaphorically to serve their team. How would a leader use a hammer? Perhaps to nail down the details of plans. How would a leader use a saw? Perhaps to cut through the bureaucracy to help team members get the resources they need. Have fun with it—add to the list of tools and discover some interesting analogies.*

TOOL	USE BY TEAM LEADER
1. Hammer	1.
2. Saw	2.
3. Drill	3.
4. Screwdriver	4.
5. Vise	5.
6. Chisel	6.
7. Pulley/lever	7.
8. Bubble balance	8.
9. Sander	9.
10. Duct tape	10.
11. Crowbar	11.
12. Pliers	12.
13. Awl	13.
14. Paintbrush	14.
15. Ladder	15.
16. Wrench	16.
17.	17.
18.	18.
19.	19.
20.	20.

External Team Consultants

While this book is aimed primarily at internal organization members attempting to facilitate team excellence, occasionally the use of external team consultants is appropriate. Table 2 outlines the responsibilities of an external team consultant assisting work teams and helping individuals better fulfill their role as leader. Such consultants in an organizational setting should be sure to stop at influencing—and consciously avoid managing the situation or serving as the proxy leader of the team. Metaphorically speaking, they should be helping team leaders learn how to fish, rather than merely giving them some fish. While fulfilling their responsibilities, they need to find ways to ensure that their knowledge and skills are left behind in the hands of the internal leaders. They may find it difficult to intentionally work their way out of a job, but it is crucial that the teams and leaders they interact with end up being self-reliant.

Summary

The collective action of teams can be enhanced by the individual actions of leaders at several levels in an organization. Take some time to reflect on what you have learned in this chapter about yourself as a potential leader. Why are you in the position you are in? What do you need to learn to do more effectively? What developmental opportunities would serve you and your organization well? To help in this effort, complete the after-chapter review that follows.

TABLE 2

Chief Responsibilities of an External Team Consultant

1. **Gather information to help the parties take an honest look at themselves and their situation**
   - Conduct discussions, focus groups, confidential interviews, surveys, observations, etc.
   - Feed back a summary of the collective information to those who provided it but protect individuals' confidentiality and anonymity
   - Clarify expectations the parties have of one another and get them to agree on which roles they would like you to play in the change effort

2. **Identify and clarify options for what could be done about the situation**
   - Get the team and associated leaders to think about goals, options, strategies, etc.
   - Describe approaches other teams have used in similar situations
   - Clarify the steps involved
   - Warn of the pitfalls and potential problems of each option

3. **Get responsible team members to make free and informed choices**
   - Facilitate a discussion of the options
   - Ensure that the people responsible are making the decisions

4. **Help develop a broad commitment to choices made and assist with implementation**
   - Establish an action plan
   - Coach the parties on how to communicate the plan
   - Get people involved
   - Provide training and facilitation as needed

5. **Gather data to help assess whether the plan is working**
   - Conduct more interviews, surveys, etc.
   - Protect the confidentiality pledges
   - Facilitate the planning of adjustments and the institutionalizing of the change effort

---

AFTER-CHAPTER REVIEW

Now that you have completed reading this chapter, it is time for you to challenge yourself to see what you remember, establish what it is you learned, and decide where and how you are going to apply what you learned. The outline provided below can help you get started. The relevancy of this chapter may necessitate that you expand on your thoughts elsewhere. Make sure you benefit from your reading by capturing your thoughts and turning them into actions.

1. Describe at least five things you remember from the material in this chapter.

-
-
-
-
-

2. Identify the insights you gained from reading the material in this chapter. These insights may have come directly from the points raised or by stimulating recollections of your own experiences.

-
-
-

3. Identify at least one situational opportunity for applying what you learned and describe the steps to be taken (including who will do what with whom, where, and when).

Situational opportunity:

Steps to be taken:

-
-
-
-

CHAPTER 2

YOUR NATURAL LEADERSHIP STRENGTHS

Capitalizing on Your Knowledge, Skills, and Personal Qualities

•

Rhino Records has produced a compilation enti-
tled *Golden Throats: The Great Celebrity Sing-Off*.
It features talented movie and TV stars singing
rock, folk, and blues classics. It includes William
Shatner (of *Star Trek* fame) singing "Lucy in the
Sky with Diamonds" and "Mr. Tambourine Man";
Jack Webb (of *Dragnet* fame) singing "Try a Little
Tenderness"; Sebastian Cabot singing "It Ain't Me
Babe" and "Like a Rolling Stone"; Andy Griffith
singing "House of the Rising Sun"; and Leonard
Nimoy (also of *Star Trek* fame) singing "Proud
Mary" and "If I Had a Hammer." The album is
listed in Rhino Records' comedy collections sec-
tion. These talented actors can sing perhaps bet-
ter than I can, but they sure don't sound like the
legends that originally performed these classics.

•

Leaders should not expect to be talented in all phases of their industry and, frankly, they shouldn't even try. For you to be an effective leader, helping your team help itself, you need to focus on your natural strengths. You are not going to be good at all things. This chapter will help you to take a look at yourself and decide what talents you bring to the table. It will ask you to develop plans to more consciously capitalize on those natural strengths and discover how to cover the other skills your team must have to excel.

Talent = Knowledge, Skills, and Personal Qualities

What knowledge, skills, and personal qualities are likely needed to provide leadership in a team-based organization? A training needs assessment survey used by one of my clients was included in chapter 1 (see exercise 3). It represents the client's determination of what skills should be considered for team leaders at their facility. A more thorough list is provided below. What knowledge, skills, and personal qualities do you have that might be useful in your efforts to help teams in your organization? In this chapter we will examine this question from many perspectives: those of the last one hundred or so teams I have worked with; those provided by models of leadership developed by leading researchers; and those of data-based leadership assessment instruments from leading companies in the field. Use the sections in this chapter, as well as the following list, to help identify your particular talents and the areas where you are going to need some help.

Knowledge needed for success as a leader:
- Knowledge of the organization's plan for a team concept (goals, roles and responsibilities, procedures, etc.)
- Knowledge of company rules and/or the union contract
- Technical knowledge associated with the work being produced by the team

- Knowledge of the culture and the politics of the organization
- Knowledge of who to go to for what kind of information
- Understanding of people and individual personalities

Skills needed for success as a leader:

- Communication, especially listening skills
- Problem solving
- Facilitation of meetings, discussions, and decision making
- Motivation
- Planning and organizing
- Presentation/speaking in front of groups
- Time management
- Report writing
- Conflict resolution
- Diplomacy
- Networking
- Keeping people accountable

Personal qualities needed for success as a leader:

- Honest
- Trustworthy
- Compassionate
- Inspirational
- Direct
- Committed
- Open to new ideas
- Nonprejudicial
- Respectful
- Responsive
- Resourceful

- Patient
- Creative
- Sincere
- Persistent
- Fun loving/humorous
- Approachable/unintimidating
- Risk taking

Are you responsible for managing a team? For decades textbooks have identified the four main functions of the manager of a team or organization as

- Planning (i.e., goal setting and identifying the steps, procedures, and time frames in which to accomplish the goals)
- Organizing (i.e., assigning people to tasks and procuring resources)
- Leading (i.e., motivating people)
- Controlling (i.e., monitoring progress and making corrective actions accordingly)

Noted scholars such as Warren Bennis have emphasized that companies in the U.S. suffer from being overmanaged and underled. We need good management to deal with the complexities of organizational life. Good managers bring order and consistency, while leadership allows us to cope with the realities brought about by our rapidly changing, competitive world. John Kotter (1999) of Harvard University points out the three key differences between leading and managing: (1) leaders set a direction more than engage in planning and budgeting; (2) leaders align people, whereas managers organize systems and staff them with people; and, perhaps most important, (3) leaders motivate people, whereas managers engage in controlling and problem solving. You need to be a leader even if your job title is manager if your organization is to benefit from having a team concept.

Leadership Effectiveness Analysis

Many instruments are available from publishers and consulting firms to help leaders (and leaders-to-be) assess their strengths. Kouzes and Posner (2002) have developed the Leadership Practices Instrument, which provides a self-assessment on what the authors feel are the five practices and the ten commitments of leadership. Buckingham and Clifton have worked with the Gallup organization to identify thirty-four potential strengths a person may bring to a leadership position.

The Management Research Group out of Portland, Maine, has gathered assessments on over thirty thousand leaders and identified six sets of behaviors that can be assessed by the individual and his or her bosses, peers, and direct reports. They have produced what they call the Leadership Effectiveness Analysis (LEA) instrument. The elements of the LEA instrument are summarized in table 3 and discussed below.

1. Creating a Vision

How talented are you at helping teams create a vision that will orient their efforts? Some achieve this by using lessons learned in the past to determine what should be happening now. Others are more innovative and willing to help people extend their thinking in addressing the rapid changes in the environment. Technical expertise could be emphasized in efforts to identify a preferred future. Some leaders take sole responsibility for creating a vision, while others emphasize a more collaborative approach. The LEA also assesses the degree to which the leader pushes for a long-term, wide-ranging approach to planning for the future. What approaches do you typically use to create a vision?

TABLE 3

Leadership Behaviors Identified on the
Leadership Effectiveness Analysis (LEA) Instrument

1. Creating a vision

- *Conservative:* studying problems in light of past practices to ensure predictability, reinforce the status quo, and minimize risk
- *Innovative:* feeling comfortable in fast-changing environments; being willing to take risks and to consider new and untested approaches
- *Technical:* acquiring and maintaining in-depth knowledge in one's field or area of focus; using one's expertise and specialized knowledge to study issues and draw conclusions
- *Self:* emphasizing the importance of making decisions independently; looking to oneself as the prime vehicle for decision making
- *Strategic:* taking a long-range, broad approach to problem solving and decision making through objective analysis, thinking ahead, and planning

2. Developing followership

- *Persuasive:* building commitment by convincing others and winning them over to one's point of view
- *Outgoing:* acting in an extroverted, friendly, and informal manner; showing a capacity to quickly establish free and easy interpersonal relationships
- *Excitement:* operating with plenty of energy, intensity, and emotional expression; having a capacity for keeping others enthusiastic and involved
- *Restraint:* maintaining a low-key, understated, and quiet interpersonal demeanor by working to control one's emotional expression

---

TABLE 3 CONT'D

3. Implementing the vision
- *Structuring:* adopting a systematic and organized approach; preferring to work in a precise, methodical manner; developing and utilizing guidelines and procedures
- *Tactical:* emphasizing the production of immediate results by focusing on short-range, hands-on, practical strategies
- *Communication:* stating clearly what one wants and expects from others; clearly expressing one's thoughts and ideas; maintaining a precise and constant flow of information
- *Delegation:* enlisting the talents of others to help meet objectives by giving them important activities and sufficient autonomy to exercise their own judgment

4. Following through
- *Control:* adopting an approach in which one takes nothing for granted, sets deadlines for certain actions, and is persistent in monitoring the progress of activities to ensure that they are completed on schedule
- *Feedback:* letting others know in a straightforward manner what one thinks of them, how well they have performed, and if they have met one's needs and expectations

5. Achieving results
- *Management focus:* seeking to exert influence by being in a position of authority, taking charge, and leading and directing the efforts of others
- *Dominant:* pushing vigorously to achieve results through a forceful, assertive, and competitive approach
- *Production:* adopting a strong orientation toward achievement; holding high expectations of oneself and others; pushing oneself and others to achieve at high levels

---

TABLE 3 CONT'D

6. **Team playing**
   - *Cooperation:* accommodating the needs and interests of others by being willing to defer performance on one's own objectives in order to assist colleagues with theirs
   - *Consensual:* valuing the ideas and opinions of others and collecting their input as part of one's decision-making process
   - *Authority:* showing loyalty to the organization; respecting the opinion of people in authority and using them as resources for information, direction, and decisions
   - *Empathy:* demonstrating an active concern for people and their needs by forming close and supportive relationships with others

---

Source: Management Research Group, *Leadership Effectiveness Analysis* (Portland, ME: Management Research Group, 1998).

2. Developing Followership

Some leaders develop followership through persuasion, convincing others to adopt their point of view. Followership can also be developed by being friendly, informal, and outgoing. Some display a lot of energy, and their enthusiasm keeps others involved. Still others try to be the calming influence and develop followership by minimizing potentially destructive emotional displays. How do you create followership among members of your teams?

3. Implementing the Vision

Having a vision for your team is one thing, but implementing it is another. Do you naturally take a systematic, organized approach to the work of your team? Do you focus on the team's step-by-step tactics to accomplish goals? Do you dedicate considerable time for clearly communicating what is expected and ensuring a constant flow of information to and from your team? Or are you a delegator, one who recruits talented members to the team and then turns them loose to do their work? How do you help your team implement its vision?

4. Following Through

The two issues here are control and feedback. Control refers to setting clear deadlines and closely monitoring whether those deadlines are met. How much are you willing to take for granted? In giving feedback, to what extent do you let others know precisely what you think of their work performance?

5. Achieving Results

To what extent do you emphasize that you are in charge and use this authority to direct the efforts of others? Dominant leaders are assertive and encourage the competitive urge to achieve. Others get results by setting high expectations for themselves as well as others. How do you help your team achieve results?

6. Team Playing

How cooperative are you? As a leader, are you willing to accommodate the needs of team members even if that means deferring performance? To what extent are you a consensus builder? Do you make sure everyone's input is used in making decisions? How respectful of authority are you? Are you loyal and respectful to the point that you would defer decision making to those in charge? Do you develop close relationships with team members by demonstrating an understanding of their needs? What is your approach to being a team player?

Determining Your Natural Talents and Strengths

There is no one best way to assess yourself as a leader. You could purchase and complete one or more of the many instruments available on the market for such purposes. You could engage in a 360-degree feedback process and have your boss, your peers, and the team members you are trying to help fill them out about you too. All I can do is assure you that effective leaders in team-based organizations own their talents and strengths:

- They have a high level of self-esteem but are not narcissistic—they can tell you what they have to offer without bragging
- They are excited to be working with team members who also have great talents and strengths
- They recognize their relative weaknesses but do not try to be all things to all people
- They are neither intimidated nor defensive about working with others who know more than they do in certain areas
- They have discovered their own talents and encourage their team-mates to do the same
- They use training and development opportunities to become competent in areas where they are naturally strong—not expect-ing to be great in all skill areas

Many types of knowledge, skills, and personal qualities have been identified over the last several pages. Which of these represent particu-lar strengths that you provide in your organization? Use exercise 5 to list your particular strengths and identify some opportunities to make more effective use of these strengths and clarify the steps you will take to do so. Also list your areas of relative weakness—areas in which you may never become great, but where you may need to become more pro-ficient. Do not work on more than two or three areas of weakness at any one time. Spend more time utilizing your strengths than working on your weaknesses.

How do you know which are your natural strengths? Buckingham and Clifton (2001) suggest some telltale signs to look for. Use the descriptions of the leadership behaviors provided in table 3 to help with this reflection.

1. **Pay attention to your immediate, spontaneous, "top-of-mind" reactions to situations.** Is your first impulse to figure out how to accommodate people's needs (cooperation)? Do you tend to refer to past precedents to cover the current situation (conservative)? Do you immediately think, "What will my boss want to happen here?"

EXERCISE 5

Identifying Your Natural Talents and Deficiencies

Directions: *To be an effective leader in a team environment, you need to own up to your strengths and confidently, though not arrogantly, apply them for the sake of the team and the organization. Reread the previous pages to remind yourself of things you know, things you can do well, and personal qualities that you can bring to your role. Identify your natural strengths, followed by your deficiencies.*

Knowledge: What do you know? What bases of knowledge have you mastered that could be applied to the work you are facing?

-
-
-
-
-

Skills: What are you capable of doing? What technical skills do you own? What interpersonal skills do you own? What skill bases have you mastered that could be applied to the work you are facing?

-
-
-
-

Personal qualities: What qualities personify you? These are not about your knowledge or skills. They include traits such as trustworthiness, openness, kindness, and so on. Which of your personal qualities could be applied to the work you are facing?

-
-
-
-

EXERCISE 5 CONT'D

Deficiencies: What knowledge, skills, or personal qualities do you lack that may present a problem for you in successfully fulfilling the work you are facing?

-
-
-
-
-

Plans for the future: Develop plans for better applying your talent — knowledge, skills, and personal qualities. Remember, it is more important to deliver your strengths to the situations you face than trying to be great at all things. However, spend some time developing a plan to reduce one of your areas of weakness, too.

(authority). Do you find yourself becoming detached and analytical? Think about situations you have faced recently and try to notice your first, immediate response. This should give you some clues about your natural strengths and tendencies.

2. **Think about what you have yearned for since early in life.** Were you the kind of kid who always wanted things neat and orderly (structuring)? Have you tended to value unplanned events where going with the flow seemed to spontaneously produce good things? Pehaps some long-term yearnings have been unfulfillable until you took on the responsibility of team leader. Notice which things you seem to do naturally now that may be manifestations of inclinations you have had for years.

3. **Become aware of the things you seem to learn very easily.** Rapid learnings offer another clue as to what your talents really are. Maybe you never thought you would be interested in budgeting information but now find yourself going over the numbers and figuring out

things quickly. Maybe you never thought of yourself as a public speaker but are now finding words just flowing out of your mouth at team presentations. Many people have not allowed themselves to consider their hidden talents, having received discouraging messages from parents and teachers for a long time. What have you enjoyed learning lately? Was there anything that you were surprised to learn easily?

4. **Recognize those things that are particularly satisfying to you.** If it feels good to see a team member become more effective because of a tip you provided, maybe you have a talent for developing people. Perhaps it may indicate that you have a natural talent for breaking down complex situations and identifying the specific details involved (tactical). Buckingham and Clifton would warn you, however, to pay attention only to the positive satisfactions. If you find yourself gaining great satisfaction in telling management "I told you so" when your ideas work, this might not be a talent that will be useful in becoming a leader in a team-based organization. If you take pleasure witnessing others' pain, don't mark that as one of your natural strengths.

Personalities, Teams, and Leadership

Thus far we have concentrated on your need to identify your natural strengths, the knowledge and skills you can easily and effectively bring to the task of helping teams. However, remember that personal qualities are also an important component of being an effective leader. Your personality synthesizes your personal qualities and is one of your most important tools for you to use in your efforts to influence teams. Capitalizing on the natural strengths of your personality and enjoying interaction with people who are different from you are crucial for success. Tolerating differences in the personalities of people you work with is not enough—you need to celebrate those differences. They provide the natural strengths you may need to benefit the team.

This section will help you take a look at your personality and understand what you might find easy and natural to do. You also need to know what a team leader would like to be able to do that may be difficult for you because of your personality. Basically your choice is to try to do it yourself or find co-leaders to fill in for the good of the team. The framework we will use to understand personalities is known as the *Myers-Briggs Type Indicator*® (MBTI®) assessment. If you have never encountered this instrument, you may want to read one or more of the references listed as MBTI® Resources in the bibliography to gain a more thorough understanding. I will attempt to give you enough of a foundation here to help make use of your personality and to understand the personalities of the members of the teams with whom you will want to work.

First of all, personality traits exist in pairs of opposites. You were born with—or developed early in life—a natural preference for one or the other of each of these pairs. Think of it this way: You are either naturally right-handed or naturally left-handed—you can do things with both hands but you generally favor one or the other. The same thing holds for aspects of your personality. For example, you are capable of acting in an Extraverted manner as well as in an Introverted manner, but you have a natural tendency to favor one over the other. That tendency may be very strong and pronounced or it may be only a slight tendency. The clearer you are on what your natural tendencies are, the more able you will be to use your personality as a tool of your leadership style.

In exercises 6–9, we examine fours pairs of type characteristics, or dichotomies: Extraversion–Introversion, Sensing–Intuition, Thinking–Feeling, and Judging–Perceiving. Your job is to decide which characteristic in each pair is most natural for you. Short checklists are provided to assist you in "typing" your personality or that of your teammates. On each checklist, the answer that predominates (E or I, S or N, T or F, J or P) indicates your likely preference. When answering the questions, choose the item that describes something that is more like the "real you," rather than the one that describes how you want to be. You will be tempted to say, "Well, it depends on the situation." We all vary our behaviors to match situations to some degree. Choose the item that is more likely to occur across situations, the one that is driven more by your natural tendencies than by how you think you are supposed to behave. Note that these checklists offer only a glimpse of MBTI typology. If you have the opportunity, I encourage you to take the latest version of the MBTI assessment. You can contact the Association for Psychological Type or CPP, Inc., to obtain the names of professionals in your area who can administer the instrument to you and provide a feedback session.

Preference for Extraversion vs. Introversion

Exercise 6 is a short checklist to help you identify whether you have a natural preference for being more Extraverted or more Introverted. All of us have both Extraversion and Introversion as a part of our personality. Use the standard of the "real you" to help determine which characteristic in this dichotomy is most natural for you.

Leaders and team members who have a preference for Extraversion are externally oriented and quite aware of what's going on around them. They are more likely than those with a preference for Introversion to reveal what they are thinking and feeling. Thoughts that surface in their brain tend to be quickly transmitted through their mouth. Most Extraverts are action oriented. They like variety and want to make things happen, not just think about it. As a result, their natural strengths include getting the ball rolling on projects and keeping their eyes and ears open to what is happening beyond their own work efforts. However, they may have some blind spots, too. They may be easily distracted and interfere with the group's ability to stay focused. They may instigate action without sufficient forethought about goals and future requirements. They may also dominate team meetings and conversations. However, it is highly beneficial to have some team leaders and members with a preference for Extraversion because of the energy they bring to the team. Their "can-do" spirit is helpful in many situations.

Many people believe that leaders should be Extraverts. It is true that the role often calls for interacting with people and things and providing energy to get things going. However, people with a natural preference

EXERCISE 6

Extraverted Type (E) or
Introverted Type (I) Checklist

Directions: *For each pair of choices, select the one that*   **Circle your**
best describes your natural tendency across most situations.   **answer**

1. Is your attention directed more externally to the world of people   **E**
and things?
Or, is your attention directed internally to the world of ideas   **I**
and concepts?

2. Are you more likely to take action and then (maybe) reflect on   **E**
it later?
Or, are you more likely to think about a situation a lot and then   **I**
(maybe) take action?

3. Do you find yourself thinking out loud?   **E**
Or, do you find yourself thinking a lot before saying things aloud?   **I**

4. Do you find yourself feeling energized by interacting with people?   **E**
Or, do you find your energy being drained by interacting with   **I**
people and thus need some down time to recharge your
batteries?

5. Do you tend to have very broad interests?   **E**
Or, do you have a few deep interests?   **I**

6. Do you think of yourself as having many relationships and the   **E**
ability to meet and talk with people easily?
Or, do you make a big distinction between friends and acquain-   **I**
tances and find small talk difficult?

7. Do you tend to notice most of everything going on around you   **E**
and not mind interruptions that much?
Or, do you hate to be interrupted and are more comfortable   **I**
with silence?

8. Are you quite willing to share what you think or feel?   **E**
Or, do you tend to wait to be asked about what you think or feel?   **I**

9. Do you learn best through doing and discussing?   **E**
Or, do you learn best through reflection and "mental practice"?   **I**

for Introversion can also be terrific leaders. They are more focused on the inner world of thoughts and concepts. They bring to a team their natural tendency to think before acting. They can help a team by insisting that what the team is attempting to accomplish be well planned and that matters have been thought through in depth. Their blind spots might include appearing secretive or overly intense as a result of all their interior thinking. They often wait to be asked for their opinion and don't typically want to provide it off-the-cuff. Team members who want immediate answers may find this frustrating. However, it is important to have some team leaders and members with a preference for Introversion because they help the team stay focused and can provide a healthy cautiousness delaying actions that others may not be prepared to support.

Remember, everyone has the capacity for both Extraversion and Introversion—here we are simply trying to determine your natural tendency. This tendency forms the basis of your personal style. However, situations call for behaviors that may be far from what is natural or comfortable. Any natural Introvert who becomes a leader knows he or she will have to deal with people. Any natural Extravert knows that as leader he or she will need to develop plans and write reports. Your choice as a leader may be to attempt to exhibit behaviors and skills that do not feel natural or to team up with someone whose personality fits the demands of the task. What is your strategy to capitalize on your strengths and to benefit from the tendencies and talents of your teammates?

When you need to deal with people who have the same preferences as you do, it is likely to be relatively easy for you to understand one another. Yet, conflict can still occur. People with similar type preferences may end up competing for the same kind of responses. Extraverts may not like all the attention other Extraverts are receiving. Introverts may become frustrated with other Introverts who spend more time thinking about plans and not coming to the same conclusions that they have.

When people need to deal with people who have opposing preferences, conflict may arise due to lack of understanding. Extraverts tend to become frustrated with Introverts who do not respond quickly to questions at team meetings. Extraverts wonder, "Why can't we just give it a shot rather than sitting here and thinking about all this stuff?" Introverts get uncomfortable with the desire to act simply for the sake of acting. They tend to zone out at team meetings when Extraverted teammates bounce from one topic to another. Leaders of both preferences need to learn to adjust in order to match their message to all members of the team.

If you are a natural Extravert, provide some quiet time for team members to think before stating their points of view. If you have key issues you need input on, try to announce those issues prior to your team meetings so that the Introverts can think before speaking. If you simply open the floor to responses to questions you present to the team, you will probably hear mostly from the Extraverts. Instead, you might use the round-robin technique. Announce the question on which you want team input. Let members think silently for a couple of minutes and then go around the circle and ask each person to comment. Let members know that if they really don't have anything to contribute on the issue, they can pass when it is their turn.

If you are a natural Introvert, expect your Extraverted teammates to speak out on issues beyond the subject matter currently on the agenda. A leader can effectively deflect off-agenda ideas that come up using the "parking lot" charting method, capturing ideas and yet limiting team meeting time to address them. This method requires that a flip chart or white board be available in the meeting room. When an issue or concern is raised that is not strictly tied to the agenda item being discussed, the leader records it somewhere on the "parking lot" flip chart or white board so as not to lose sight of it. The group is asked to return to the current agenda item and agrees to look for an opportunity to address the "parked" issue at a future time.

Preference for Sensing (S) vs. Intuition (N)

What is your preferred approach to understanding the world around you? Do you rely primarily on your five senses—seeing, hearing, smelling, tasting, and touching (Sensing)? Do you tend to take things in and discern patterns to intuitively make sense of what is going on (Intuition)? All of us use both approaches. Use exercise 7 to help determine your natural preference in this dichotomy.

Leaders and team members who have a preference for Sensing zero in on the facts and details. They want to know what is "actually" going on. They want to focus on today's realities and use their common sense to understand the situation. Those with a preference for Intuition tend to look at situations and quickly speculate on the possibilities. They notice what could be happening, focusing on the connections and patterns between the details more than on the facts themselves. They tend to look beyond the current situation and use their creativity to focus on the future.

The work world tends to have many more Sensing types than Intuitive types. But a team will generally have both types. Those with a preference for Sensing are often frustrated by the idealism of those with a preference for Intuition. They aren't very interested in the theories and concepts underlying the business strategies. They want to know the specific steps and responsibilities to be undertaken right away. Intuitive types may find themselves frustrated by what they perceive to be resistance on the part of the Sensing types to think "outside the box." Why don't they speculate more about what could be and what should be? Intuitive types want to find the strategies for long-term success and often don't appreciate the Sensing types' focus on short-term bottom-line results.

When you are working with Sensing types, it is important that you develop the case for the need for change before presenting the new idea. Show respect for the past and don't be quick to condemn the traditional approach team members have been using up until now. Work with them to see the facts that led you to believe that something is broken and needs to be fixed. You might try to break down the change concept into its component parts; you will need to work with the Sensing types to identify a step-by-step implementation plan and a realistic time frame for the steps. Allow them to "try before they buy." Introduce innovations on a trial, pilot basis. Allow time at team meetings to pay attention to the details.

EXERCISE 7

Sensing Type (S) or
Intuitive Type (N) Checklist

Directions: *For each pair of choices, select the one that*   **Circle your**
best describes your natural tendency across most situations.   **answer**

1. Are you more interested in the actual facts of a situation?   **S**
   Or, are you more interested in the possibilities of the situation?   **N**

2. Do you tend to notice the details?   **S**
   Or, do you tend to notice the patterns?   **N**

3. Are you more patient with routines?   **S**
   Or, are you more patient with complexity?   **N**

4. Do people describe you as sensible, practical, pragmatic, and   **S**
   down-to-earth?
   Or, do they describe you as imaginative, innovative, creative,   **N**
   and idealistic?

5. Are you more present oriented and thus attend to what is   **S**
   happening here and now?
   Or, are you more future oriented and thus keep thinking about   **N**
   what could be?

6. Do you mistrust your intuition and try to prove things to your-   **S**
   self and others in a careful, step-by-step fashion?
   Or, once your intuition tells you what the answer is, are you   **N**
   even willing to ignore some facts and go with your hunches?

7. Do you consider yourself to have a lot of common sense and   **S**
   prefer people who also have a lot of common sense?
   Or, do you consider yourself creative and prefer people who   **N**
   also use a lot of creative thinking?

8. Do you find yourself responding to what people literally say?   **S**
   Or, do you find yourself reading between the lines and figuring out   **N**
   what they mean?

9. Do you value practical, hands-on experience as the best way   **S**
   to learn?
   Or, do you value learning that comes from inspiration and   **N**
   conceptualization?

When you are working with Intuitive types, allow time for brain-storming. Encourage them to look beyond what they are doing currently and speculate on far-reaching and intriguing possibilities—run wild with a discussion of what could be. Make sure time is spent on keeping things real before going forward but try not to throw a wet blanket on innovative thinking too soon. Challenge the Intuitive types to find the connections between the actions that need to be taken. Encourage them to discover the unified whole underlying team tasks and activities. Having both Sensing and Intuitive types on a team can be a dynamite combination, especially when it comes to planning and problem-solving activities. Intuitive types can help push the envelope and creatively develop new products, processes, and pathways for the team to consider. The Sensing types can take the wild and crazy speculations and identify the obstacles that need to be addressed and the steps to take to move the idea from the drawing board to reality. Both parties need to participate in "what if" thinking. Ideas need to be wiggled and shaken until a clearer image emerges and a road map to the goal is established.

Preference for Thinking vs. Feeling

The third dichotomy identified in the Myers-Briggs® typological framework has to do with how one naturally goes about making decisions. Use exercise 8 to help determine whether you have more of a natural preference for Thinking or Feeling, but remember, we are all capable of using either.

Leaders and team members who have a preference for Thinking value logic above all else. They want to use the principles of logic to come to conclusions wherever possible. They are more comfortable arguing and critiquing ideas and concepts being discussed. They can enjoy analyzing issues without taking things personally. They are often nonchalant about good work—their own as well as that of others. "Heck, isn't that what we are paid for?" This may establish a very impersonal tone and reduce the energy needed to build enthusiastic support for a change idea.

EXERCISE 8

Thinking Type (T) or
Feeling Type (F) Checklist

Directions: *For each pair of choices, select the one that best describes your natural tendency across most situations.*

Circle your answer

1. Do you prefer to use the principles of cause-and-effect logic to make conclusions?   **T**

Or, do you prefer to apply your values and beliefs to make conclusions?   **F**

2. Do you you prefer to decide whether things are either true or false and thus have a more objective orientation?   **T**

Or, do you prefer to decide first whether you agree or disagree with something and thus have a more subjective orientation?   **F**

3. Do you tend to come across as impersonal even when that is not your intention?   **T**

Or, do you tend to come across as naturally friendly unless your values are offended?   **F**

4. Do you tend to be analytical, skeptical, and questioning?   **T**
Or, do do you tend to be trusting and maybe overly accepting?   **F**

5. Are you likely to choose truth over tact and thus state things bluntly?   **T**

Or, are you likely to choose tact over truth and thus try to smooth over negative comments?   **F**

6. Do you appreciate a good argument because it allows an opportunity to get both sides of an issue out in the open?   **T**

Or, do you tend to dislike (even fear) conflict and try to keep things harmonious?   **F**

7. Is your idea of justice to treat everyone the same?   **T**
Or, is your idea of justice to treat people according to their needs?   **F**

8. Do you tend to be nonchalant about good work, your own as well as that of others?   **T**

Or, do you express appreciation readily and tend to want it, too?   **F**

9. Are you more concerned with being reasonable and focusing on the task?   **T**

Or, are you more concerned with being compassionate and focusing on relationships?   **F**

Those with a preference for Feeling tend to use their values and beliefs to come to conclusions. They examine problems and issues from a "people" point of view and think about who will like the idea and who will be against it. They are very good at letting people know they are appreciated, but they also need to feel appreciated themselves. They prize harmony and try to help establish an inclusive team spirit. They want the team to feel like one big happy family—everyone agreeing with everyone else. However, if an expressed point of view contradicts their values and beliefs, look out! They can be self-righteous, get angry, or become depressed.

When you are working with Thinking types, try to allow time to analyze and question the ideas and activities. Make sure the discussion is focused on what the problems and options are rather than who is to be blamed. Try not to get discouraged if the Thinking types calmly agree with you but fail to show much enthusiasm, or to take their criticisms personally. Be sure the discussion includes analysis of the risks involved in not taking a certain action, not just whether the action has potential flaws. Attempt to channel their competitive urge toward defeating the obstacles interfering with accomplishing team goals, not toward defeating people and other teams. Be prepared to examine the objective realities associated with your team's situations, not just your hunches and opinions.

When you are working with Feeling types, listen attentively and show respect. Be aware that sarcasm and cynicism may not be well received. Encourage Feeling types to help the team establish ethical guidelines for decision making. Feeling type leaders and members can be good at encouraging everyone to contribute. Try not to discount concerns about the stylistic and aesthetic issues associated with the situation even if you think the only thing that is important is the substance. Encourage Feeling types (especially the Extraverts) to take on the role of presenting the team's case to others in the organization. Their enthusiasm can arouse support beyond the logic underlying the case.

Preference for Judging vs. Perceiving

The final dichotomy of the Myers-Briggs typological framework identifies an important life-style attitude. Use exercise 9 to help determine whether you have a natural preference for Judging or Perceiving. Remember again that we all use both preferences to some extent.

Leaders and team members who have a preference for Judging tend to want decisions made quickly. They want to have things decided up front and then have the team fulfill those expectations. They are decisive and purposeful. They want the team to have schedules and use to-do lists. They believe in deadlines and often try to accomplish tasks early. Their greatest pleasure comes from finishing things, and they prefer a planned and orderly approach.

Those with a preference for Perceiving want to keep the team's options open as long as possible. They think life should be experienced and well understood. Their greatest pleasure comes from starting things. They contribute to team discussions by generating options to consider. However, they may come across as indecisive because they are more interested in gaining more information and possibilities than in coming to conclusions. They prefer a spontaneous approach to projects and to go where the work takes them. They are more interested in the journey than the destination. After decisions have been made, they can be prone to second-guessing.

As with all the dichotomies, neither type is better or worse—they are just different. Their differences can lead to frustration, but together they cover both ends of the spectrum. Team leaders and members who have a preference for Judging may cut off information too quickly to get the group to make a decision. When working with Judging types, set aside a sufficient time period for discussion of options to ensure that decisions are not made prematurely. Another approach is to insist that a team come up with no fewer than three options for solving the problem before it makes a decision. When Judging types know that there will not be an endless discussion of possibilities, they have a deadline to look forward to and can trust that their desire for conclusion will be satisfied.

EXERCISE 9

Judging Type (J) or
Perceiving Type (P) Checklist

Directions: *For each pair of choices, select the one that best describes your natural tendency across most situations.*

Circle your answer

1. Do you tend to push for closure in situations?   J
   Or, do you tend to push for understanding in situations?   P

2. Do you get your greatest pleasure from finishing things?   J
   Or, do you get your greatest pleasure from starting things?   P

3. Do you tend to be more decisive and purposeful?   J
   Or, do you tend to be more flexible?   P

4. Do you prefer to make the decision?   J
   Or, do you prefer to generate the options?   P

5. Do you prefer a planned and orderly approach to things?   J
   Or, do you prefer a more casual and spontaneous approach to things?   P

6. Do you like schedules and to-do lists and try to stick to them?   J
   Or, do you like to respond to things as they arise?   P

7. Do you want things decided well in advance and stick to those expectations?   J
   Or, do you want to keep your options open?   P

8. Do you take deadlines seriously and try to get things done early to avoid last-minute stress?   J
   Or, do you use deadlines as a stimulus to get started and feel energized by last-minute pressures?   P

9. Do you cut off information and make decisions quickly?   J
   Or, do you seek out lots of information, maybe even more than you need?   P

When you are working with Perceiving types, you may find that they are happy to have others make the decision as long as they can be involved in generating acceptable possibilities. Even Perceiving types begin to feel overwhelmed when there is a never-ending stream of information and possibilities. It may also help to have set time limits for brainstorming followed by procedures to rank the utility of the ideas generated. However, it may be important for the team to set a ground rule that once the decision is made, team members must not denigrate the selection outside of team meetings.

Personality Type and Leadership Style

The Sensing–Intuition (S–N) and Thinking–Feeling (T–F) dichotomies represent cognitive functions underlying one's personality. Several researchers, including Nutt (1986) and Haley and Pini (1994), have found that a person's preferences on these two dichotomies explain much about his or her approach to problem solving and decision making. Since these are core behaviors of influencing individuals and teams, it can be particularly helpful to look at the four resulting preference combinations (ST, SF, NF, NT) when examining leadership style. Exploring these combinations can help you understand some of the strengths and potential blind spots of your personality type.

"Sensible Technicians" (STs): Preferences for Sensing and Thinking

Leaders with preferences for Sensing and Thinking (STs), the "Sensible Technicians," are down-to-earth types who tend to focus on completing the list of tasks assigned to them. They tend to provide stability to a team and usually are reliable types other members can depend on. They would rather help the team fix its problems in a step-by-step fashion than throw out what the team has been doing and invent a whole new system. Sensible Technicians love common sense and want the team to deal with what is real rather than dream about the ideal. They prefer to look at facts and details. They may not love bureaucracy but they can survive it better than other types. They like things to be organized and well documented.

No one personality type demonstrates the perfect set of traits and preferences required to succeed as a leader. Many Sensible Technicians are prone to be too short-term oriented. They are so pragmatic that they tend to focus solely on the here and now and often fail to produce the long-term plans that require thinking "outside the box." They are not likely to embrace change unless they are first convinced that the system is broken. When trying to help a team with a change effort, they may take an overly cautious approach to guard against catastrophe. Their matter-of-fact manner and tendency to take good behavior for granted may fail to inspire other members of the team. Their focus on details may lead them to nitpicking and micromanaging the team's efforts.

Table 4 provides more detail about the organizational tendencies of Sensible Technicians. It utilizes the 7-S model of organizational effec tiveness described by Peters and Waterman in their book *In Search of Excellence* (1982). The model outlines ST preferences for business strat egy, structure, systems (i.e., what procedures they promote), staff (i.e., how they treat their people), style, skills, and shared values. It also pro vides a list of weaknesses Sensible Technicians may bring to the team they are trying to lead.

Sociable Facilitators (SFs): Preferences for Sensing and Feeling

Leaders with preferences for Sensing and Feeling (SFs), the "Sociable Facilitators," are often very good at helping people feel like they belong. They build teams inclusively, connecting members with other members having similar interests. They try to make sure everyone has some input. They are "people persons" and commonly care more about the relationships on the team than the tasks. Sociable Facilitators take plea sure in rescuing teammates.

TABLE 4

Organizational Tendencies of Sensible Technicians (STs)

Sensible Technicians prefer

- *Strategy* that is systematic, detailed, practical, sensible, fair, slow but steady, patient, heavily documented, and focused on one step at a time

- *Structure* that is logical and organized, hierarchical, bureaucratic, and centralized, and that has clear channels, checks and balances to reduce risks, and legalistic job descriptions

- *Systems* that include clear business procedures, routines, formats for reports, systematic data gathering, formulas for decisions, and a reliance on hard data and experience

- *Style* that conveys dependability, logic, patience, fairness, formality, decisiveness, bluntness, objectivity, and accountability; that is realistic, detail and fact oriented, matter-of-fact, and impersonal; and that plans—and then follows the plan—and reinforces compliance

- *Staff* to be managed with an awareness of headcount, categorization of employees, and clear selection criteria for each job; and hire people who respect rules and regulations, demonstrate logic and stability, and display common sense

- *Skills* that emphasize being thorough and efficient in meetings and reports, absorbing and using details and facts, and performing routines and measurement activities such as operational analysis and accounting

- *Shared values* such as logic, conservatism, stability, dependability, orderliness, practicality, punctuality, fairness, objectivity, competitiveness, efficiency, compliance with rules, and security

---

TABLE 4 CONT'D

Sensible Technicians may have weaknesses such as

- Treating strategy as an end, not as a means

- Overguarding against catastrophe

- Missing the forest for the trees; being short-sighted

- Being too impersonal and matter-of-fact

- Favoring rigid and legalistic structures, making change difficult

- Compartmentalizing in a way that leads to overspecialization

- Overrelying on formulas for conducting decision making

- Nitpicking

- Resisting innovation; having difficulty dealing with uncertainty

- Being impatient with complexity

- Forgetting to stroke people; taking staff for granted

- Rigidly adhering to plans

SF tendencies can also produce blind spots. In leadership positions Sociable Facilitators may be perceived as softhearted and suckers for lost souls. They enjoy socializing and tend to know a lot about everyone. Sometimes they are accused of being busybodies or gossipers. Sociable Facilitators tend to be uncomfortable with conflict. This leads them to overuse strategies of avoidance and accommodation to smooth over conflicts. Table 5 further elaborates their organizational tendencies including strengths and possible weaknesses.

TABLE 5

Organizational Tendencies of Sociable Facilitators (SFs)

Sociable Facilitators prefer

- *Strategy* that emphasizes values and considers personal reactions; that is also detailed, systematic, slow but steady, down-to-earth, present oriented, and based on verifiable facts and experiences

- *Structure* that is family oriented and centralized; one with many channels to funnel input and clarify expectations and decision-making procedures

- *Systems* in which routines are established and followed; where reports follow a format but include a personal perspective, and where input—including facts, details, opinions, examples, reactions, and so on—is sought from the people, not impersonal sources of information

- *Style* that conveys consideration, compassion, thoroughness, fairness, dependability, tolerance, participation, support, practicality, compromise, and an attitude of live and let live; that is slow but ensures that all members have their say

- *Staff* to be managed with an awareness of headcount and whether people feel they belong; and mold people to accept company values, emphasize training and development opportunities, and facilitate interaction among staff members

- *Skills* that emphasize absorbing and using details and facts about people, human resources and development, marketing and customer service, interpersonal relationships, developing routines, and patching up systems

- *Shared values* such as affiliation, fairness, appropriate behavior, trust, loyalty, harmony, pragmatism, the golden rule, tradition, cooperation, and a sense that anyone can succeed if they only try

---

TABLE 5 CONT'D

Sociable Facilitators may have weaknesses such as

- Treating strategy as an end, not as a means
- Being overconcerned with people and having softhearted tendencies
- Resisting change
- Perpetuating positions beyond their usefulness
- Oversimplifying problems
- Nitpicking
- Avoiding conflict
- Naïvely believing that all you have to do is work hard
- Missing the forest for the trees; being short-sighted
- Being a busybody, trying to please everybody, or playing favorites
- Being uncomfortable with complex or abstract situations
- Being passive-aggressive or self-righteous when offended

Noble Funlovers (NFs):
Preferences for Intuition and Feeling

Leaders with preferences for Intuition and Feeling (NFs), the "Noble Funlovers," tend to focus on the big picture and the values of the organization. They believe in the cause and in people's important role in forwarding that cause. They are often terrific communicators and can inspire their followers, provoking change and cheering on efforts to do what is right. They want systems that are aesthetically and ethically pleasing, and they want us all to have fun while doing so. They are strong supporters of training and development opportunities for their people.

TABLE 6

Organizational Tendencies of Noble Funlovers (NFs)

Noble Funlovers prefer

- *Strategy* that is innovative, creative, based on values, future oriented, communicated to all, and people oriented; that emphasizes development and relationships, acquires resources, and has contingencies built in to cover personal concerns

- *Structure* that is ad hoc, loose, organic, flat, and decentralized; that includes growth-oriented job descriptions

- *Systems* that are flexible and unstructured; that allow for personal judgment and hunches, use brainstorming sessions to discover alternatives, and promote open channels to facilitate quick and easy communication between all levels

- *Style* that is idealistic, enthusiastic, charismatic, dramatic, sociable, and personable and includes high-energy bursts; that promotes democratic participation, evolution, compromise, the smoothing over of conflicts, the expression of appreciation, and leaving decisions open to modification

- *Staff* to be managed by pushing development and the use of potential, selecting people who fit in, and finding the good in all

- *Skills* such as communication, empathy, and the ability to see both sides of issues; those with a customer service or public relations bent

- *Shared values* such as harmony, cooperation, loyalty, creativity, development, stimulation, variety, autonomy, authenticity, and the belief that people are good and important

TABLE 6 CONT'D

Noble Funlovers may have weaknesses such as

- Having a high need for approval; avoiding conflict
- Being overly emotional or dramatic
- Being moralistic
- Overextending
- Creating dependencies
- Having difficulty enforcing discipline; trying to rescue lost souls
- Being naïve or overly trusting
- Overemphasizing enthusiasm; working in bursts
- Being poor at noticing the details
- Having too many direct reports
- Being too flexible and/or inconsistent
- Reinventing the wheel
- Failing to follow through and meet deadlines
- Being overly influenced by personal likes and dislikes
- Talking too much

NFs typically have some blind spots, too. Their attraction to aesthetics and inspiration may overwhelm the substance of the tasks to be performed. The idealism of these Noble Funlovers may turn into self-righteousness when they confront members who violate their personal standards. Their flair for being fun loving and/or dramatic may turn off or frighten their more staid teammates. While they can be great communicators, sometimes they just talk too much. Table 6 further elaborates their organizational tendencies including strengths and possible weaknesses.

Novel Transformers (NTs):
Preferences for Intuition and Thinking

Leaders with preferences for Intuition and Thinking (NTs), the "Novel Transformers," seek more perfect systems. They are often visionary leaders dissatisfied with the status quo—constantly thinking about what a team or organization could be or should be like. They are the architects of progress, designing frameworks and systems to produce results. They prize and demand competency in themselves and others, with high standards and a focus on the big picture and the future.

Like all leaders, Novel Transformers have their blind spots, too. They tend to find it hard not to show disappointment, even disdain, for repeated mistakes. They are often accused of being too idealistic and too demanding because their mind races ahead and keeps escalating expectations of the team. They may seem more interested in the challenge than in savoring successes. Table 7 further elaborates their organizational tendencies including strengths and possible weaknesses.

You now have a foundation for understanding your personality through the framework of the *Myers-Briggs Type Indicator* instrument. Your personality will show up in your efforts to provide leadership to your organization and your team. You have been provided ideas regarding what your natural strengths and weaknesses may be. You have also been provided suggestions on how to work with various type preferences on teams. What will you do with what you have learned? Use exercise 10 in conjunction with the after-chapter review to plan how to capitalize on what you now know about your personality.

TABLE 7

Organizational Tendencies of Novel Transformers (NTs)

Novel Transformers prefer

- *Strategy* that is goal and future oriented, innovative, theoretical; that takes calculated risks and sees the big picture; that provides a plan for others to execute

- *Structure* that is complex, decentralized, transitional; that provides enough order to encourage productivity

- *Systems* that are flexible but rational, focus on results not procedures, gather information fast and use it to gain a sense of progress; that expedite information to the decision makers

- *Style* that conveys confidence and a sense that anything is possible; that is blunt, impersonal; that provides meaning and direction; and act as the architect of progress/ideas, the revolutionary, and frequently ask the question "Why?"

- *Staff* to be managed in an impersonal way that demands competency, indicates high expectations, and is responsive to new ideas; that can execute plans

- *Skills* that emphasize research and development, logic, efficiency, planning

- *Shared values* such as change, innovation, competency, nonconformity, logic, need for achievement, appreciation for profound and complex solutions

---

TABLE 7 CONT'D

Novel Transformers may have weaknesses such as

- Losing interest

- Being elitist

- Failing to follow through or meet deadlines

- Being restless

- Escalating standards

- Being confrontative and argumentative

- Being critical and impatient with repeat mistakes

- Finding it difficult to shift focus

- Spending too much time planning

- Leaving structures and procedures too vague

- Requiring praise while forgetting to praise others

Summary

This chapter covered what people in the field feel are the important bases of knowledge, skills, and personal qualities (including personality) that a leader brings to a team. No person can possess all that talent. The key to using this chapter is to identify your strengths and extend them to help your team members help themselves. You can also use this chapter to recognize the talents of your teammates. Instead of trying to be all things to all people, partner with others and maximize the use of the collective talents available. Leadership in a team environment is a collaborative, participative process.

EXERCISE 10

Capitalizing on Your Personality Preferences

Directions: Answer the following questions about your personality in the space provided.

1. **Describe your personality**—not just the letters of your Myers-Briggs type, but the qualities of your personality that you feel best describe your natural tendencies.

2. **Identify situations** where your natural tendencies are likely to help improve a situation or a relationship on your team.

3. **Produce a plan** that includes a scenario of how you will approach a situation or a relationship and apply the natural tendencies of your personality.

4. **Identify a situation** where the natural tendencies of your personality or those of one of your teammates might produce an obstacle to success. What could you do to improve this situation?

AFTER-CHAPTER REVIEW

Now that you have completed reading this chapter, it is time for you to challenge yourself to see what you remember, establish what it is you learned, and decide where and how you are going to apply what you learned. The outline provided below can help you get started. The relevancy of this chapter may necessitate that you expand on your thoughts elsewhere. Make sure you benefit from your reading by capturing your thoughts and turning them into actions.

1. Describe at least five things you remember from the material in this chapter.

-
-
-
-
-

2. Identify the insights you gained from reading the material in this chapter. These insights may have come directly from the points raised or by stimulating recollections of your own experiences.

-
-
-

3. Identify at least one situational opportunity for applying what you learned and describe the steps to be taken (including who will do what with whom, where, and when).

Situational opportunity:

Steps to be taken:

-
-
-
-

EFFECTIVE TEAMBUILDING

Launching or Growing Your Team

•

Sometimes you get to choose who will be on your team and other times the team's members are inherited. It can be compared to running a sports team, where the general manager, with input from the coach, has three strategies to choose from: (1) use the draft or obtain free agents to staff the team; (2) keep the existing members but reassign them to positions that better fit their skills; or (3) spend a lot of time and attention on the development of members' skills at their current position.

The Detroit Red Wings hockey team went from being one of the worst teams in the eighties— locals referred to them as the "Dead Wings"— to perennial contenders for the Stanley Cup in the nineties and beyond. General Manager Ken Holland and owner Mike Illitch helped Sergei Federov defect from Russia and become a star center for the team. They brought along top draft choices to ensure that all four lines had the ability to contribute. They acquired free agents including Brett Hull to fill out an all-star lineup. And they appointed Steve Yzerman captain to set the tone of hard work and excellence. Finally, they recruited the most successful head coach in the league, Scotty Bowman, to establish a system to utilize the talent. They selected the people they felt would produce a successful team.

In 1968 baseball's Detroit Tigers finally made it to the World Series after many years of frustration. They had accomplished this feat with a shortstop who could field his position well but who was barely hitting his weight (i.e., under a .200 batting average), and they had four very good outfielders, including Al Kaline and Mickey Stanley, but only three outfield positions to fill. In their quest to become a world champion, they decided to reassign Stanley, a good hitter, to play shortstop during the World Series. He played flawlessly, and this bold move benefited the whole team—they won the World Series. They brought a team to excellence by placing the players they had in positions that best benefited the team.

George Wills devotes a whole chapter in his book *Men at Work* to Cal Ripken Jr. of the Baltimore Orioles—a great example of a player developing his skills at his position to help make his team great. Ripken built a batting cage in his own basement to practice hitting all year long. During the season, he would dedicate ten to twenty minutes of practice time each day to fielding difficult

ground balls in the hole instead of having balls hit
right to him as most players do. Although Ripken
was the most recognizable star on his team, he
continually worked hard at improving his skills to
help his team move toward excellence.

•

A team can achieve excellence by selecting people who will bring success to the team, by placing current members in positions that will
best benefit the team, or by having members continually develop the
skills needed to become great at their position. Which strategy would
be best for building your team?

Definition of Team

If you are a leader in an organization hoping to benefit from a team
concept, it is inevitable that you will be asked to recruit and/or help a
group of individuals become a more effective team. The word *team*
comes from the Latin root *deuk,* which means "to pull." A group of
individuals is not a team unless they pull together to reach a common
goal. *Team* tends to be used loosely in many organizations, where
management often blithely declares, "We are all one big team." While
the sentiment for cooperation may be admirable, such statements do
little to produce the behaviors needed to really succeed as a team.
Other companies claim to have a team concept, but all they have done
is change the word they use to describe a unit from *department* to
team. It's even more disturbing to see organizations anointing any
group that meets on a somewhat regular basis as a team. It may be a
good idea to share information across individuals and functions, but
let's not call a group a team unless it requires the *interactive* use of the
skills of a *small* group of people working in an *interdependent* manner
to accomplish *common* goals. If these features do not exist, you don't
really have a team.

The Three Types of Teams in Organizations

Three types of teams have had a decent track record in helping organizations succeed: problem-solving teams, self-directed work teams, and leadership teams. Problem-solving teams are probably the most prevalent, though they are known by many names (e.g., rapid improvement teams, employee involvement teams, etc.). Basically they are permanent committees or temporary task forces bringing together the diverse skills, knowledge, and backgrounds of people to identify and analyze organizational problems and make recommendations for what could improve situations. They typically only have the right to make recommendations, while management reserves the right to decide whether to go forward with their ideas. Since the 1980s this type of team has become common in business practice. The old practice of separating the doing of the work from the thinking about the work is finally fading away in most organizations. Workers today are less likely to be required to "check their brains at the plant gate." Managers realize they benefit from the wisdom of those people closer to the action. Your job as a leader may be to facilitate the formation, development, and maintenance of such teams.

During the 1990s and into this century, we have also seen the rise of so-called self-directed work teams (SDWTs). These are groups of employees brought together to make things or deliver services. They are given the power to make decisions, not just recommendations, at least within the parameters established by management. No team operates independently from the realities of the organization that formed it. Thus SDWTs appear quite different depending on the organization in which they reside. Here are some of the ideal characteristics of SDWTs:

- Being collectively responsible for an identifiable piece of the business
- Receiving clear metrics daily to verify progress
- Consisting of members with varying skills, abilities, and problem-solving strategies

- Exhibiting little or no status differences among members
- Providing opportunities to interact—to meet easily and frequently
- Establishing interdependent job responsibilities
- Offering cross-training or at least cross-education for all jobs on the team
- Having the authority to make decisions on how to get the work done
- Providing a mixture of individual and group rewards
- Making available the help and encouragement of external coaches and resource people

In some companies, SDWTs have reduced or eliminated the need for supervision and have distributed the duties formerly fulfilled by representatives of management across the team members themselves. Oftentimes the team is expected to elect a peer to be the point person interacting with other departments, teams, and levels of management. The organization may provide an area manager who oversees the work of several SDWTs and helps resolve any disciplinary issues that arise within any of the teams. Studies have shown that on average SDWTs outproduce traditional work groups. However, success is dependent on how these teams are implemented. If you are in an organization utilizing the SDWT concept of teams, are you prepared to help them grow and mature? If you have been recently elected team leader, are you prepared to influence your peers?

The use of a leadership team at the top of an organization has also become more prevalent in recent years. The CEO (or facility manager) and his or her direct reports attempt to use their collective wisdom in the development of strategies to run the business. In some unionized settings, a joint steering committee is formed to gain the input of top union leaders and top-level managers. The idea is that one's business strategy must represent the integration of the perspectives of all the functions. Business life is more complex than ever—no one person can be an expert in so many areas. Allowing each area to run its own function has produced isolated silos and failed to gain the synergy needed to compete in today's marketplace. Teams of leaders are asked to pull together to produce strategic plans and make organizational decisions. Many of the tools provided throughout this book can help make these powerful teams succeed. Chapter 11 is dedicated to examining the unique issues in providing leadership for these leadership teams.

Teambuilding and the Stages of Team Development

Effective leaders match their style and behavior to the situations they face. Hersey and Blanchard (1996) point out that when teams are new to the situation and do not know each other very well, it is better for the leader to be able to tell people what needs to be done and how to do it. As the team matures as a unit and gains experience in doing the tasks, the leader should shift to selling ideas about how to do things and to work together. Once the team becomes familiar with the work and each other, the leader participates with the team, identifying problems and options but ensuring that the input of team members and the leader is utilized in any decisions affecting activities. Ultimately, the leader delegates responsibility to the team to decide how to get the work done in a collaborative manner, while the leader skillfully provides the connection with the larger organization by clarifying expectations, gaining resources, and recognizing the team's accomplishments. Thus the level of maturity of a team determines which leadership style is most effective.

All teams tend to go through various stages as they develop. Perhaps the best-known model for these stages was developed by Tuckman and Jensen (1977), as follows:

1. **Forming:** Clarifying the task and getting the members acquainted

2. **Storming:** Encouraging the expression of different points of view in a constructive manner and resolving the natural competition for influence among the team members

3. **Norming:** Establishing the team's standards for performance and the unwritten rules that govern members' behaviors

4. **Performing:** Accomplishing the tasks and fulfilling the team's mission

5. **Closing:** Disbanding the team

In reality, things are not quite that cut-and-dried, but the model does serve as a useful framework for determining the help teams may need as they mature. Whenever the organization provides a deadline for accomplishing a task, the team will attempt to jump to the Performing stage. The model lays out the kinds of things teambuilding sessions should facilitate to produce a team capable of delivering up to its maximum potential when performing.

Helping Teams Through the Forming Stage

If you are being asked to help launch a new team in your organization, you will need to identify the team's membership and its purpose. Chapter 4 will provide you with valuable tools, such as team chartering, to identify purpose, goals, responsibilities, procedures, and ground rules to get the team off on the right foot. As a leader, you need to provide a means for getting the team organized to accomplish the tasks it was formed to achieve. You need to help the team understand why it exists in your organization.

The other side of the Forming stage is recruiting and selecting the members of the team. You need to help identify people to handle the job responsibilities and to build respectful and trusting relationships with each other. If you have the opportunity to influence who will be on the team, you will want to ensure that the range of technical skills needed to accomplish the tasks is represented. In addition, thought should be given to which constituencies are likely to be affected by the work this team will be asked to do. To gain political clout and the subsequent commitment to implement the ideas generated by the team, representatives from these stakeholders could be included. Politics will always be involved to some extent in the selection of team members, especially on committees and task forces. Don't forget to include an examination of the interpersonal skills needed to help your team succeed. This is especially important if you are hiring new employees to form this team. If your organization is serious about using a team concept as a key strategy and structure for building a better company, then you need to include team skills as part of your selection procedures as you search for the "right" people to join the team. What talent, knowledge, and personal qualities are needed? What protocol and organizational politics should be kept in mind when selecting members for the team? Table 8 lists some things you should consider in the selection of team members.

The first meeting of your new team should have both a task and a relationship component. The task component would involve having the members understand (or establish/negotiate) the team's charter. It would be useful to have a representative from senior management attend this portion of the meeting to further establish the importance of the team being formed. The establishment of a team charter will be covered thoroughly in chapter 4. The other half of this first team meeting should be dedicated to having the members get acquainted with each other. There are many ways to do this. You might consider having team members pair up and interview each other and then act as a "designated bragger" for their new teammate. This reduces the inhibition of having to say great things about oneself and it establishes that everyone needs to speak up at team meetings. I have found that even shy team members want to make sure they do not let their new-found friend down.

A more common practice is to have members introduce themselves to their teammates. It is useful to establish a document that captures the collective talents that exist on your team. It is motivating to see that you are part of a body that includes so much knowledge and talent. Here are a few questions to help inventory the talents of the team:

- What knowledge bases exist on this team?
- What skill bases exist on this team?

TABLE 8

Selecting Members for the Team

With the purpose of the team firmly in mind, the following guidelines can help you get the "right" people on the team. What talent, knowledge, and personal qualities are needed? What protocol and organizational politics should be considered?

- Who should select the members of the team?
- Can selectees decline the opportunity?
- How will the criteria for membership be established?
- In addition to subject matter expertise, are there other skills and qualities that should typically be considered when selecting members for a team?
- Should there be different categories of membership (e.g., resource people, full members, team leader, etc.)?
- How should those selected be notified?
- How should managers of the selectees be notified?
- Since membership on a team will require time away from members' other duties, what should be done to clarify priorities and enhance members' ability to manage time?
- To what information should team members have access to help them serve as a representative on a cross-functional team?
- How should the activities of members on a team be considered when performance reviews are administered?
- What organizational systems should routinely be examined to ensure alignment when launching a new team?

- What knowledge and/or skill bases might be missing? To whom can we turn to fill in the gaps?

Exercise 11 provides another way for members to get to know each other. It asks each member to develop a personal "coat of arms" as a

EXERCISE 11

Personal "Coat of Arms"

The purpose of this exercise is to get team members to reveal information about who they are as a person in a fun and symbolic manner.

Directions for team members:

1. Draw a coat of arms divided into four sections as shown, enlarged to fill an 8½ x 11" sheet of paper. The sections could be designated in advance by the facilitator, or team members could be asked for their preferences.

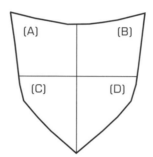

Examples:

- (A) key relationships, (B) work experience, (C) education, (D) values or personality

- (A) past, (B) present, (C) short-term future, (D) long-term future

- (A) skills, (B) knowledge, (C) personal qualities/values, (D) aspirations/hopes/dreams

You might also make up your own four sections.

2. Fill each portion with drawings, small pictures cut out of magazines, and a key word or two.

3. Present your personal coat of arms to the other participants and explain the symbolism behind the things you included.

4. Respond to questions from the other participants.

5. State what you learned about yourself and what you learned about the others who participated.

means of sharing personal information with others. Directions should be provided to team members in advance so that they can prepare their coat of arms and use the meeting time to present it to their new teammates. You can also make this a fun activity for everyone to do at the session itself. Bring in lots of magazines from which people can cut out pictures—many people are inhibited about drawing pictures. Do what you can to produce a friendly, supportive atmosphere. Remember, the purpose of this exercise is for members to get acquainted, not to judge artistic talent.

Helping Teams Through the Storming Stage

It is natural for teams to experience some conflict. A major benefit of using a team approach is having differing points of view to consider. This leads to competition for influence. As a leader, you can help the team learn how to handle constructively the resulting arguments and discussions. You can help by letting the team know that conflict is natural. You can help by channeling members' competitive urges toward the accomplishment of the team goal instead of toward each other. The more specific the goals, the easier this will be. Training sessions for developing conflict resolution skills may be required. Chapter 7 provides material and tools for such sessions.

Helping Teams Through the Norming Stage

The best teams choose how they are going to conduct business. They have a methodology for how they will hold meetings, solve problems, make decisions, and go about their tasks. While there is no one best way to do any of these procedures, discussing and agreeing on an approach to them and then seeing that everyone on the team actually uses it helps build belief in the team. Trust is developed through actions, not words, so here is a chance to gain members' trust. Team members with a high need for achievement may be reluctant to count on the team to deliver. They may secretly feel, "If it is going to be, it is up to me." Later they may complain that others are not doing their fair share of the tasks. Perhaps the real problem is that the team does not have norms for how to conduct these procedures or standards for performance. Your job as leader is to help them establish these norms and standards, perhaps by

- Updating the team charter
- Sending team members to training sessions on problem solving, decision making, and running effective meetings, and then expecting them to practice what they learn in the sessions
- Providing awareness and feedback about the processes that have already evolved

Table 9 includes a list of team norms I have helped teams identify about themselves. Some they have wanted to keep and some they have decided to try to change.

Have your team use this list as well as its own observations to determine which norms describe how it operates. Many norms and procedures seem to materialize unconsciously. Your job is to help your team become conscious of them. Facilitate a discussion about whether the team wants to continue following the norms identified or to change them. What standards does your team want to live up to? How can members of the team monitor whether their behavior is living up to these standards? Help your team help itself.

Helping Teams Through the Performing Stage

Team members need to know the score. As a leader in a team environment, what can you do to help the team know whether it is accomplishing the goals and progressing according to plan? Many companies are providing boards near each team's work space with more information on productivity and quality than was traditionally provided to the workforce. What can you do to help team members comprehend the information provided? How can you help ensure that information is updated in a timely fashion? How can you remind members of the commitments they made during problem-solving efforts? The key to the leader's role during the Performing stage is letting members do their

TABLE 9

Norms Commonly Found on Teams

- Our team outproduces any other team.

- Meetings must start and end on time.

- Seniority rules.

- If someone misses a meeting, a person is designated to bring the absent person up to speed.

- Don't touch each other's belongings.

- Meetings should be kept informal.

- Getting it done is more important than getting it right.

- Let's not have any arguments.

- If someone looks unhappy, leave him or her alone.

- As long as you seem to be trying hard, results aren't that important.

- If you don't say anything at the meeting, you must have agreed with whatever was decided.

- The boss ultimately decides.

- Everyone should have to do an equal amount of undesirable work.

- All decisions must be voted on.

- If we can't decide unanimously, then we postpone the decision.

- Never snitch on a teammate.

- Don't volunteer.

TABLE 9 CONT'D

- You only need to show up at a meeting if you are responsible for presenting something.

- Always follow the chain of command.

- Stick with your own kind.

- Don't take things too seriously.

- If things are going wrong, it must be management's fault.

- We may have ten people on this team, but two of us do most of the work.

- Just show up.

- You don't have to follow the agenda if there is something you really want to bring up.

- Swearing, sarcasm, and cynicism are tolerated.

- We keep getting better and better.

---

work and providing feedback on the team's progress against the expectations. Chapter 10 provides more detailed advice on the data that should be collected for evaluating the outcomes and processes of your team during the Performing stage.

Helping Teams Through the Closing Stage

Tuckman and Jensen's (1977) revised model of stages of group development suggests that there are common behavioral reactions to the realization that a team will soon be disbanded. When the team has completed its task, the leader can help bring about positive closure to the team's experience in a number of ways. The team should feel appreciated for its efforts and be recognized by management for the degree to which it has accomplished its tasks. Problem-solving teams will also

TABLE 10

After-Action Review

After each significant event in a team's life, 15–60 minutes should be dedicated to documenting and learning from the experience. The six questions listed below, modeled after the U.S. Army's approach, can be used to match the needs and opportunities presented by the team concept in your organization.

- What was the intent of the action that was taken?

- What actually happened?

- What did we learn from that experience?

- What do we do now, knowing what we know?

- What is our detailed plan to put our learning into practice?

- Who should we tell about what we have learned, and how do we get that story to them?

want to feel assured that their ideas will be implemented. Perhaps most important, team members and the organization as a whole will benefit from spending time identifying the lessons learned, which could be used to improve future team efforts.

But you really shouldn't wait until the Closing stage to identify these lessons. Many organizations now insist on teams adhering to a system that regularly identifies lessons learned and makes those lessons available to other teams as well. The U.S. Army's procedure known as "after-action review" is now being copied by many business organizations (see table 10). The after-chapter reviews in this book are based on it. Establishing some sort of debriefing system will help your organization learn from the experience of its teams and make members feel that they are part of the system.

It should be noted that the Closing stage of a team's existence may produce changes in the behavior of some members as the time approaches to disband the team. Some members may experience separation anxiety. Others who have been relatively inactive may suddenly try to contribute ideas as they see the opportunity slipping away. Sometimes teams come to the point where they have solved those problems within their control but now see other problems they wish the organization would address. This may produce frustration. If members continue to meet and focus on what cannot be addressed, they may become angry or depressed. This is not conducive to the future success of the team concept. If you cannot get management to expand the scope of the team's charter, you may need to suggest disbanding the team. Again, the best you can do is provide a sense of genuine celebration for what has been accomplished and the opportunity to learn from the team's experience. Leaders sometimes have to help people experience the wisdom of letting go. Help them understand and address the things they can control and understand and let go of the things they cannot—and feel the wisdom of knowing the difference between the two.

Experiencing the Magic of Teams

Sometimes teams just seem to magically generate the right "chemistry," but there are reasons for the magic. It doesn't just happen. As team leader, your job is to help team members understand the task and develop the procedures and relationships needed to succeed. Teambuilding is not just a matter of getting people to get along with each other—and effective teams do more than solve problems and do their jobs. A balance between being task oriented and relationship oriented is required. Don't think of one being more important than the other. In fact, as leader, you will need to be both task and relationship oriented at the same time. Leadership is the X-factor. As leader, you should be aware of the seven key components of team excellence:

1. **Clear goals and sense of direction.** The purpose is clear, the goals are challenging and stated in specific terms, and all members are committed to accomplishing them.

2. **Identification of talent.** You determine what talent exists on the team and whether it is being utilized and continually developed.

3. **Clear roles and responsibilities.** Each member knows his or her role on the team and how it helps the team succeed.

4. **Agreed-upon procedures.** These are established for getting tasks done, for planning, for making decisions, for holding meetings, and especially for problem solving.

5. **Constructive interpersonal relations.** Members show each other respect, differences are celebrated, everyone communicates, and conflicts are resolved.

6. **Active reinforcement of team-orientated behaviors.** Recognition is provided for members' living up to their responsibilities, especially for helping out teammates.

7. **Diplomatic external ties.** The team purposely nurtures positive relationships with other teams, key managers and union leaders, and key "customers."

Components 1, 2, 3, 4, and 6 are more useful in dealing with the task aspects of team development. On the relationship side, components 5 and 7 are the most important.

Motivations Underlying Team Development Sessions

When is the right time to do teambuilding? The real answer to this question is that teambuilding (or team deteriorating) is happening all the time. Any time you and team members become aware of how the group of individuals is attempting to pull together and learn from that awareness, you are engaged in teambuilding. However, in most organizations teambuilding is perceived as an event, a series of events, or perhaps team training sessions. There are some very admirable motivations for arranging such events and some devious ones, too. Hopefully, the overriding reason to engage in a teambuilding activity or event is to develop a more effective and satisfying group that is working together to accomplish something. This should involve evaluating where the team is and planning for what may be next. It is often offered when the team is first formed to sell the members on the benefits of working as a team or to get acquainted with each other and the expectations the organization has for the team. Another popular time to offer teambuilding is when the team seems to be stuck. Someone perceives that there is a problem, the team engages in some diagnostic activity, and it then develops the plans needed to remove the pain it is experiencing.

Remember, effective teams have both a task and a relationship function to fulfill. It is best if every teambuilding effort reflects both orientations. In many, if not most, organizations, *teambuilding* is a code word for developing better relations—and often involves resolving some conflict between members or to help the members "bond." I am aware of work and leadership teams being sent to outdoor adventure camps together where they have to discover how to scale walls and get their team across difficult terrain. I know of organizational teams that have been sent to car race tracks and expected to learn how to operate as a pit crew and as race drivers. These activities can be fun and exciting and may provide people with a whole new framework for viewing one another. Breakthroughs can occur and people may learn to appreciate members whom they did not respect before. Teammates can see how they need to pull together to solve problems and to overcome difficult obstacles.

However, if you use these methods of teambuilding, be sure that sufficient time is spent analyzing what was learned about the team and how the members will apply what they learned to the assigned organizational tasks they are expected to perform on the job. Too often, teambuilding adventures are fun (or scary) escapes from work that do not result in improvements in performance and satisfaction levels. Some personality types thrive on the excitement, while others feel threatened. If you are going to invest in this type of approach—often an expensive investment—be sure the learning is applied. The structured significant emotional events this approach provides can create attitude changes and a sense of bonding, but that does not ensure that the team will be better at doing its assignments, better at holding meetings, or better at resolving conflicts.

Another warning may be in order here. Some organizations provide teambuilding efforts involving all the members when really the issue is that there is one weak member or one or two people in conflict. Conflict resolution strategies are discussed in chapter 7. You may want to consider using some of the tools provided there instead of a teambuilding event involving all members. Otherwise, it may feel like teambuilding is a punishment that members must endure because one or two people are causing problems. It may also feel like the best way to get attention in this organization is to be a squeaky wheel. I have seen many times where teams spend 90 percent of their energy dealing with 10 percent of their members. I have also seen team members give up if one or two fellow members seem to be getting away with doing less work. Certainly equity and accountability are important, but performance management techniques such as those described in chapter 8 may provide more appropriate interventions than the kind that take up everybody's time at some teambuilding event.

Teambuilding events have also been used by organizations to soften up members prior to negotiations or some major change that may adversely impact them. Teambuilding events have been scheduled because customers have insisted on their suppliers offering such events. Teambuilding has been offered because some certification desired by the organization requires documentation that such events have occurred. Business fads come and go, and sometimes teambuilding events are offered because it seems like a "cool thing to do." It is an attempt to reward people with some fun. I have seen companies designate dinners, trips to ball games, picnics, and happy hour at the local bar as their teambuilding efforts. I am not suggesting that these events cannot be helpful. I am only asking that you question whether people learn something through your event that they then can be expected to use when they return to their jobs. Take teambuilding seriously.

The best teambuilding efforts are conceived as an ongoing process to establish or apply some systematic approach to getting people to work together successfully. The events must be grounded in the work the team is expected to accomplish. The events are like practice sessions similar to the practice sessions sports teams use to prepare for game day. My earlier book *Tools for Team Excellence* (1996) includes some exercises and activities for addressing each of the seven key components of team excellence in addition to those provided here. Since the publication of that book, I have conducted many training sessions for team leaders and trainers. I have facetiously asked them to go to the mountaintop, consult with any burning bushes, and come down with the "Ten Commandments for Teambuilding." Table 11 presents a composite of some of their best thinking.

It has already been emphasized that teambuilding efforts need to be a series of ongoing events. Exercise 12 provides an opening exercise to be used in every session after the first one. Every session is a test of whether actions are following words. Thus each session becomes a great opportunity to gain credibility for the team concept at your company.

Summary

The use of teams in organizational settings is no longer a new strategy. However, there are as many poor examples of the use of teams as there are good ones. Problem-solving teams, self-directed work teams, and leadership teams have proven to be successful business strategies for many companies. But when management merely declares that "we are

---

TABLE 11

The Ten Commandments of Teambuilding

  I. Thou shalt not form teams for teams' sake.

  II. Thou shalt address the task and the relationship side of
  every team effort.

  III. Thou shalt conduct a needs assessment before proceeding
  with teambuilding.

  IV. Thou shalt use a model of team effectiveness (e.g., the seven
  key components of team excellence) to ensure that all team
  elements are considered.

  V. Thou shalt tailor each teambuilding effort to the needs
  of the team.

  VI. Thou shalt prepare the organization and its systems to
  benefit and support the teambuilding effort.

  VII. Thou shalt have the whole team present for each team
  building session.

  VIII. Thou shalt not make the teambuilding a one-shot effort.

  IX. Thou shalt not count on training alone to build effective
  teams.

  X. Thou shalt not expect perfect teams—continuous improvement is the religion of success with teams.

---

all one big team" or that former departments are now to be known as teams, they are doomed to failure. Teams must be built and maintained. This chapter has described elements for leadership to emphasize at various stages of a team's development. Your ability to help a team examine and improve on the seven key components of team excellence provides the X-factor for success. Help your teams help themselves.

EXERCISE 12

Teambuilding As an Ongoing Effort

Directions: *Answer the questions below individually and as a team at the beginning of each teambuilding session. Keep in mind that the first session provided the opportunity to learn more about each team member, examine collective strengths and weaknesses, and develop some plans, and for each individual to commit to some behaviors that would help this team. The following questions are a follow-up to ensure that the team is on the right track.*

1. What was something you learned (or relearned) about yourself, a teammate, or this team in general during the previous session?

2. What attitudinal and/or behavioral changes have you attempted since our last teambuilding session to help this team become a bit more effective or satisfying? What were the consequences of your efforts?

3. Which teammates have you seen attempting things to help this team? What did they do? What were the consequences?

4. What do you now believe are the key strengths and the key weaknesses of this team?

5. What needs to happen in today's session to help this team to continue to improve?

AFTER-CHAPTER REVIEW

Now that you have completed reading this chapter, it is time for you to challenge yourself to see what you remember, establish what it is you learned, and decide where and how you are going to apply what you learned. The outline provided below can help you get started. The relevancy of this chapter may necessitate that you expand on your thoughts elsewhere. Make sure you benefit from your reading by capturing your thoughts and turning them into actions.

1. Describe at least five things you remember from the material in this chapter.

   •

   •

   •

   •

   •

2. Identify the insights you gained from reading the material in this chapter. These insights may have come directly from the points raised or by stimulating recollections of your own experiences.

   •

   •

   •

3. Identify at least one situational opportunity for applying what you learned and describe the steps to be taken (including who will do what with whom, where, and when).

   Situational opportunity:

   Steps to be taken:

   •

   •

   •

   •

CHAPTER 4

KNOWING WHY
THE TEAM EXISTS

Leading the Way to Clear Goals

•

At one organization, management and the union agreed to form a series of committees to enable all employees to influence key decisions in its operations. They established production committees to determine product mix and production goals to meet customer needs. They established personnel committees to participate in hiring, performance review, and promotional decisions. And they established "advisory" committees to review budget information and strategic planning in each department of the company.

But advisory committee work became ambiguous. Some department heads shared budgetary information regularly, and some waited to be asked. In a couple of departments, the advisory committee collected money for a "flower fund" for members and their families in times of sickness and death or at celebratory times such as weddings and births. In some departments, the advisory committee emerged as the committee in charge of scheduling major meetings for planning or for holiday celebrations. In fact some departments started referring to their advisory committees as "welfare committees." Other committees chose improving morale as their key goal, but meetings became complaint sessions about managers. The union became concerned that advisory committee members were taking over the stewards' role. Over time, fewer people wanted to be on the advisory committee. Ultimately, advisory committees became the weak link in this company's team concept.

•

The story above includes several valuable lessons. First, it is important that the purpose of each team established be made clear. Second, as things evolve over time, management (and union leadership, if any) must continue to manage. You cannot set up teams—even self-directed teams—and then let them get involved in whatever way they want. Third, it helps if the name given to the team clearly reflects its mission. This chapter provides ideas and tools for ensuring that every team in your organization has a clear sense of direction. This is the most important component in any team system seeking excellence.

Developing a Clear Sense of Direction: The Team Charter

The single most important thing you can do as team leader is to help in clarifying your team's goals. Teams exist in organizations to accomplish something, whether as task forces, committees, work teams, departments of salaried employees, or executive teams. If your company is creating teams for teams' sake, get out if you can. Without a sense of purpose, without clear goals and objectives, your team will flounder. As a leader, help your team by finding out what management expects of it. Find out what the team members think they can accomplish. This chapter will help you help your team establish a charter that will clarify its sense of direction. A team charter can be used to clarify expectations about all the components needed for the team to achieve excellence. It can also guide the development of specific team goals. There is no one best way to do this, but never forget: Your team needs to know why it exists and what it is to accomplish—and your organization must know these things, too.

A charter legitimizes a team. Much like a franchise agreement, it must first be established generically for all like teams in the system and then specifically for each team actually launched. It clarifies not only the reason for the team's existence, but also its operational boundaries. The organization employing a team concept needs to decide these matters prior to the actual launching of any teams and then make sure each team can live up to its charter. This is the role of top-level leadership: upper management in most organizations, or a joint steering committee if the firm is unionized. Leadership at the top has the responsibility to establish the policies surrounding the use of a team concept as a business strategy and structure. Are teams being formed to solve problems within their functional departments? Are cross-functional teams being formed to address issues that cut across the organization's structure? Are work teams being formed to self-manage a significant portion of the business? What is the purpose of forming teams in your organization? What are the rules and boundaries your teams must abide by?

The team charter needs to be specific enough to focus the team's attention. As the Susan Orlean character announces in the award-winning movie *Adaptation*, "There are too many ideas and things and people. Too many directions to go. . . . The reason it matters to care passionately about something is that it whittles the world down to a more manageable size." The team charter announces what the members need to be passionate about as a team and it provides a focus. It helps make team members feel empowered to do something meaningful instead of making them feel like galley slaves. Empowered teams need to know what they are resourced to conquer. Goals that are challenging yet attainable provide the greatest motivation.

The team charter defines the team. It describes the purpose of the team's existence, identifies the responsibilities of its leader, sets the milestones and the timeline the team is expected to follow, and clarifies the resources the team has available to accomplish its tasks. Teams exist to do the work of the organization. The team charter clarifies expectations between senior leadership and the team about the nature of that work. Table 12 provides a list of management guidelines your team can use in establishing a team charter.

The team charter also exists to clarify expectations among team members. It must clarify the team's mission, but it should also describe a vision of what the team will look like when it is performing at its best. The charter could contain sections covering any or all of the seven key components needed to achieve excellence:

1. **Clear goals and sense of direction** (by establishing the mission, reason for existence, goals, objectives)

2. **Identification of talent** (by justifying who is on the team by clarifying what knowledge and skills are needed to accomplish its tasks)

3. **Clear roles and responsibilities** (by establishing what is expected from each member and from the leader)

4. **Agreed-upon procedures** (by outlining the rules governing meetings, problem solving, decision making, and other team actions)

5. **Constructive interpersonal relations** (by establishing a code of conduct to ensure respect for differences, communication between members, effective conflict resolution, etc.)

6. **Active reinforcement of team-oriented behaviors** (by providing recognition and appreciation for these behaviors and the means to hold members accountable for fulfilling expectations)

TABLE 12

Management Guidelines for Establishing a Team Charter

- Senior management decides whether to invest in the establishment of a team—or to continue support for a team—to make something, provide a service, or solve some problem for the organization.

- A team leader is selected by the sponsoring senior manager, or the team members elect a leader according to rules established by senior management.

- A review of the stages of the team process is provided if necessary.

- Senior management articulates the mission of the project and its vision of where it could lead.

- The team leader and senior management draft a strategic plan including a rough timeline for the project or the output to be measured if the team is ongoing, as well as an expiration date for the charter and a description of the process for renewal or modification.

- The support functions that must be involved and the resources needed are identified by the team leader and the representative from senior management.

- Senior management ensures alignment between this project and other projects and functions in the organization.

- Senior management announces the birth or rebirth of the project or work team to all managers and directs them to provide support.

- The leader and the senior manager agree on the process and the frequency of reports from the team.

7. **Diplomatic external ties** (by establishing methods of communicating with key managers, union leaders, and heads of functions
that are either suppliers or customers of the team)

There is no one best way of establishing a team charter. The guidelines and elements described in the previous sections represent the
domain to consider. Your organization needs to consider how thorough
it wants these charters to be. The more thorough they are, the clearer
the expectations will be, but the more time it will take to develop them.
In addition, these charters will serve to establish the credibility of the
organization's use of the team concept. This is an opportunity to take
teams seriously; it cannot be merely an exercise. The team can draft the
charter with your help as a facilitator, or the organization can provide a
model for the team to fit to its unique circumstances. Either way, the
charter must be negotiated and approved by senior management. That
is why it is useful to include members of upper management in the
charter development session. This may relieve the competitive nature of
subsequent negotiation and approval-seeking sessions. Exercise 13
includes a series of questions used with a newly established team, and
the key managers enabling that team, in a manufacturing setting. Use
these questions or modify them as you facilitate a chartering session for
your team.

Following is an example of a team charter that was established in a
pharmaceutical research facility. The names and some specifics have
been modified to ensure confidentiality.

Charter for the A Team

Mission of the Team
*The A team is being formed to investigate the viability of the B compound
for use as a drug to reduce hemorrhoids. The team is to take the investigation through the preclinical stages, at which time a review will be undertaken by senior management to decide whether to go through with clinical
studies. Company C is under contract with company D to conduct this
investigation and report the results to them in the next twelve months.*

Developing Your Team's Charter

Directions: *Use the following questions or adapt them to your situation in guiding the development of your team charter.*

1. **Purpose:** What is the purpose of your team? Why does this team exist?

2. **Goals:** What are the priority goals that need to be accomplished in the next twelve months? Establish "SMART" goals for this particular team. For which goals will the members of this team be held collectively responsible? How?

3. **Responsibilities:** What are the responsibilities of each team member? How will individual team members be held accountable?

4. **Procedure:** What procedures (e.g., meeting, planning, scheduling, budgeting, information sharing, decision making, problem solving, project management, task assignment, progress evaluation, etc.) need to be established for this team to be effective, satisfying, and efficient? What rules, principles, and guidelines for team procedures have worked well for you on teams in the past? Is the team willing to make a consensus decision regarding adopting any of them?

5. **Ground rules:** What will be this team's interpersonal code of conduct? What are the ground rules of behavior that each member of this team will agree to abide by?

Leadership Responsibility

Mr. E will serve as the sponsoring senior manager. He will update the team regarding any changes in the contract for the B compound, review minutes of team meetings, and be available for consultation upon the request of the team leader. He will also assist in efforts to gain the needed support from line managers and will also be expected to provide significant input for the performance review of the team leader.

Ms. F will serve as the A team leader, since she is familiar with the earliest efforts to investigate the B compound. She is responsible for identifying the expertise needed to take the investigation through the preclinical stages. She is to recruit members from the needed line functions and to convene regular meetings of the team and will chair the meetings in a manner that ensures cross-functional input—but she is free to offer her own facts, opinions, and suggestions as well. Ms. F will meet periodically with the sponsoring senior manager to update him and to negotiate additional resources (people, lab equipment, databases, etc.) as needed. She will be the primary author of all formal reports but must include the input of the various points of view expressed on the team. At this point, she is expected to devote 20 percent of her work time to this project. She is also expected to provide input regarding the contributions made by members of the team. The team leader is expected to attend the team development process training session as soon as possible.

Coordination/Alignment Issues for This Project

Company C research is currently investigating two other compounds for possible relief of hemorrhoid symptoms. It is imperative that Ms. F meet with the leader of the team investigating the other hemorrhoid compounds to share insights and report progress. Information regarding these investigations is to be considered confidential. Reports are to be shared only with company C team members and senior managers.

While the B compound is not considered a top-priority project, it does represent an important contract to the organization. In order to fulfill the obligation of completing the preclinical investigations in the next twelve months, Ms. F is empowered to excuse herself from another team assign-

ment to be able to dedicate 20 percent of her time to this project. Objectives listed on her current performance review are to be changed to reflect this change of assignment.

Since resources in the G function (e.g., chemistry or toxicology) are currently being utilized to near capacity, the A team is expected to schedule its need for those studies ninety days from now. If this presents a major problem, the team can recommend outsourcing one or more of these studies to a laboratory that can conduct these studies when needed to ensure fulfillment of the contract.

In addition to developing a written charter, leaders need to be able to succinctly verbalize the mandate for their team's existence. Be sure you regularly remind team members of their purpose. Make sure others in the organization—other managers, human resource staff members, engineers, members of other teams, and so on—understand your team's charter, too. You won't be reading the charter to these people and explaining all its nuances, so you must be able to capture in a few sentences the essence of what your team is attempting to accomplish and how they are set up to operate. You may enjoy completing exercise 14 as useful practice. It asks you to pretend you are in an elevator when a key vice president steps in and happens to ask you about your team. Can you capture the key elements of your team's charter in the thirty to sixty seconds you would have on this elevator ride?

Team Goal Setting

The team charter clarifies the sense of direction for the team, providing a long-term, broad understanding for the team and the organization. But teams also need to know what to focus on this week, this day, and this hour. Without clear goals, you are basically building teams for teams' sake, making it likely that the organization will not receive a good return on the investment of having a team concept and the team members themselves will likely feel frustrated. They need clear goals to

EXERCISE 14

Composing an "Elevator Speech" About Your Team

Directions: *Visualize being in an elevator with a key manager or union official from your organization. After pleasantries are exchanged, this person
congratulates you for being willing to lead the efforts to establish a team
approach to work. Pretend he asks you, "What is the purpose of the teams
you are associated with? What are they supposed to accomplish? What is
expected of the members, and what should they be able to expect from
the organization?"*

*You have only 30–60 seconds to reply before he reaches his floor and exits.
What will you say? Feel free to use the following outlines to help you organize what you want to say and then write out your short speech in the space
provided at the end.*

Key points on *purpose of the team:*

Key points on *what the team is supposed to accomplish:*

Key points on *what is expected of the members:*

Key points on *what members can expect from the organization:*

Your completed "elevator speech":

know what they are collectively responsible for accomplishing. Leaders need to make sure that goals are established. As long as they are reasonable, they can be announced to the team by management, or the team can play a role in establishing them. The goals must be perceived as challenging yet attainable. Teams also need to be able to look at a scorecard and assess whether they are "winning."

Research by Edwin Locke and Gary Latham (1990) strongly supports the need for goals, which help provide the following:

- Focus
- A means to channel behaviors
- Motivation
- A chance to fulfill the need for achievement
- Challenge
- Clarification of priorities

Doesn't it seem like the need for clear goals is an easy case to make? Then why is it that managers, group leaders, and group members themselves often resist establishing clear goals? Why have you resisted setting goals? The most common answer is that once goals are set, someone might be held accountable for accomplishing them. Many people in organizations consciously or unconsciously leave goal statements vague. They may honestly feel that accountability is important, but they end up spending time justifying what happened and what didn't. They have become skilled at explaining things after the fact. Members may also fear that if goals are established and the team succeeds, it will only lead to ever-escalating expectations. However, if we don't know what we are trying to accomplish, how will we ever figure out what we are supposed to be doing? As Yogi Berra, former New York Yankees all-star catcher, once said, "We're lost, but we're making good time." Sometimes we seem to confuse effort with accomplishment. How can we ever expect teams to succeed and feel fully satisfied unless we clarify the goals they are to achieve?

"SMART" Criteria for Well-Written Goal Statements

If you really want to make the team concept succeed, you must help the team take the steps needed to establish well-written goal statements. You must help establish "SMART" goals in advance to guide the actions the team needs to take to fulfill its charter. Research verifies that goals are motivating when they are written in a manner that fulfills five specific criteria. The acronym "SMART" helps us remember what those criteria are:

S = **Specific.** The goal is described in a detailed manner that is clear and unambiguous.

M = **Measurable.** The goal is quantified or easily documented as to whether it was achieved.

A = **Attainable.** The goal is perceived to be challenging but within reach of the team.

R = **Relevant.** The goal is perceived to be within the purview of the work of the team.

T = **Time bound.** The timeline for accomplishing the goal is established.

Team goals should obviously include statements clarifying what outcomes are expected. But in addition to production and service quotas, expectations regarding quality, safety, cost, morale, and housekeeping standards should be established. Additional standards to include on a team's scorecard are reviewed in chapter 10. Meanwhile, let's examine some poorly written goal statements and contrast them with well-written, "SMART" statements.

Poor statement: *The team is expected to produce parts that are of first-class quality.*

SMART statement: *The team is to produce parts that fit into the cylinders in the module provided by our customers. The diameter of the base must be within .001mm of the dimensions shown in the blueprint accompanying each order. Every tenth part produced must be measured by an opera-*

tor on this team, and 99 percent of all parts measured must satisfy this criterion every hour within every production run.

Poor statement: *The team is expected to conduct efficient and satisfying meetings.*

SMART statement: *The team will hold weekly meetings using our agreed-upon five-item agenda. The meeting will begin on time and end after no more than fifty minutes. A team meeting satisfaction survey will be administered during the last five minutes of each meeting. The scores on this survey must average 4.0 or higher out of 5 each month. If the average goes below this number, a team facilitator will be assigned to attend the next meeting and help the team identify strategies and tactics to achieve the 4.0 average rating.*

Notice how the SMART statements clearly provide a focus for the team. A well-written statement leaves little subsequent doubt. Your teams will know when they are succeeding and when they are not. Clearly written goal statements provide teams with a very clear sense of direction.

Hitting Moving Targets

Knowing what they are expected to accomplish provides teams with some sense of security. However, the world is changing. In his popular book *Who Moved My Cheese?* Spencer Johnson (1998) provided an analogy for how we must prepare our teams. To gain continuous reinforcement of our efforts, we must strive for continuous improvement. This frustrates many team members and even makes them suspicious of the organization's use of the team concept. Is the company just trying to get more and more work out of them? The reality of global competition is that we must improve productivity or at least add value to everything we do—or someone else will. Leaders need to make sure teams do not rest on their laurels.

Coaches of sports teams live in fear of complacency. They know they must motivate the players to push for better performance or the chances for a championship season will be lost. Your ability to reinforce progress and use the challenge provided by your company's competitors provides the balance between losing out and burning out. This is not an easy task. You need to lead by example. You can't expect team members to continually improve by working smarter if you do not do the same. Are you able to show them how you are pushing yourself to improve your approaches to helping them help themselves? What are you doing to become a more effective team leader? Does your team know your goals for development? What are you trying to do to help your team rejuvenate itself? How are you reinforcing its past successes? Are you providing compelling arguments for the need for change? Are you helping team members gain the external perspective needed to know if they are doing "well enough"? Are you helping them become aware of changing times and encouraging them to find ways to stay on top?

Getting Your Team into the Flow

We've all experienced moments when things seem to be flowing extremely well. Sometimes this experience occurs for the whole team. In those moments everyone on the team is doing their part. Coordination happens seamlessly. Team members' egos just disappear as they unite to conquer the team's tasks. Time flies by, and at the same time they clearly see each action and have no trouble keeping up. They feel like the team is in control, is concentrating, and truly "has its act together." They are focused on the moment and not worried about the future nor upset about the past. Those are wonderful moments.

Mihaly Csikszentmihalyi (1990) and his associates have studied the experience of "flow" with thousands of individuals. He has speculated about the application of his findings to the design of jobs and the management of organizations. I believe his findings can be applied to helping teams feel the wonderful feeling of flow more frequently, too. The first thing he discovered about flow experiences is that the goals were very clear. He points out that having clear goals does not mean knowing only what the end result must be—it involves knowing the tasks to be accomplished moment to moment. People need to focus on savoring the steps along the way, not just the completion. For flow to occur, we must receive feedback immediately so that we know that we know what we are doing. The thrill of flow occurs when there is a match between the challenges of the situation and the skills and knowledge we possess to meet the challenge.

Have you ever watched a slow-motion replay of a successful football play? Every player is in sync. They know the goal of the play, and each man knows the step-by-step movements that must be executed. They find out immediately whether their blocks or pass patterns are producing the desired results. They apply their skills to overcome the challenges posed by the opposing team, the weather conditions, and the time remaining on the clock. They are in flow. If you want your teams to experience flow at work, get their goals clarified. It won't be enough to clarify the long-term mission. The goals of the moment must be clear and in sync with that overall mission. Ensure that your teammates are receiving immediate feedback regarding what is working. Help them have that revelation that they truly know what they are doing even under difficult conditions. When goals challenge team members to exhibit their skills, the satisfaction of being in flow can occur.

Summary

This chapter has emphasized the supreme importance of making sure your teams have a clear sense of direction. Team charters spell out the reasons for the existence of the team and what is expected of its members. Leaders provide the X-factor by communicating upward with management to ensure that the mission and vision for the team are clear. Leaders must also communicate with the team members themselves to establish SMART goal statements that enable them to know whether they are in flow. You know what is needed (a clear sense of direction) and you will need great negotiation and communication skills to get there.

AFTER-CHAPTER REVIEW

Now that you have completed reading this chapter, it is time for you to challenge yourself to see what you remember, establish what it is you learned, and decide where and how you are going to apply what you learned. The outline provided below can help you get started. The relevancy of this chapter may necessitate that you expand on your thoughts elsewhere. Make sure you benefit from your reading by capturing your thoughts and turning them into actions.

1. Describe at least five things you remember from the material in this chapter.

   -
   -
   -
   -
   -

2. Identify the insights you gained from reading the material in this chapter. These insights may have come directly from the points raised or by stimulating recollections of your own experiences.

   -
   -
   -

3. Identify at least one situational opportunity for applying what you learned and describe the steps to be taken (including who will do what with whom, where, and when).

   Situational opportunity:

   Steps to be taken:

   -
   -
   -
   -

COMMUNICATE, COMMUNICATE, COMMUNICATE

Sharing, Listening, Providing Feedback

•

Do you have friends or relatives who talk a lot but say very little? Relate detail after detail but somehow never seem to get to the point? Tell the same stories at every family get-together? Or do you know people who repeatedly complain about every little way they have been slighted or wronged but never seem to bring up how they may have contributed to the situation? How about people who gossip about everyone else—into everyone else's business but unable to take care of their own? Or do you have a friend or relative who announces a schedule to the group like an activity director on a cruise line? Or do you know someone who talks and socializes and never helps with whatever needs to get done or cleaned up? Or someone who sits at the table and doesn't speak unless spoken to and then only gives one-word answers?

> Most families and circles of friends include one
> or more of these characters. We usually put up
> with them; in fact, we actually love them (most
> days). We have grown to accept their idiosyn-
> crasies because we know these people are likely
> to be a part of our life for years to come.

•

Things are often much the same on teams. However, our teams are members of our work organization and we need to get things done. We need to develop levels of acceptance similar to those we have with our eccentric family members and friends while somehow making our communications more productive. This chapter focuses on helping you to gain more specific insight about the communication problems on your team and to help members past the obstacles, without expecting perfection.

Importance of Communication

Virtually every team I have worked with has complained about a communication problem. I never doubt that their complaints are valid, but when they say, "We have a communication problem," that doesn't tell me enough. In fact, this has become a fashionable way for organizations to express concern in a way that doesn't point the blame at any one individual. Nevertheless, the ability to communicate is a crucial skill for leaders and members alike to create the synergy of which teams are capable. Your ability as leader to communicate will determine to a large extent your potential for helping a team help itself.

Three Basic Communication Skills

Management's ability to communicate the team's charter, up-to-date business information, and any subsequent changes in expectations is crucial for launching and sustaining successful teams. Of course, effective communication is never a one-way phenomenon. Team members, leaders, and organizational staff members associated with the team's efforts must all be proficient in the three basic communication skills:

- Sharing information
- Listening effectively
- Providing feedback

Let's examine each of these in turn.

Sharing Information

How good are you at sharing information? Can you provide facts in a meaningful and useful manner? Can you attract the attention of team members without pushing yourself on them? Do you separate opinion from fact? Do you help information come alive by providing examples and analogies like a good storyteller? Are you better at sharing information to one person at a time or to the whole group? Can you present information in written form as well as verbally? Can people tell what you are passionate about? Do people see you as credible when you share information?

There are many things you could do to improve your ability to share information in your organization, and some are probably obvious. Following are a few ideas, but you are urged to choose no more than three to apply. Unless you are focused in your self-improvement efforts, it is unlikely you will internalize your intention and turn it into action.

- **Share a greeting.** Always say "Hi," "Good morning," or "How ya doin'?" or some such greeting as you pass people in the hallway or aisle. There may be a million things on your mind but don't miss the opportunity to provide recognition. Another way to put this is, never take the chance that people may think you are snubbing them.

- **Tell the truth.** It is said that you never have to remember what you told people if you told them the truth. When you start stretching the truth and telling lies, you have to work at remembering what you told to whom. Sharing information with people provides you with an opportunity to gain their trust. Don't blow it.

- **Ask questions.** Instead of always stating your point of view or telling people what you know, make it a point to frequently ask questions. "What is going well today?" "What are your thoughts on what came up in our meeting?" "What's our biggest challenge today?" "How are people getting along lately?" Show people that you want sharing information to be a two-way street. Show them that you respect and want their point of view instead of just wanting to sell your own.

- **Use stories, analogies, and pictures.** When making a presentation to your team, liven things up by getting your points across through stories, analogies, and pictures. Help people see things as well as hear things. Instead of merely saying, "We need to increase production five hundred units a week," describe a week when those numbers were reached. What was going on then, and what did they do differently? If the new production goal is beyond what they have ever reached, paint a picture in their head about what a successful week would look like. For example:

  > By 10 o'clock on Monday, the first bin would be filled and shipped off to the docks. By noon we would have all the second bin components lined up and ready for final assembly after lunch. By Tuesday afternoon we would know if any of our customers returned parts produced on Monday and we would adjust our rotation accordingly. On hump day we would get pizza shipped in for our afternoon break to celebrate that we are ahead of schedule. On Friday, the first round is on me at our favorite pub because we beat the goal that management is challenging us with.

- **Repeat yourself.** Here's an old adage for presentations: "Start by telling them what you are going to tell them. Then tell them. Finish by telling them what you told them." Prepare people for the information you are going to share with them. Tell them how many points you need to get across to them. Explain each point. End the talk by reciting the list of the points they need to remember.

- **Separate opinion from fact.** Facts are friendly. People are better off knowing what they have to deal with than not knowing. State the facts and where you got them. You might also want to share your point of view of what you think is going on, but make sure it's clear that's what you are doing. You may have insights from interactions that did not involve the person to whom you are now providing information. Let people know what you think may be happening and then ask them what their view is. "Collectively, we might figure things out. Let's do that together."

- **Never bring up more than seven.** The human brain tends to organize blocks of information in units no larger than seven. In fact we are lucky to remember lists even that long. If you need to raise more than seven issues, try to categorize them so that the final outline is not longer than seven items. Ideally, don't share more than five things at a time—use the fingers on one hand to stress each point.

What are you going to do to improve your ability to share information with team members, your boss, or other members of your organization? Football and basketball coaches frequently decide what the team's first plays are going to be even before the game begins. Sometimes circumstances cause the script to be abandoned, but the team goes into the game with the confidence of knowing what they are supposed to do. This is known as scripting the plays. Exercise 15 can help you become more aware of your intentions as you script tomorrow's activities.

Listening Effectively

How good are you at listening? Listening is actually even more important than sharing information as you attempt to communicate with the teams you are helping. Listening is key to understanding, respectful relationship building, problem solving, and learning.

EXERCISE 15

Scripting the Start of Your Day

Directions: *Script the first three or four interactions you hope to have at the beginning of tomorrow's workday. As you walk into your place of work, who are you likely to see and who are you intentionally going to seek out? What information are you going to share with these individuals? How are you going to share this information in a more skillful manner?*

You might want to rehearse these interactions on the night before. Highlight points in your mind during your drive to your office, factory, restaurant, or school. Remember, things may not go according to plan, but put your best foot forward instead of winging it. Purposely work on your ability to share information more effectively. Share it in a way that gets information across and builds better relations.

SCENARIO #1

- Who will you encounter?

- What are the main points you want to share with each person?

- Which of the tips outlined in this section do you want to incorporate to attempt to share information in a more skillful manner?

- How will you determine if this was successful?

SCENARIO #2

- Who will you encounter?

- What are the main points you want to share with each person?

- Which tips do you want to incorporate to attempt to share information in a more skillful manner?

- How will you determine if this was successful?

EXERCISE 15 CONT'D

SCENARIO #3

• Who will you encounter?

• What are the main points you want to share with each person?

• Which tips do you want to incorporate to attempt to share information in a more skillful manner?

• How will you determine if this was successful?

Most adults are lousy listeners. As little kids, we naturally hear what is being said, but somehow in the process of growing up we seem to jump to trying to respond rather than to listen. The first thing out of our mouth after someone has shared a thought with us is "I agree," "I disagree," or "Here's what I think." Or perhaps: "Ah, that's nothing—you should hear what happened to me." We fail to describe what we have heard before we evaluate it. Our brain can process information so quickly (much faster than anyone can speak), that we already move on to our reactions, our issues, our responses. Showing someone that you actually heard what he or she said is a powerful way to show respect. It turns sequential monologues into potential dialogues. It is a way to connect. What could you be doing to improve your listening skills? You will never be a perfect listener, but that shouldn't stop you from trying to improve. As a leader in a team environment, you will have no more important skill than listening. Let's examine some tips to consider. Pick one or two that you can commit to using today.

- **You must really want to listen!** Aren't there some people at work you really don't look forward to listening to? The two of you won't team up successfully until you break through and respectfully listen to each other. Leaders are often tempted to control situations by talking instead of listening, but the power of listening is what creates the bonds on great teams.

- **Pay attention and show attention.** If you are looking at your watch or flipping through the pages of a report or newspaper, you are giving signals that you don't really want to listen to the other person. Give respectful eye contact. Look friendly. Encourage the other person to say what they are thinking. Avoid interrupting her before she finishes her thought. The more you show you are listening, the more you will hear.

- **Hear what the person actually says.** The adult mind hears a few words and starts to process it. While we're analyzing and interrupting what we're hearing we miss whole sentences, even paragraphs. Listening is a two-phased process: a descriptive phase and an evaluative phase. Don't jump to the evaluative phase too quickly. If you dedicate yourself to being able to describe everything you hear before you put your two cents in, you will become a better listener overnight.

- **Feelings are not right or wrong.** Just listen to what the person is feeling. Avoid telling the person, "You should be happy" or, "You shouldn't feel upset about that." You don't have to agree with people's feelings—just make sure they know that you heard how they do feel.

- **Take the listener's needs into account.** Remember who you are listening to and what you know about his personality or situation. If he has a preference for Introversion, be sure you give him some time to collect his thoughts before you expect him to respond. If he is under a lot of pressure, use a calm tone of voice and show some patience. Sometimes it is helpful to report your own feelings. This can create a supportive and open atmosphere. However, beware of the tendency to steal the spotlight.

- **Watch for nonverbal signals.** People attempt to tell us a lot by their body language and tone of voice. They may be telling you how strongly they feel about the information they are sharing with you. Take into consideration any contradictions between what they are saying and what they are showing.

- **Clarify the situation.** Check things out instead of making assumptions. You might misinterpret the person's body language. A person's foot wiggling fast when a certain topic comes up may indicate he is sensitive about the topic or that he is excited about it, or it may just mean he has to go to the bathroom. The same body signal can mean different things. Clarify what you hear as well. Don't pretend that you understand everything being said. Show that you care to get it right.

What will you do to improve your listening skills? Exercise 16 provides a log to help you to monitor your listening efforts and to chart your progress.

Providing Feedback

Providing feedback completes the two-way loop of effective communication. The team concept will not work without people being able to give each other feedback. At its most basic level, providing feedback is just good descriptive listening. It entails stating that you heard what the person said or noticing what the person actually did. Beyond being a verification process, it may include some judgment and reinforcement. It is an opportunity to praise behaviors or stated intentions you want to see continued or to point out some need for change. Here is another opportunity to be the X-factor in your team's efforts to be excellent. As a leader, you need to model providing feedback in an effective manner. You must have the courage to give constructive feedback. You also need to encourage team members to give their fellow team members feedback.

Following are seven tips for improving your ability to provide feedback. While they are all important to this crucial skill, remember that improving your ability is enhanced when you focus your efforts. You are

Monitoring Your Listening

Directions:

Use the log below to collect data from the next three phone calls you place (not receive). For each call, use a stopwatch to measure how much time you spend listening and the total time of the call. Then calculate the percentage of time you spent listening. Identify which listening tips you attempted to practice during the call.

After completing this log, monitor the next three face-to-face interactions you have at work. Instead of using a stopwatch for these, merely record which listening tips you used and what you could have done better as a listener. Look for patterns regarding your listening skills and what impact they are having. Develop an action plan to continue your progress.

PHONE CALL #1:

• Who did you call, and what was the purpose of the call?

• Percentage of time spent listening:

• Listening tips you found yourself practicing:

• What could you have done better as a listener in this phone call?

PHONE CALL #2:

• Who did you call, and what was the purpose of the call?

• Percentage of time spent listening:

• Listening tips you found yourself practicing:

• What could you have done better as a listener in this phone call?

EXERCISE 16 CONT'D

PHONE CALL #3:

- Who did you call, and what was the purpose of the call?

- Percentage of time spent listening:

- Listening tips you found yourself practicing:

- What could you have done better as a listener in this phone call?

FACE-TO-FACE INTERACTION #1:

- Listening tips you found yourself practicing:

- What could you have done better as a listener in this interaction?

FACE-TO-FACE INTERACTION #2:

- Listening tips you found yourself practicing:

- What could you have done better as a listener in this interaction?

FACE-TO-FACE INTERACTION #3:

- Listening tips you found yourself practicing:

- What could you have done better as a listener in this interaction?

PATTERNS AND IMPACT:

- What patterns do you see emerging from the data you collected in this log?

- What impact are these having on your efforts to be a better listener?

- What is your plan for continuing to improve your listening skills?

urged to choose the one to three tips that you believe are most deserving of your time and energy.

- **Time it well.** Try to give feedback as soon as possible after the behavior occurred or the intention was stated. It is important that these things be fresh in the mind of the person to whom you are trying to provide feedback. Since imposed feedback is usually less effective than requested feedback, you need to quickly read the person's reaction and receptivity. Be prepared to suggest a time when it may be more convenient and a location where the two of you can continue the discussion in private. Be empathetic and sensitive to the feelings of the recipient.

- **Describe before you evaluate.** State the facts. Describe what you saw or heard. Do not say that you liked or disliked it. Ask the person if she saw it the same way. Unless the two of you agree about the facts of the situation, the likelihood of your coming to the same conclusions is not high. When it comes time to state your judgment of the behavior or statement, be sure to honestly praise the elements you genuinely liked. In fact, you should be trying to positively reinforce behaviors far more often than offering criticism. People who receive praise from you on a regular basis are more likely to accept negative feedback from you on the occasions where it is needed.

- **Be specific rather than general.** Provide details. Be clear about the actual behavior you are trying to reinforce or change. Don't be vague by saying things like "I am having trouble with your attitude." Pinpoint the concern (or the positive judgment) by giving examples. "I noticed that you said, 'Yeah, right,' after every point I raised in the meeting we just left. Am I correct in assuming from your tone of voice that you don't believe I will do what I was proposing?"

- **Disagree with behaviors rather than judge the person.** Do not attack, discount, or demean the person to whom you are giving feedback. Deal with behaviors, not personalities. If you are going to criticize someone, make it clear that you disagree with what he said or did, not that you think less of him as a person.

- **Don't critique for the sake of critiquing.** Direct your feedback toward things that the receiver can address and things in which you and the team have a stake in the outcome. Does it really matter, or do you just want to vent? Remember that the purpose of providing feedback is either to positively reinforce or negatively "deinforce" behaviors. Your role is not to declare a person guilty of something. Provide feedback so that the person is motivated to repeat, or use more frequently, the positive behaviors you noticed. Or provide feedback on behaviors that are creating problems and that the person can change if she is willing. There must be options. Give the receiver the first opportunity to identify the options that might produce a different result. Add options for her to consider but make sure you are helping her help herself. (Additional information on this form of coaching is provided in chapter 8.)

- **Summarize agreements.** If the feedback leads to agreement, summarize who will do what with whom by when. Offer any assistance you are willing to provide to make the change successful. Be sure that both of you know what to monitor to verify that the feedback was put to use. If the only agreement the two of you can reach is to talk about it some more, make sure you set up a time to get back together.

- **Receive as well as give feedback.** Ask for feedback on how your effort to provide feedback went. Ask what you did that helped and what you did that could have been handled better. Here is your chance to model a nondefensive approach to feedback. Make the giving and receiving of feedback be seen as a learning opportunity.

Your teams need effective communication, and you need to be a leader in attempting to set the standard of continually improving everyone's ability to communicate. Interpersonal communication really breaks down to the three basic skills described earlier: sharing information, listening effectively, and providing constructive feedback. What has experience taught you regarding your ability to demonstrate these skills? Experience can be a great teacher if you pay attention to it.

Exercise 17 is designed to guide you through the process of reflecting on what lessons you have learned from your efforts to communicate with a team. While you can complete this exercise individually, it is even more powerful if you complete it with another team leader. This will create the opportunity to practice sharing information, listening effectively, and providing constructive feedback. It can also provide you with the opportunity to learn vicariously through the experiences of another team leader.

Thus far, we have focused on your ability to communicate. What can you do to help team members communicate more effectively with each other? You could arrange a communication skills training session for the team and hand members copies of tips for improving listening and feedback skills. We all form communication habits. Helping team members become aware of their communication strengths and weaknesses is an important first step. You could share the tips provided in this chapter and ask each member to apply one to three tips for each skill just as you are doing. Help team members identify their own set of expectations for communicating with each other. They may be more committed to live by self-selected rules than by rules imposed on them. You may wish to dedicate a whole team meeting to the topic.

Meetings, Bloody Meetings

If you are going to have a team concept in your organization, there will be meetings. In addition to sending a shiver down the spine of many people, meetings are the single most expensive social technology used in organizations. Yet they provide a very important opportunity for the team concept to succeed—and they represent a crucial communication tool that you as a leader must know how to use effectively. However, we have all been frustrated in a meeting at one time or another. Following

EXERCISE 17

Assessing Your Communication Skills

You can complete this exercise alone or with a fellow team leader.

Directions:

1. First, find a private space and remove all distractions (turn off cell phones, let the answering machine pick up any messages, place a do-not-disturb sign on the door, etc.).

2. You will be reflecting on a series of questions. If by yourself, you might want to write down your answers in a journal. If you are doing the exercise with a fellow team leader, each of you should be given the opportunity to answer each question, but make sure the other party provides descriptive feedback so that you hear your answer reflected out loud. Alternate who goes first for each question.

3. For all questions listed below, reflect on a recent experience where you attempted to communicate with a team (or an individual team member). Focus on what you did and could have done, not on what others should have done.

   • What things did you do that helped people understand what you were trying to say?

   • How might you have been more successful in your efforts to share the information?

   • Did you listen to people's responses as you shared the information? What did you do well as a listener?

   • Did you respond to what team members said? When you responded (i.e., gave feedback), did you start off descriptively, or did you react in a judging fashion by saying whether you agreed or disagreed with their comments?

   • If you had to go through the same experience again, what would you do differently?

Now that you have reflected on some lessons learned from that past experience, look for another opportunity to communicate with a team in the near future. Try to apply these lessons to this upcoming experience.

are some of the more common problems and frustrations associated with meetings.

Meetings Turning into Complaint Sessions

Members just get together and point out everything they don't like. They complain about management. They complain about the equipment. They complain about each other. While it is important for members to be aware of the problems related to the successful use of the team concept, it is crucial that they take responsibility for using their knowledge and skills to address the problems within their control. Complaint sessions must be turned into problem-solving sessions.

Meetings Turning into Demand Sessions

Members go beyond complaining by figuring out what they want but then use the meeting to demand that management take care of it. Meetings become an alternative to negotiation, where teams try to get what they can through other means. While management support is crucial, teams will not become empowered unless they work on issues and problems within their own control. It must be made clear to teams that meeting time is to be spent on identifying what the team can do to make things better in collaboration with the rest of the organization.

Members Failing to Participate

If some resistant members attend meetings but sit there without saying anything, you cannot gain the collective wisdom of the team. If some members rebel even further by reading the newspaper or falling asleep, management will lose faith in the team concept. Even the teammates of the resistant members will become resentful or cynical. It must be made clear that the responsibilities of team members include participation. It may help to make attendance mandatory, though as they say, "You can lead a horse to water but you can't make it drink." You need everyone there and you need leadership capable of encouraging involvement.

Members Becoming Frustrated by a Lack of Follow-Through

Even when members participate and generate solutions to the team's problems, if talk does not result in action, members will declare the meetings useless. Before you launch your team concept, make sure it is clear that teams must work on problems within their control and/or influence and that there is a structure in place to identify and allocate resources to assist them. Trust in the team concept is developed through actions, not words.

Members Sharing Whatever Pops into Their Head

If the team meeting is not organized and focused, frustration is the likely result. You want to encourage free speech and open communications, but that doesn't mean you want to make meetings a free-for-all. An agenda must be established, and someone must be charged with the responsibility to enforce rules so that the agenda is followed. Topic jumping allows for some venting of feelings but typically does not produce the desired results.

A Couple of Members Dominating

Some people talk more than others. Some people don't want to fight for airtime. You don't truly have a functioning team if most of the discussion is generated from just a few of the members. You need the perspectives of all, or nearly all, members to gain the full wisdom of the team, as well as the team's full commitment. Don't assume that just because you have a group of smart people in a room you will get good results— you still need some rules to make the most of the meeting opportunity. The leaders can suggest techniques such as silent brainstorming and round-robin participation to ensure that all members have an opportunity to gather their thoughts and contribute to the discussion.

Meetings Lasting Too Long

The human brain (and seat) can only take so much. Make sure that the agenda is focused and the purpose for discussing each item is clear. Sometimes the information being provided is not subject to debate. Sometimes the team being asked to prioritize problems or options is not being asked to decide what actions will actually be taken. It may not be easy to schedule team meetings and still carry on production. But it doesn't help to have one long meeting every month or so if the amount of information is going to be overwhelming. You may need to provide short "huddles" for the team in addition to formal meetings. If the meeting needs to last more than an hour, it should closely follow the rules of systematic problem solving (see chapter 6).

Too Many Interruptions Occurring

While some interruptions can't be helped, if certain members are constantly being called in and out of the meeting to converse with others outside the team, you can't blame team members for feeling that the meeting must not be very important and that they aren't very special. At a minimum cell phones and pagers should be set on vibration mode and members instructed not to take the call unless it is an emergency. Instructions should be given to others that the meeting is not to be disturbed. If a member anticipates he may need to excuse himself at some point, he should be expected to let the group know at the beginning of the meeting. Meetings are an expensive investment in terms of labor costs. Interruptions siphon off this investment.

People Using Meetings to Show Off

As if at a "dog and pony show," team members come in and report how great things are going within their area of responsibility. Each person puts on his little show. There is little or no discussion. Members usually listen politely and are respectful (though I have seen examples where people just show up for "their" spot on the agenda and then leave). While one function of teams is to keep people informed, frequent reliance on dog and pony show meetings will result in very little gain for the organization. The team concept is at its best when the team members are expected to produce something that requires interaction and interdependency. In addition, these polite shows tend to suggest that there are no problems, there is no need for change, and conflict is unlikely. This does not match the reality of most organizations today.

Meetings Being Used to Justify the Organization's Claim of Having a Team Concept

Football teams have locker-room meetings, but the real work of the team is done on the field. A very small fraction of your team's time together is meeting time. If you are calling a work group a team just because it meets together every Monday morning, you are not likely to see much benefit. If the members of your team are located far apart, you had better find other ways they can connect on a regular basis beside meetings. Meetings show some commitment because people must dedicate the time to get together to work on things in addition to their time spent in other productive activities, but it is only one communication tool among many.

Four Keys to Effective Communication Through Meetings

Think of effective communication as a function of abilities, motivation, and opportunity. Team meetings represent a major opportunity to have effective communication. While you probably want to keep your meetings friendly, you still need to keep them orderly. A disciplined approach to meetings does not have to be cold and formal, but it does require certain elements to be in place.

Clear Purpose and Agenda

At a minimum, the overall purpose of the meeting should be announced at the beginning of the meeting. Or, if desired, the purpose of each item on the agenda could be announced. Purposes might include sharing information, discussing information, soliciting options and input, making decisions, building better relations, and so on. Be very clear on the purpose and ask all members to act accordingly. Ideally, the agenda is provided to team members in advance or at least posted at the beginning of the meeting and includes some items solicited from the team prior to the meeting. The estimated time to be devoted to each item on the agenda should also be announced.

Clear Roles and Responsibilities

Each attendee should understand and fulfill his or her role and responsibilities.

- The *chairperson* convenes the meeting, keeps the team focused on the purpose and the agenda, and identifies who has the floor to speak.

- The *recorder* keeps the minutes for the meeting. It should be determined in advance whether to keep both an internal and external form of the minutes. At a minimum, the minutes must include all decisions made or announced at the meeting, but they can also include information regarding problems raised, options considered, data gathered, and so on. It may be wise not to share ideas generated during brainstorming sessions with people outside the team. The team must feel safe to consider all ideas but hold itself responsible for those ideas on which it makes decisions.

- *Team members* must commit to attending and contributing. Those charged with the responsibility, or having volunteered, to bring materials to the meeting must deliver.

- The *facilitator,* if one is designated by the team, focuses on the process more than on the content of the meeting. He or she has the responsibility to try to keep everyone involved and to intervene if a few dominate. The facilitator should be the friendly but firm enforcer of the team's ground rules.

- *Ex-officio members* of the team may attend as a source of information the team needs to resolve an issue. They may be members of management (or union leadership) attending to show their support for the team and to gain insight regarding the issues the team is addressing. They may simply be observers trying to learn what the team does well so that they can help their own teams in another part of the organization. Typically, the responsibility of ex-officio members is to provide voice, not vote. That is, they are there to provide information, observations, and questions for the team to consider, not to participate in the team's decision-making process.

Clear Ground Rules

Every team should have a clear set of ground rules regarding members' behavior at team meetings to encourage mutual respect and effective decision making. Often these rules are included in the team charter. Some common examples for personal behavior include "No personal attacks" and "Only one person is to speak at a time." Procedural rules could include "Meetings are to start and end on time" and "The chair will declare when the team is to engage in brainstorming and when it is to engage in debate." A separate section should be provided for the rules of brainstorming.

A special section on decision-making rules should be provided as well. This could include statements clarifying that the team is only to make recommendations and that management has the final decision. Or, that the team may make decisions on matters within stated boundaries and that those decisions must be made by consensus—in which case there should be further rules regarding how the team is to verify whether a consensus is in fact reached. The team may use some form of majority rule in its decision making such as, "For a decision to be final, 80 percent of those in attendance must be in favor." (See chapter 6 for more help on decision making.)

Do not have ground rules that not all members are expected to follow. Agreement and enforcement of these rules partly determines whether your team concept is credible.

Evaluation and Feedback

Members must be given the opportunity to comment on the way team meetings are being conducted. There are several ways to do this: a written form can be provided to solicit anonymous feedback from team members; time can be allocated at the end of each meeting for members to comment on how they felt about the meeting; or an observer can be assigned to a team meeting and later tell members what he or she saw occurring. In all cases, the key is making sure that the feedback is listened to and used to improve future team meetings. I have found it very useful to have teams dedicate at least a meeting a year—and more in the early stages of a team's development—to systematically address the problems associated with their meetings. (A problem-solving system proven to be a particularly helpful way to organize these sessions is provided in chapter 6.)

Alternatives to Team Meetings

In addition to the traditional meeting involving all members and including a multiple-item agenda, some exciting alternatives exist for you to use occasionally. One such alternative, serial one-on-one sessions, requires more time from the team leader than it does the members. The leader arranges for individual team members to be relieved from their current duties for fifteen to thirty minutes to meet with the leader alone. The leader asks each member five to seven questions and records their answers. The leader is committed to keeping each individual's responses confidential but provides a summary of the themes that emerged across the membership for each question asked. The findings are reported at the next team meeting in a manner that protects the anonymity of the respondents, and the team can use the report to engage in a team development planning session. Members are encouraged to keep their responses short (two to four minutes for each question) to stay within the time frame dedicated for each session. While the questions you use should vary according to your circumstances, here is a generic set to help you get started:

- What have you noticed about our team lately (especially about how we communicate with each other)?
- What do you think our team does well?
- What do you think our team needs to do better or differently?
- How is this organization helping our team become more effective?
- What obstacles exist that might interfere with our team becoming more effective?
- What could you do to help this team become even more effective and satisfying?
- What could I do to help?

Dialogue As a Tool for Teams

Did you know that the word *discussion* stems from the Latin *discutere,* which means "to smash to pieces"? Traditional discussion, therefore, can be seen as a form of conversation oriented toward advocacy that promotes fragmentation. People discuss to "win." It is a dismal way to conduct teamwork, not just because it undermines cooperation, but because ideas and solutions rarely get the consideration they deserve.

Contrast this with *dialogue,* which comes from two Greek roots, *dia* (meaning "through" or "with each other") and *logos* (meaning "the word"). It carries a sense of "meaning flowing through." The key is getting the group to purposefully adopt a spirit of inquiry instead of the typical advocating for a certain point of view. In a dialogue the team is asked to pay attention to the assumptions taken for granted that underlie their points of view. Dialogue is a proven strategy for stepping back from individualism and developing an environment—a container or field of inquiry—to pull together collective assumptions, shared intentions, and the beliefs of a group.

If dialogue can be defined as "a sustained collective inquiry into everyday experience and what we take for granted" (Senge et al., 1998), its goal is to break new ground by establishing a setting that enables people to become more aware of the context around their experience, and of the processes of thought and feeling that created the experience. If your team discussions seem to be turning into complaint sessions, where members don't seem to be gaining any useful insights, you might want to arrange for a *dialogue* session as refined by Senge et al., summarized as follows.

> *The team sits in a circle and shares their points of view while examining aloud the assumptions underlying their perspectives. The facilitator makes it clear what is to be the subject matter of the dialogue. All members are allowed to "check in," that is, to state how they feel entering this session and a brief summary of their point of view. Only one person at a time is allowed to speak, and all must speak to the center of the circle as if they were depositing their wisdom into a container. After the check-in, a device is used to control who can speak: the speaker must have possession of the "talking stick." This idea is borrowed from a Native American tradition, where the council of elders literally passed around a stick that determined who was to speak as all the others listened. Your team can use a tennis ball or a pen or any device to serve as your talking stick. Group members can nonverbally signal that they would like to speak next and receive the talking stick. A teammate might pass the stick to another hoping that he or she will take the opportunity to speak on the topic.*

People must be given the choice to participate, and the rest of the team must pay close attention to what is said and what is meant. Dialogue encourages people to suspend their assumptions, to refrain from imposing their views on others, and to avoid suppressing or holding back what they think. The word *suspension* means "to hang in front." Hanging your assumptions in front of you so that you and others can reflect on them is a delicate and powerful art. It means exploring assumptions from new angles: bringing them forward, making them explicit, giving them considerable weight, and trying to understand where they came from.

Stages of Dialogue

Briefly, the three stages of dialogue are surfacing assumptions, displaying assumptions, and inquiry, where you invite others to see the new dimensions in what you are thinking and saying. Part of the value of suspending assumptions is honoring the passion that underlies each participant's viewpoint while refusing to allow that passion to become a roadblock. Do not ask anyone to give up their views, allow one view to be imposed on the team, or expect team members who disagree with the prevailing wisdom to remain quiet. The assumptions hang in front of the room, available for all to question and explore. Suspending assumptions is difficult. Differences must be celebrated rather than overcome. The group needs to develop an excitement for learning how different people came to a different understanding of the same things (Senge et al., 1998).

A dialogue session, which should last for at least an hour, allows team members to agree to disagree. It is not intended to solve problems or help members reach decisions, but rather to provide team members the luxury of examining an issue in depth. It encourages deep thinking and feeling but not convincing each other of anything. The hope is that the sharing will produce collective wisdom. As leader, you must help your team understand the purpose and procedures of dialogue. You might arrange a problem-solving or planning session to follow a dialogue after sufficient time has passed to reflect and learn from it. A dialogue session is a powerful communication tool that helps a team experience a balance between inquiry and advocacy in its efforts to deal with the issues it faces.

Closing the Dialogue

As leader, you need to declare when the dialogue session is over. This should be determined either by a preset time limit or the recognition that the energy of the group is so low that new comments are not surfacing. Generally speaking, you should gain a commitment to hold a series of dialogues (at least three) before asking the group whether it wants to continue to use this method or abandon it. It is important to identify what the members gained from the session. Have a flip chart or a white board available for this purpose. What are the lessons learned from the collective wisdom they generated? Remember, this is not a tool to be used to convince people what is right or what is wrong, but a means to focus on what everyone learned about the issue and especially what they learned by examining the assumptions underlying their perspectives.

Summary

To succeed with a team concept, we must communicate, communicate, and communicate some more. We all learned to talk as babies but have we learned to communicate as adults? This chapter asked you to examine your basic communication skills. How well do you share information, listen effectively, and provide constructive feedback? What are you doing to improve these skills? The effectiveness of your team's communication does not rest solely on your shoulders. Are your team members trying to get better at it, too? How effective are your team's meetings, and what can be done to improve them? This chapter also introduced some less common communication alternatives. Are you willing to suggest trying them? If you and your team want your communication patterns to evolve and improve, the team must attempt to change. And change requires some risk taking. Who, better than you, should initiate the effort?

AFTER-CHAPTER REVIEW

Now that you have completed reading this chapter, it is time for you to challenge yourself to see what you remember, establish what it is you learned, and decide where and how you are going to apply what you learned. The outline provided below can help you get started. The relevancy of this chapter may necessitate that you expand on your thoughts elsewhere. Make sure you benefit from your reading by capturing your thoughts and turning them into actions.

1. Describe at least five things you remember from the material in this chapter.

   •

   •

   •

   •

   •

2. Identify the insights you gained from reading the material in this chapter. These insights may have come directly from the points raised or by stimulating recollections of your own experiences.

   •

   •

   •

3. Identify at least one situational opportunity for applying what you learned and describe the steps to be taken (including who will do what with whom, where, and when).

   Situational opportunity:

   Steps to be taken:

   •

   •

   •

   •

CHAPTER 6

PROBLEM SOLVING AND DECISION MAKING

Establishing Defined Procedures

•

I have a favorite hardware store near where I live—Stadium Hardware in Ann Arbor, Michigan. The people who work there are great problem solvers. I had a drainpipe that needed to go around a corner. They showed me three options that would work and ultimately custom-made a small sleeve that got the job done inexpensively. Another time I told them that I had too many squirrels and raccoons on my bird feeders. After eliminating the options of trapping or poisoning the critters, I was told to try using safflower seeds instead of sunflower seeds, and voilà! I now can enjoy just about as many birds as before and no squirrels or raccoons go near my feeders.

The staff at Stadium Hardware is knowledgeable and motivated to solve people's problems. Sometimes my problem is solved by a single clerk, but I notice that most of the employees get

their greatest pleasure from bouncing ideas off
their co-workers and coming up with solutions to
my home and yard issues that no individual
employee (and especially not me) could have
thought of by himself. They are good problem
solvers because they listen to figure out what the
problem really is—and what might be causing it—
before they start pointing out solutions. They are
good problem solvers because they want to solve
the problem, not make me feel bad for being part
of the reason why the problem exists. They are
good problem solvers because they generate
options and then let me as the customer decide
which one to try.

●

Do you know some good problem solvers? Are the people on the team
you are trying to help good problem solvers? If I could nominate just
two procedures for a team to be skilled at, they would be problem solving
and decision making. This chapter will give you a system and a set of tools
to help your team succeed at both. Let's help your team become like those
employees at my favorite hardware store.

Your Team's Two Most Important Plays

You have been warned repeatedly that organizations that have teams for
teams' sake are foolish. Rather, build your team to gain the synergy
available from bringing together the minds and skills of diverse talents.
People are being paid to function well on your team—they are professionals. Sports teams have plays designed by their coaching staff. They
outperform pickup teams primarily because they have a discipline to

their approach for getting their work done. For your business to benefit from having a team concept a business strategy and practice, your
team needs to have plays to increase the odds that it will be particularly good at problem solving and decision making.

Having a systematic approach to performing these key procedures
not only increases effectiveness and efficiency, it also helps build trust.
When team members see that problems are solved and decisions are
made in accordance with what has been established in the team charter,
they begin to believe that they can depend on their teammates. This is
especially important on teams of high achievers. High achievers hate to
depend on others. They feel that "if it has to be, it better be me." Do you
ever feel that way? Don't fall into the trap of trying to get the team's
work done on your own. Also, be careful not to overrely on the most talented or most reliable team members. Being asked to be involved in all
aspects of the team's work may be flattering to them at first, but later it
may produce burnout or resentment. Teams exist to gain collective wisdom. Problem solving and decision making need to be done in a manner that capitalizes on the brainpower of the many, not the few.

Teams need to be able to make decisions to complete the problem-
solving process. They need to have systematic problem-solving procedures in place to make wise decisions. These two processes represent the
ebb and flow of success—teams must be adept at expanding their thinking to include many points of view and then narrow their thinking by
coming to a conclusion that all members are committed to implement.
To expand their thinking, they need to be skilled in the use of brainstorming and other problem-solving tools. To narrow their thinking,
they need to be skilled at decision making.

Team Decision-Making Issues

Teams frequently have trouble making decisions, which can be very
frustrating for members. At various times in the problem-solving
process, a team needs to decide to focus on a particular problem; decide

on the root causes of that problem; decide on the best strategy to address those root causes; and decide what actions need to be taken to implement the strategy. Later the team will need to decide whether the actions taken have successfully addressed the root causes and decide how to express appreciation to those people who made the resolution possible. Teams need to make lots of decisions. Yes, it is important to communicate and hear everyone's point of view, but ultimately it must get beyond the diplomacy of "agreeing to disagree." Ultimately the team must unite around a set of decisions to make a difference in the work they must perform.

Traditionally we think of decision making in business settings as a logical, step-by-step process. We lay out our options, assign values or probabilities to those options, and then logically—almost mathematically—come to a conclusion. Yet, human beings are not computers and businesses do not operate in a sterile laboratory protected from outside forces. The reality is that many factors, some logical and some not, affect decision making. There are more unknowns than knowns in most business decisions. No one can truly predict the future, but we make decisions to attempt to produce a better one. Your team will not be able to produce perfect, risk-free solutions. But your team can become aware of the factors affecting its decision making. It can dedicate itself to using a systematic problem-solving process and follow through on the rules of decision making that it establishes for itself.

What are the factors affecting decision making, and how can the team manage them? Dr. Frank Yates (2003) of the University of Michigan has identified the ten cardinal decision-making issues:

- Need
- Mode
- Investment
- Options
- Possibilities

- Judgment
- Value
- Trade-offs
- Acceptability
- Implementation

The team begins the process by deciding whether a *need* to make a decision exists. How much is the current problem costing the organization and its people? Some rely on the argument that "if it ain't broke, don't fix it." However, that doesn't mean team members shouldn't consider examining something that is currently working well. They may want to see if others are doing it even better than they are. They may want to examine whether their current approach is likely to be successful in satisfying the demands the team anticipates facing in the future. The point is that there must be a need to make a decision. Don't waste the team's time on "academic" exercises.

The second cardinal issue is *mode*. Who should be making this decision, and how should it be investigated? Should the decision be made by your team? Is the subject matter of the decision within the boundaries established in your team charter? Should the decision be made in conjunction with others in the organization? How will this be determined? Is there a methodology that should be utilized?

Then there is *investment*. What resources does your team have to address the problem? Are there additional resources available within your organization that might help? How much do you need of which resources? Who should explore the availability of these resources? What is your business case for the investment of these resources?

Next consider the *options*. This is particularly important during the "alternatives" step of the problem-solving process (see table 13, p. 142). What are the strategies and actions that could be taken that might make a difference? Have all the options been considered? This issue is not to be confused with the fifth issue, *possibilities*. Possibilities are things that could be set into motion if action is taken. If we resolve the matter by choosing option X, what might the ramifications be? What might be the side effects? Are these things that we should care about?

The next cardinal issue is *judgment*. To what extent is it likely that these effects would actually happen? It is especially important to consider those effects that we really care about. This leads to the issue of *value*. Would people really care if the expected effects actually occurred? Who would be upset by the decision, and who would be happy? To what extent are the actions consistent with the values of the people who will be affected by the decision?

Since no decision is going to be perfect, what *trade-offs* should be considered? What combination of solutions might best capitalize on the various strengths and weaknesses available among the options? Can we package these trade-offs to help us with the next cardinal issue, *acceptability?* Who needs to buy into this decision and our decision-making process? Is it acceptable to all team members? To management? To the "customers" of the product or service our team will produce as a result of this decision?

The final cardinal decision-making issue is *implementation.* Who and what must be involved in putting the idea into practice? The team should not wait until the end of the process to address this issue. It is of no value to have a team produce a decision that it can't actually implement.

Your team needs to keep all ten of these issues in mind as it approaches the task of decision making. No wonder decision making is a difficult responsibility. It is easy to criticize the decisions of others. Allowing teams to wrestle with the difficulties of decision making makes them insiders instead of sideline critics. Team decision making provides an opportunity to learn about how the organization operates. Team involvement in decision making also provides collective wisdom from people close to the action.

Team Decision-Making Methods

There are several ways teams can make decisions. Unfortunately, on many teams decisions are made by those who speak out the most. The team operates under the assumption that silence means agreement. What is wrong with this assumption? It doesn't verify the commitment of each team member to support the decision. I have seen numerous examples of team members not acting in accordance with a decision made at a meeting. When confronted, these members say things like, "You guys thought that was the best way to go. I never said I agreed with that." To operate as a united team, you need a procedure for checking how each and every member feels about the option the team is considering. This can be done in a variety of ways.

Democratic Decision Making

The democratic approach to decision making is to use voting procedures. A civil and open debate is conducted, and then members declare which option they think is best. The majority rules. We expect our legislators to operate in this fashion. I hope your team does even better than our government officials. Your team's charter should specify its decision-making standards. It should state whether a simple majority is all that is needed to make the decision or whether a higher standard, such as a two-thirds or four-fifths majority, is required. Open debate must be respectfully continued until the vote satisfies the team's majority rule.

If your team chooses the democratic voting approach, you must include three other rules in your charter. First, the size of a quorum must be determined. Is the number of votes needed decided by the number of members who attend a particular meeting or by the number of people identified as team members in the charter? Second, it should be stated that all team members agree to abide by any decisions made in accordance with the majority rules approach whether they were in attendance at the meeting or not. Your team may allow for absentee ballots, although the downside of this is that those people will be voting without the benefit of hearing more of the debate. It is crucial that all team members agree to act in accordance with the decision and further agree not to bad-mouth the decision outside team meetings. Third, the team needs a rule regarding how long a decision can be delayed in order to gain the needed majority. Some teams I have worked with operate under the rule that a decision can be postponed up to three times if the needed majority is not achieved. After that, the option receiving the highest number of votes (i.e., the plurality choice) is to be accepted. These same three rules should also be included in team charters that insist on consensus decision making.

Consensus Decision Making

Ideally, teams come to consensus decisions. Consensus decisions require that each and every team member agrees to support a plan of action that represents to the team the best among imperfect options. The research on consensus decision making by teams is clear: Consensus decisions produce higher quality solutions to complex problems and build a sense of ownership and commitment to follow through with appropriate actions. However, to truly reach a consensus, team members must be patient. They must be open to fully understanding the spectrum of ideas and opinions associated with the issue. Beware that some team members may go along with the decision advocated by the more vociferous members simply to avoid arguments. As team leader, you need to help confirm whether everyone on the team truly believes that the option chosen is the best among the ideas generated by the team. Decisions that involve merely averaging, compromising, and finding the middle ground do not represent true consensus.

I have been on jury duty twice and was proud to see that we, ordinary citizens, can apply the principles of consensus decision making to come to difficult but just conclusions. In both cases, the jury sat through the presentations of evidence and testimonies without comment. The system requires the separation of listening to facts and testimony from the process of making a decision. When we got to the deliberation stage, we went around the circle stating a fact or two we thought the other jurors should keep in mind. We did this without revealing how we were going to vote. Then we passed around sheets of paper and conducted a secret ballot straw vote to discover our collective decision at that point. We used a secret ballot so that members would not feel the need to dig in their heels and defend their point of view during subsequent discussions. We explored the key facts and after a couple of hours voted again. In both cases we reached a unanimous verdict.

What if one member of your team holds out? Consensus decision making actually provides veto power to each team member. You don't want members giving in just for the sake of getting the meeting over with and you don't want to have people digging their heels in just to save face. If one member, or a small minority of team members, disagrees with the option preferred by the rest of the team, ask the dissenter(s) for suggestions on how to modify the option to make it more palatable without undoing the essence of the option. You may have to declare a brainstorming period in which all members can speculate on ways to adjust the option without yet committing to the ideas thus generated. After the brainstorming, you need to push the team back to the work of making the decision. This is another situation where you may need to use the rule in the team charter regarding how long you can afford to postpone decisions before achieving the consensus. Deadlines must be met. Remember, the purpose is not to achieve an ideal state. The purpose is to choose among imperfect options generated by the brainpower of the diverse perspectives of team members in a manner that gains their commitment to follow through on the decision.

Consensus decision making takes time. But the investment is worth it if the process educates all members of the team about the complexity of the issues. It is especially worth it if the process gains the united commitment of the whole team to follow the same path. Consensus decisions are almost always better than the decision that would be made by the average member (which is basically the same thing as majority rule). When teams incorporate the wisdom of its many members, they may achieve synergy. Then the decision is better than what could have been produced by any one member. Exercise 18 offers some fun in an activity you can use with your team to prove the value of consensus decision making.

It should be noted that sometimes a team might not have the power to actually make decisions. In many organizations, the team charter calls for the team to make recommendations and then for management to decide whether to accept and implement the recommendations made. Management must manage and be held accountable to the stakeholders involved. Customers demand time frames and quality standards. Investors expect cost-effectiveness and productivity. Other work teams in the same company may be impacted by the decision, and thus someone must help coordinate these decisions. While it is generally true that people closer to the action have insights that may lead to wiser decisions, management must ensure that the decisions are in accordance with agreements made with the relevant constituencies. However, it would be foolish of management to institute a system where teams are making recommendations that are not usually accepted.

Teams must be educated on the criteria the organization must use in its decision-making processes. Again, the team charter must be clear regarding these criteria. While consensus decisions might be preferred, provisions must be made for those circumstances where management (or a joint committee in a unionized setting) must decide to gain closure on an issue. The key to whether people will accept and act on such decisions lies in the manner in which the discussion and debate were handled. People must feel their voice was respectfully heard even if they were unable to control the final outcome. The use of teams to aid the business decision-making process must have practical considerations. The use of teams in organizational settings is not an academic exercise.

Systematic Problem Solving

The other key procedure team members need to agree on is how they will solve problems. Systematic problem solving enables a team to make wise decisions, raising it far above the level of "sandlot" teams that address problems in a free-form manner. This is the *mode* issue that Dr. Yates identified earlier in the section on decision making. How does your team go about problem solving? Does your team seem to jump quickly to solutions without spending the time to understand the problem first? Do team members act as if their job were merely to identify problems and expect management to solve the issues associated with them? These tendencies turn meetings into complaint or demand sessions, and people spend a lot of time figuring out whom to blame rather than what should be done about the matter.

A key ground rule that makes a significant difference is to allow teams to work only on problems within their sphere of influence.

EXERCISE 18

Consensus Decision Making:
The Significant Inventions Exercise

Make copies of this exercise so that each member can participate individually.

Directions: *Rank the fifteen significant inventions listed below by date (1 = oldest; 15 = newest) individually without any consultation with teammates and record your answers in column 1. After everyone has completed this task, work as a team to make a consensus decision regarding the rank assigned to each item. Record your team's answers in column 2. Finally, turn to page 140 to find out how the experts ranked these items; transfer their answers to column 3.*

INVENTION Rank from 1 to 15 (1 = Oldest; 15 = Newest)	1. Your Individual Ranking	2. Your Team's Ranking	3. Experts' Ranking	4. Difference Between Cols. 1 & 3	5. Difference Between Cols. 2 & 3
A. Word processor					
B. Jet aircraft					
C. Soft bifocal contact lenses					
D. Sputnik satellite					
E. Xerographic copier					
F. Robotics					
G. Rocket					
H. Hard bifocal lenses					
I. Frozen food					
J. Laser					
K. Video home system (VHS)					
L. Personal Walkman					
M. Bar code system					
N. Dental plate					
O. Microcomputer					

EXERCISE 18 CONT'D

Experts' Ranking of Significant Inventions

Ranking from Oldest to Newest	Date	Inventor/Country of Origin
1. Rocket	1100	China
2. Hard bifocal lenses	1784	Benjamin Franklin
3. Dental plate	1817	Anthony A. Plankston
4. Frozen food	1923	Clarence Birdseye
5. Jet aircraft	1939	Hans von Ohain
6. Xerographic copier	1950	Halvid Co. (USA)
7. Sputnik satellite	1957	USSR
8. Laser	1958	Charles A. Townes
9. Robotics	1962	Rand Corporation (USA)
10. Word processor	1965	IBM (USA)
11. Bar code system	1970	Monach Marking/ Plessey Telecom
12. Microcomputer	1973	Trong Truong
13. Video home system (VHS)	1975	Matsushita/JVC (Japan)
14. Personal Walkman	1979	Sony (Japan)
15. Soft bifocal contact lenses	1985	Softsite Lens Lab (USA)

Source: Scanlon Leadership Network. Used with permission.

Scoring the Exercise

The sum of the absolute differences between columns 1 and 3 identifies your *individual accuracy score*. The sum of the absolute differences between columns 2 and 3 identifies your *team accuracy score*. The sum of members' *individual accuracy scores* divided by the number of team members represents the average *individual accuracy score* on your team.

The lower the score, the more accurate it is. In over 90 percent of cases, the *team accuracy score* will be better (i.e., lower) than the average *individual accuracy score* on the team. This proves that team decisions are better than the average individual's decision.

Did any individual have a better (i.e., lower) accuracy score than the team's accuracy score? If not, your team achieved synergy. If so, discuss why that person was not able to influence the team's efforts to rank these items more accurately.

Sometimes in management's effort to show that they support the team concept, they oversell the opportunity. Yes, you probably want to make sure you let people know that their ideas are respected by the organization. However, you don't want to encourage a system where a team in one part of your facility spends its time deciding how others should do their business. You want your teams working on the subjects of their own expertise—their own business. The team charter needs to be clear on which issues are within the domain of consideration for the team and which are out of bounds. The charter should also clarify which procedures are to be used in problem solving and who gets the final say as to whether the solutions identified are to be implemented.

There are many models of systematic problem solving that your teams could use, but be sure the approach is not so detailed that they cannot commit it to memory. If team members can't remember the steps involved, they probably won't be using it on a regular basis. In *Tools for Team Excellence,* I introduced the "4-A" method of problem solving. Since then, hundreds of teams have adopted this approach and have found it simple yet useful and systematic. However, we have found that it helps to add two follow-up steps. Table 13 presents the "4-A Plus 2" model for systematic problem solving.

Using the "4-A Plus 2" Model for Problem Solving

Effective team problem solving involves a systematic application of four key steps—*awareness, analysis, alternatives,* and *action* and then two follow-up steps, *assessment* and *appreciation*—to turn action into results. Each step is initially addressed in a manner that expands the group's thinking and then shifts to gain a focus by narrowing the group's thinking. The leader needs to use tools such as brainstorming to orchestrate the expansion of thinking in the first half and the focusing in the second half. In essence you are helping ensure that team members separate idea generation from idea judging and deciding.

TABLE 13

The "4-A Plus 2" Model for Problem Solving

1ST A: AWARENESS

Expand your thinking to include all the problems to consider
- Brainstorm (no criticism or discussion allowed)
- Chart all ideas

Narrow your focus to the one problem you will work on now
- Use specific criteria to review each problem
- Write a one-sentence problem statement

2ND A: ANALYSIS

Expand your thinking to all possible causes of the problem
- Brainstorm or use "fishbone" diagramming
- Design an experiment to gather data for identifying causes of the problem

Narrow your focus to the one to three core causes
- Use specific criteria to review each cause
- Apply the Pareto principle (i.e., 80% of the problem results from 20% of the factors) and highlight the chief cause(s)

3RD A: ALTERNATIVES

Expand your thinking to all solutions to the chief causes
- Provide individual quiet time for writing down ideas
- Encourage creative thinking and use round-robin brainstorming

Narrow your focus to the best strategy available
- Use specific criteria (e.g., effectiveness, cost, etc.) to screen the alternatives
- Seek consensus decision making to select which option to try

4TH A: ACTION

Expand your thinking to all possible implementation actions
- Specify what might have to happen concretely
- Be sure the implementation plan is real, not just philosophical

(continued)

TABLE 13 CONT'D

Narrow your focus to who is to do what with whom by when for each step
- Clarify individual responsibilities
- Chart an implementation timeline

PLUS 1: ASSESSMENT

Expand your thinking to identify all data that maybe should be tracked
- Establish metrics/documentation that might help determine if the problem has been alleviated
- Identify strategies that could be used to gather this evaluative data

Narrow your choices and choose the data/documentation that best builds your case
- Determine which data will be tracked and where they will be posted
- Determine who is responsible for gathering the data and how they will do it

PLUS 2: APPRECIATION

Expand your thinking regarding who should be thanked for their role in this effort
- Verify who helped with the problem identification, analysis, planning, and implementation
- Decide what can be done to let these people know their efforts are appreciated

Narrow your choices regarding whom to recognize for what
- Decide who will be honored by whom, when, and how
- Devise a way to provide individual recognition without detracting from the team's effort

1. Awareness

The first "A" of problem solving is *awareness*. The goal is to identify all possible problems the team might want to address and then pick one to work on in the meeting. You can use exercise 19 applying the rules of brainstorming to make sure that you have identified the whole range of problems that might deserve attention. Insist on a few minutes of quiet time for all members (especially the Introverts) to collect their thoughts and encourage them to jot down some notes to themselves. Go around the circle of team members and ask each to contribute an idea for the group to consider. Remind members to state problems, not solutions, at this step. Do not allow any team member to criticize the consideration of any problem during this brainstorming phase. Ask team members to state only those problems they think the group might be chartered to address without long-winded explanations or justifications. Chart all problems your team identifies.

After you produce a list of problems, have the team review the list to decide which problems deserve your attention. Now is the time to encourage civil debate. You should ask the team to use specific criteria when screening the list. For example, you might give priority attention to all problems that are both important and something the team can influence. Then, the group must pick the problem to focus on for that meeting using whatever decision-making rules have been established in the team charter. Before you leave the awareness step, write a one- or two-sentence definition of the problem and check with team members as to whether it captures their thinking.

2. Analysis

The second "A" of problem solving is *analysis*. Use exercise 20 to help orchestrate a broadening of team members' thinking by having them brainstorm all the potential causes of the problem identified at the end of the first step. Why does this problem exist? What things happened prior to the problem that might be its cause? You may want to use a technique such as "fishbone" diagramming to make sure you have covered all likely

EXERCISE 19

Step 1 of the 4-A Plus 2 Model: Awareness

Directions: *Record team members' responses to document the use of the* awareness *step of the model.*

1. Brainstorm a list of problems, procedures, projects, or issues that this team needs to work on together.

   •

   •

   •

   •

   •

   •

   •

   •

   Etc.

2. Choose one item for the team to work on today using the following criteria:

   • It must be within the control (at least the strong influence) of this team

   • It must be specific enough that we can discuss it thoroughly in the limited time we have available

   • It is an issue that affects nearly every person on this team

   Item chosen:

3. Write a one-sentence statement of the problem your team is agreeing to work on below:

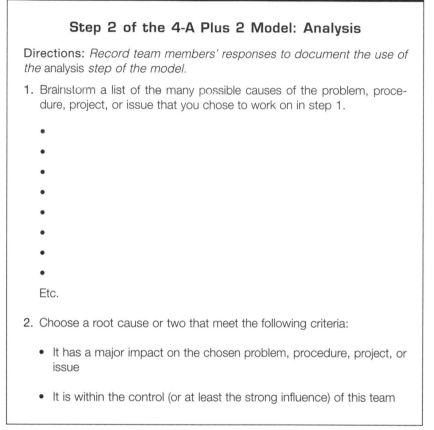

EXERCISE 20

Step 2 of the 4-A Plus 2 Model: Analysis

Directions: *Record team members' responses to document the use of the* analysis *step of the model.*

1. Brainstorm a list of the many possible causes of the problem, procedure, project, or issue that you chose to work on in step 1.

-
-
-
-
-
-
-
-

Etc.

2. Choose a root cause or two that meet the following criteria:

- It has a major impact on the chosen problem, procedure, project, or issue

- It is within the control (or at least the strong influence) of this team

---

categories of problem causes. After you have a long list of all possible causes, systematically analyze each cause to clarify the extent to which it actually contributes to the problem. This may necessitate gathering some data and charting them in a systematic manner (e.g., Pareto analysis). Attempt to identify the one to three root causes that, if addressed, would generate a significant reduction in the problem. Remember, you are trying to identify causes, not solutions, at this stage.

Alternatives

The third "A" of problem solving is *alternatives.* Use exercise 21 to help free up team members' creative potential. Ask members to suspend all

EXERCISE 21

Step 3 of the 4-A Plus 2 Model: Alternatives

Directions: *Record team members' responses to document the use of the* alternatives *step of the model.*

1. Brainstorm a long list of the many strategies/solutions that might eliminate or significantly reduce the root cause(s) chosen in step 2. Be creative and encourage members to identify anything they think might help address the root causes.

    •

    •

    •

    •

    •

    •

    •

    •

    Etc.

2. Choose the best strategy/solution using the following criteria:

    • It would have a major positive impact on the problem and its root cause(s)

    • It is likely to be affordable

    • It could be implemented in a timely manner

    • It would involve nearly all members of this team

judgment and identify a list of the many strategies and approaches you might take to address the root cause(s) of the problem you are attempting to solve. Encourage them to come up with wild and "outside-the-box" solutions. Do not have them discuss or debate the alternatives they dream up until they have all the possibilities charted. Then shift the thinking toward narrowing the possibilities. Use some criteria (e.g., Will it do away with the chief cause? How practical is the solution? Can we afford it? Is it something we can control and/or influence? etc.) to identify thetwo or three key strategies the team will commit to use to do away with the causes underlying the problem chosen. Use your team's decision-making rules and remind the team that it is very im-portant that every member agrees to implement the alternatives chosen.

Action

The fourth "A" of problem solving is *action.* Too many problem solvers stop after they have identified the solution and fail to detail a plan for how to implement that solution. This has led to the demise of many team concept efforts. Don't let this happen in your organization. Make sure your team invests the time and effort to spell out an implementa-tion plan. Use exercise 22 to help the team identify the many actions that may have to be taken to implement the strategy that was selected as the best hope for solving the problem. Remind team members that they need to include themselves in the implementation to be truly empow-ered. After all the actions and steps have been identified, specify who is to do what with whom by when and how to make your solution real. It is best if each step is activated or at least monitored by a member of the team.

The Need for Follow-up

We have now covered the four "A's" your team needs to systematically apply its problem-solving and decision-making skills. To ensure the completion of the action plan and to help reinforce the continuous use of the team's problem-solving process as a business practice, two fol-low-up steps are required: *assessment* and *appreciation.* These steps also help shift a company culture from that of playing "CYA" blame games to that of continuous improvement and learning.

EXERCISE 22

Step 4 of the 4-A Plus 2 Model: Action

Directions: *Record team members' responses to document the use of the* action *step of the model.*

1. Brainstorm a list of the actions that might need to be taken to implement the alternative chosen in step 3.

-
-
-
-
-
-
-
-

Etc.

2. Identify the steps that will be taken to implement the strategy/solution. For each step, specify who will do what with whom by when and how. The team should attempt to ensure that every member plays a role in the implementation of the solution/strategy.

-
-
-
-
-

Assessment

While it is important that your team develop a detailed action plan for implementing its carefully chosen solutions, you still need to find out if the solutions had their intended effect after the implementation. The first follow-up step is *assessment*. Again, have team members start by expanding their thinking; use exercise 23 as a guide. Have them

EXERCISE 23

Follow-up Step 1 of the
4-A Plus 2 Model: Assessment

Directions: *Record team members' responses to document the use of the* assessment *step of the model.*

1. Brainstorm a list of all the data that should be tracked to help determine whether the problem has been reduced or eliminated. Also brainstorm a list identifying the methods that could be used to gather this evaluation evidence.

Reactions

-

-

-

Results

-

-

-

Cost-Effectiveness

-

-

-

Learning

-

-

-

EXERCISE 23 CONT'D

Methods for gathering evaluation evidence

-
-
-

2. Specify:

- Which data will be tracked, and when

- Where they will be posted

- Who is responsible for gathering which portion of the data

- Which method is to be used to gather each portion

---

brainstorm all the metrics that could be used to verify that the root causes of the problem have been eliminated or at least significantly reduced. Metrics obviously vary depending on the nature of the problem being addressed. At least four categories of assessment metrics warrant consideration:

- **Reactions.** First, help them identify what they would expect to hear if the problem were successfully resolved. Are your customers happy? Are workers pleased with the strategy employed? Has the solution increased or decreased stress levels? How are people feeling about the actions taken?

- **Results.** Did the actions result in improvements in production? In quality? In delivery time? Did they reduce accidents? Absenteeism? The metrics once again depend on the problem addressed, but they should also be tied to your team's scorecard. Chapter 10 will provide many ideas about what to include on a team scorecard.

- **Cost-Effectiveness.** Next, your team needs to find out whether the solution was cost-effective. What were the costs associated with the implementation of the solution? What were the direct and indirect benefits of the results? What dollar figures can be assigned to these benefits? Basically, your team needs to find out if it was worth it.

- **Learning.** Don't forget to include some assessment of what was learned through the team's problem-solving and decision-making efforts. What technical knowledge was gained through the analysis and implementation? What did team members learn about themselves, their teammates, and other functions in the organization through the four steps of the problem-solving process? What business knowledge do they have now that they didn't have before? What have they learned about what it takes to work as a team?

Before leaving the assessment step, team members need to narrow the scope of the metrics to be used. They need to make some decisions and commitments. Which metrics for reactions, results, cost-effectiveness, and learning would best prove or disprove whether the problem has been resolved to a sufficient degree? Who will gather the data? What methods (e.g., surveys, interviews, observations, company records, etc.) should be employed? When should the data be gathered? Are there any previous records that can be used to verify that current metrics indicate improvements? Help your team focus its assessment plan so that it verifies whether progress is being made and that it can be executed without too much extra work.

Appreciation

Systematic problem solving requires discipline and hard work. Problem solving will drain your team members' energy unless you provide heartfelt appreciation for their efforts and the results. If all this hard, systematic work is taken for granted, it is likely the team will burn out and/or become complacent. To activate this second follow-up step, use exercise 24 to get your team to brainstorm the names of all the people who helped further the problem-solving process. Team members should

EXERCISE 24

Follow-up Step 2 of the
4-A Plus 2 Model: Appreciation

Directions: *Record team members' responses to document the use of the* appreciation *step of the model.*

1. Brainstorm a list of all the people that in some small or large way helped your group in any way throughout the problem-solving process. Who helped you become aware of the problems that your team might want to deal with? Who helped define the problem that you worked on? Who provided data that helped you analyze the causes of the problem? Who helped you pinpoint the chief cause of the problem? Who provided ideas regarding alternative means of resolving the problem? Who helped you choose which solution would be recommended? Who helped with the implementation of the solution? Did anyone play any indirect role that helped your team fulfill its role as a problem solver?

-
-
-
-
-
-

Etc.

2. Specify who your team will reward and/or recognize for the help they provided. How will this reward or recognition be provided? By whom? When?

-
-
-
-
-
-

Etc.

have an opportunity to recognize teammates who made a difference. They should also use this step as a means to build better diplomatic relations with managers, union officials, staff professionals, skilled tradesmen, customers, and any other organizational members who helped the team during the various steps of the problem-solving process. Providing recognition is typically enough, but your team might want to brainstorm symbolic rewards it would like to provide the key helpers. Hats, T-shirts, key chains, gag gifts, food, certificates, and many other low-cost items can make the celebration of collaboration more special.

As has been emphasized in all steps of the 4-A Plus 2 problem-solving model, don't let your team merely speculate about whom they want to express their appreciation to, and how. Make sure they complete this last step by deciding on a focused and doable plan for who will contact whom, when and with what. Bring closure to successful problem-solving efforts but generate the energy needed for more rounds of it.

Summary

This chapter focused on the team's two most important procedures: problem solving and decision making. It pays to have a clear understanding on these matters. Without agreed-upon, systematic problem-solving and decision-making procedures, team members will become frustrated and the organization will not benefit from the collective wisdom available. Decisions made by human beings involve many factors and do not solely follow the principles of logic. You can only try to make sure that the expectations have been made clear. The 4-A Plus 2 model is a proven process to help give the team the discipline to work together and address the issues within its domain.

AFTER-CHAPTER REVIEW

Now that you have completed reading this chapter, it is time for you to challenge yourself to see what you remember, establish what it is you learned, and decide where and how you are going to apply what you learned. The outline provided below can help you get started. The relevancy of this chapter may necessitate that you expand on your thoughts elsewhere. Make sure you benefit from your reading by capturing your thoughts and turning them into actions.

1. Describe at least five things you remember from the material in this chapter.

    •

    •

    •

    •

    •

2. Identify the insights you gained from reading the material in this chapter. These insights may have come directly from the points raised or by stimulating recollections of your own experiences.

    •

    •

    •

3. Identify at least one situational opportunity for applying what you learned and describe the steps to be taken (including who will do what with whom, where, and when).

    Situational opportunity:

    Steps to be taken:

    •

    •

    •

    •

CHAPTER 7

RESOLVING CONFLICT

Turning the Blame Game into Problem Solving

•

When people think about teams, they think about competition. Sports teams compete. Debate teams compete. Players on teams compete for playing time and assignment to key positions. Competition produces conflict. If handled well, it pushes us to produce at our best. If handled poorly, people's feelings get hurt and the team and organization suffer as well.

I recently had the opportunity to work with a hospital system that was suffering from the effects of unproductive conflict. The trouble centered on the fact that occasionally in the middle of surgery it would be discovered that a needed instrument was missing from the case assigned to the operation. Sometimes whole cases of instruments were missing or arrived at the very last minute. The doctors would yell at the nurses. The nurses would get on the phone and berate the technicians in the central sterilizing room who packed the

cases. The technicians would blame the transporters in the logistics department who delivered
the cases.

The conflict was primarily between units, but the
stress of the conflict led to bickering and finger
pointing within the teams as well. In addition, the
nursing staff happened to be primarily Caucasian
females, the technicians in central sterile pro-
cessing were African-American females, the
transporters were African-American males, and
the doctors were primarily male and foreign-born.
Accusations of racism and sexism added to the
tension. The more time was spent trying to
determine who was to blame, the less progress
was made. The key to improvement ended up
being the willingness of the key leaders from
each unit—and from upper management—to analyze the process for instrument selection, sterili-
zation, and delivery and to engage in systematic
problem solving.

•

Conflicts you have experienced with teams in your organization might
not have had the life-and-death implications of my client's situation.
However, I assume you have felt the tension associated with conflict. In
fact many people shy away from taking on leadership responsibilities
because they know that at some point they will be dragged into conflict-
laden situations. This chapter is designed to provide you with tools to
help others help themselves in these circumstances. It will emphasize
the importance of reducing time spent playing the blame game and
channeling the energy toward what actually needs to be done about the
situation.

Definition of Conflict

Conflict is merely a matter or individuals or groups having different perspectives on a matter. Sorry, conflict is inevitable on a team—you just have to accept that fact. The opposite of conflict is not peace and harmony, but rather apathy. When people care about what they are working on, they speak out. Thus, there are some potential advantages of having at least some conflict on a team. Conflict generates energy and often is a prerequisite for change. People may talk about problems, but until they generate some felt need to change, typically nothing happens. Conflict often provides the felt need. It can motivate people to actually do something about the situation. Conflict between a team and those outside the team usually results in team cohesion. Members of the team often put aside their differences and unite to face the challenge. As a kid, you may have fought regularly with your brothers or sisters; but when a kid down the block picked on one of them, you may have found you and your siblings uniting as a family unit. Finally, it should be noted that conflict helps a team get beyond the overly polite stage that typically exists when a team forms. Conflict, if handled well, produces more realistic discussions and decisions within the team.

Of course, there are obvious potential disadvantages of conflict as well. Conflict can polarize a group and result in the use of political tactics rather than rational problem solving. Individuals want to know whose side you are on. Subgroups of team members meet before the meetings and arrange who will say what and who will support whom. This makes a mockery of the team meeting and may discourage genuine dialogue between the parties involved. Trusting the "other side" becomes difficult. Conflict also disrupts productive activity. We spend our time arguing over issues rather than getting our work done. Finally, it should be noted that many people are uncomfortable with conflict. Sometimes an individual will revel in the role of devil's advocate, but that generally does not result in warm-and-fuzzy feelings all around. Sometimes people who may possess the information crucial for reaching a higher-quality decision simply clam up instead of standing up to their more aggressive teammates. They just don't want to fight for airtime.

Conflict should be seen as inevitable and neither inherently good nor bad for the team. The key is how conflict situations are handled. As leader, you have the opportunity to help a team navigate these rougher waters. You can be the X-factor that makes a difference. You don't have to settle issues for people, only help the team settle on a process to resolve them. If no one steps up to bring some order to deal with the matters of conflict, a power vacuum emerges. Power vacuums encourage more competition and conflict. Unless the energy of the group is channeled toward resolving the issues, you can expect a divided membership and people scrambling to cover their behinds. What can you do to help the members choose a path to unite and move forward? Let's make sure we have an understanding of the different causes of conflict and then look at options.

Causes of Conflict

There are countless differences between people and between situations, so there is no single explanation for conflict or what to do about it. However, there are some patterns that should help you to understand the basics of conflict. Table 14 outlines some of the more common causes of conflict in organizational settings, divided into three main categories.

Competition

Competition between individuals or teams is one main cause of conflict. Anytime I want to have things my way and you want things another way, we are likely to experience conflict. I may want things a certain way because I have a strong need for control. In addition, since no organization has unlimited resources, I may be motivated to com-

---

TABLE 14

Common Causes of Conflict

COMPETITION

- For limited resources or rewards
- For control
- For accomplishment
- Between differing values, opinions, or goals

LACK OF UNDERSTANDING

- About differences in situations, experiences, or personalities
- Involving a lack of communication
- Involving rumors

IMPACT OF PAST EVENTS

- Lingering hurt feelings
- Desire for revenge
- Lack of trust
- Lack of respect

---

pete with you because I want something that you also want (e.g., a new computer, a more desirable schedule, a better office, etc.), and the organization cannot afford to satisfy both our desires. Furthermore, if our values or goals differ, I will think that my way is right and your way is wrong. Our conflict will generate behaviors aimed at determining which of us gets his or her way.

Lack of Understanding

In chapter 2 we discussed the frustration experienced by people with differing personalities when they try to communicate with each other. Personalities represent our natural tendencies, and often we are surprised that others don't think and talk the same way we do. Instead of accepting, or even trying to benefit from, these differences, we allow our frustration to turn into conflict. The same pattern can occur when the conflict stems from different backgrounds, professions, upbringing, age, race, ethnicity, or gender. We don't understand where some of our teammates are coming from because we have not had the same experiences that helped form their views on life. When we stereotype people from any given group, we complicate this problem even further. We make assumptions about the individual based on patterns that probably don't even exist. We fail to look at the actual situation and instead focus on who is involved and what group they represent to us. Lack of understanding provokes many of the conflicts experienced in organizational settings.

Impact of Past Events

Conflict involves feelings we bring to the present situation that were actually generated by past events. We spend more time with people at work than nearly any other group of people in our life. This proximity gives us the opportunity to benefit from relating with people we might not have bothered to interact with otherwise. However, it also gives us plenty of opportunities to disappoint each other. Many people are prone to remember the one time a person treated them poorly and take for granted the many times he or she treated them well. Memories of past events often put people on guard. This defensiveness shows up in lack of trust or even lack of respect. We hold onto hurt feelings and find it difficult to move forward. The likelihood of the impact of past events being the root cause of a given conflict is a function of some personal tendencies but also of how long the group has interacted with each

other. Before looking at some specific tools you can use to help teams
deal with conflict, let's look at the forms of conflict that tend to emerge
during the different stages of a team's development.

Conflict Throughout the Stages of Team Development

Conflict is natural at every stage of Tuckman's model for team development. One stage is even known for it: Storming. Table 15 will help
refresh your memory about the model by outlining the stages of development and providing a brief explanation of each.

Forming

During the Forming stage, team members get acquainted with each
other and the tasks they are expected to perform. It is typically a polite
stage. Members tend not to engage in conflict with each other. They use
the avoiding and accommodating styles of conflict resolution, and thus
some important issues may get swept under the rug. Another potential
danger during this stage is that when one or two particularly aggressive
individuals frighten the less confrontational team members, these
members may come to regret being named to the team in the first place,
even at this very early stage. During the Forming stage it is crucial for
team leaders to develop a team charter (as described in chapter 4). In
particular, the charter sections clarifying team goals and an interpersonal code of conduct may likely head off some unproductive conflict
experienced by teams early on. Leaders must also be skilled at eliciting
the perspectives of all members of the team. It is important that the
team avoid producing a "politically correct" team charter that does not
truly reflect the feelings of its members. A charter that is only a piece
of paper and not a true reflection of what the team is trying to accomplish, as well as what members can expect from one another, is not a
useful tool.

TABLE 15

Stages of Team Development

FORMING

• The team attempts to figure out why it exists

• Team members get acquainted with each other

STORMING

• Individuals compete to influence how the team will go about
  its task

NORMING

• Standards of performance for the team are established

• Unwritten rules of how the members are to behave in the
  group emerge

PERFORMING

• The team executes the plan and procedures in an effort to
  accomplish its assignments

CLOSING

• The team approaches its dissolution

Storming

As a leader, your conflict resolution skills are particularly needed to help teams through the Storming stage. Storming is inevitable when a team approach to work is used. While the team charter helps spell out *what* needs to get done, your talented and caring members still want to influence *how* things get done. This leads to differences of opinion and thus conflict. By the way, these signs of storming are often quite subtle rather than nasty (you'll find an approach for dealing with difficult people later in the chapter). Expect civil disagreements. Look for nonverbal signs from members who might not agree but aren't saying anything about it. Conflict is uncomfortable for most people. A difficult part of your job as team leader is to make sure your team is not taking the path of least resistance and agreeing to the first idea presented just to avoid friction. Look for signs of withdrawal from members who "lose" early battles on how the team is going to get its work done. They may reduce their input at team meetings, begin to show up late or not at all, or no longer volunteer to take on tasks to help the team. Most people "get even" in a passive-aggressive fashion rather than directly. They might seek to bring down the early dominators of the team. They might just sit back and minimize their contributions. They don't want to get in trouble but they may wait to be asked or told to do things instead of taking the initiative. Worse yet, they may just be waiting to play the game of "I told you so," which discourages teammates from taking the initiative in future situations.

Opposing ideas generate the energy for change. The potential for wise, innovative solutions to complex problems is highest when the group is able to hold several possibilities in its collective head simultaneously. However, the energy of conflict must ultimately be channeled toward the resolution of problems and issues in order to become useful energy. The danger of the Storming stage is that the energy may be aimed at individuals and subgroups instead of team goals. This can split a group, create fear and resentment, and generate an urge to psychologically (or physically) withdraw from the team. Remember, the opposite of conflict is apathy, not "peace and harmony." When apathy prevails, you lose virtually all the benefits of a team approach to work.

Norming

The third stage of group development is known as Norming. Members establish how hard they want to work and how important it is to achieve performance excellence. Again, don't expect explicit discussions of these matters to emerge automatically. More typically, group norms emerge subtly, even unconsciously. People learn what they can get away with as well as what is expected. The tighter-knit the group, the more norms impact behavior. I have witnessed many teams who don't care that much whether they are pleasing management or the company but will do anything to avoid the wrath of their peers. Successful navigation of the Forming and Storming stages produces team cohesion, but team cohesion does not ensure productivity. The more cohesive a team is, the less variance there will be among members. If a team is very cohesive and sets a high standard of performance, all members will strive not to let their peers down. Some teams are cohesive but establish a norm of being anti-management—you may be facing a very resistant team. If the team uses meetings to complain about things and be cynical, it makes it difficult for any member to take on a positive attitude.

As leader, you need to help team members establish a process for clarifying their roles and responsibilities and how they will be held accountable. You may also need to help team members see the connections between what the company wants and what is in their best interests. It is especially important that team members be given recognition and appreciation for team-oriented behaviors. Clarification of expectations and reinforcement of behaviors consistent with those expectations are the key themes during the Norming stage. A tool for negotiating behavior changes among and between team members is provided later in this chapter.

Performing

In Tuckman's model, Performing is the fourth stage of development for a team. However, the reality is that production teams may have to perform from the very beginning of their existence. Committees, task forces, and project teams are pushed to perform by whatever deadlines are set, whether the team has worked thorough the issues of the previous three stages or not. The model merely suggests that a team will be better prepared to perform if it has successfully formed, stormed, and normed. The team may have set its own performance standards, but ultimately performance is judged by its "customers." A customer may be the end user of the work produced by the team or it may be management or it may be the team down the line that utilizes the output as input for its own activities. Criticism from the customer either causes members to band together or to separate in a manner that covers their own behind.

As leader, you can help by developing better diplomatic ties between your team and key players outside the team. Perceptions are realities in organizational settings. What are you doing to garner a positive image of the team throughout the organization? (See chapter 9 for tools to help you become the ambassador for your team.) You can play a key role by encouraging team members to engage in systematic problem solving together rather than spend time playing the blame game. Effective and efficient team problem-solving procedures can keep production rolling. Facilitating such procedures helps a team through the Performing stage of development.

Closing

A fifth stage of group development called the Closing stage is not often discussed. It applies to those teams working on projects and assignments that have a defined end point, where the team is to dissolve once it makes its recommendations, decisions, or plans or otherwise fulfills its charter. As the end point approaches, members who have grown very close may begin to engage in behaviors that put a psychological distance between themselves and the people they anticipate missing. Consciously or unconsciously they shield themselves from the hurt of separation. This may puzzle other team members, and some may even feel betrayed. This, too, could generate some conflict.

Furthermore, a very different set of behaviors may emerge from those members who have been low participators up to this point. You may witness a flurry of effort to contribute to the project or to get to know other team members as they to begin recognize the possibility that they may have squandered an opportunity. These low contributors may be guarding against anticipated retribution when the work of the team is evaluated by management. If the team seems to be gaining recognition for having been successful, these low contributors may now want to more clearly demonstrate their connection with the team. This may produce some resentment from the team members who had been active all along. While you want the team to experience ending with a positive bang, not a whimper, the possibility of the team ending on a bad note certainly exists. One of the key things you can do as leader is to get team members to spend time recognizing what they learned from their experience working together. Facilitate an after-action review (see p. 75) and perhaps arrange a social event where team members can celebrate their accomplishments and say their fond good-byes.

Turning the Blame Game into Problem Solving

When it comes to helping teams that are experiencing unproductive conflict, the key is to help reduce the amount of time members spend playing the blame game. Members often waste considerable time trying to pinpoint who is at fault and determining who is "one up" on whom. Sometimes they point the finger directly, but often they are more subtle. In either case, they play games that are not helpful if the goal is honest and direct communication. Beware people who unconsciously play the role of prosecutor, victim, or rescuer to manipulate people during the blame game. It's legitimate to set limits on behavior and to enforce the rules much like a prosecutor would. However, if it's done solely for the purpose of making people act in accordance with personal desires and not the agreed-upon rules of the team, it is a form of power play. Guilt can be a powerful force, but it is not a recommended tool for producing compliant behavior. And it is not just the prosecutors who try to make others feel guilty. Victims often have a legitimate beef about wrongful treatment. But eliciting guilt from others is unlikely to produce effective team relationships. And rescuers sometimes keep others dependent rather than truly being helpful, as demonstrated in the following dialogue.

Team member as prosecutor: "You know I hate doing this job, and here you have assigned me to it again."

Team leader as victim: "I never do anything right as far as you are concerned."

Area manager as rescuer to the team leader and prosecutor to the member: "Hey, you elected your team leader and gave her the power to make job assignments, so quit trying to undermine her authority."

Team member as victim: "They tell me to be honest and open. They tell me this team concept will empower me, but here I am, still stuck with the crap work again."

Team leader after the area manager has left and now acting as rescuer: "Now don't tell the boss, but I will find a way that you won't have to do that task at least for the next couple of weeks."

Team leader talking with the area manager later that day and now acting as prosecutor: "I appreciate your trying to help me be the leader, but I don't want the kind of help that makes me look like a management suck-up to my teammates. Plus, I bet my teammates are over there feeling even more anti-management than before."

Area manager now as victim: "Gee, I was only trying to help, and now you kick me when I supported you."

Team member now as rescuer and overhearing this conversation: "Hey Sally [team leader], leave him alone. He was only trying to do his job."

Does this dialogue sound familiar? Things get tricky in the real world. As leader, you need to remind people that straightforward communication is essential. You occasionally have to take a risk and give constructive feedback to someone playing games. Your ability to give constructive feedback and to engage people in systematic problem solving is key in reducing the use of the blame game on your team. Your theme needs to be, "Let's move on to figuring out what the problem is, not who is at fault."

In the language of the 4-A Plus 2 problem-solving model, this chapter has so far attempted to raise your *awareness* of the problematic conflict that may occur within and between the teams you are trying to help and provided an *analysis* of the causes of such conflicts. Before we explore the many *alternatives* for how to address these sources of unproductive conflict, use exercise 25 to brainstorm a list of situations you might want to help address. Treat the remaining portions of this chapter as a toolbox and select the alternatives and actions you think might be useful for your teams. Later assess whether these tools have resolved the causes of the conflicts identified and express appreciation to those who helped you achieve the results.

Approaches to Dealing with Conflict

According to the model developed by Kenneth Thomas and Ralph Kilmann (2002), the *Thomas-Kilmann Conflict Mode Instrument* (TKI), there are five basic approaches to handling conflict: *avoiding, accommodating, competing, compromising,* and *collaborating.* Each approach has some advantages and some disadvantages. The key is to match the approach with the situation. Ideally you want all members to be able to use all five approaches. You should consider training team members in how and when to use them. Start by identifying what the participants already know about conflict. Experience is a powerful teacher if we spend time reflecting on what it has taught us. Exercise 26 asks team members to answer a series of questions to identify their perceptions regarding conflict strategies. Remind your team members that the approaches to conflict they've learned through experience are not necessarily right or wrong and that no one method will address every situation. Care should be taken to avoid overusing any one approach. Conflict resolution is more of an art than a science.

EXERCISE 25

Awareness and Analysis of the Problematic Conflicts on Your Team

Directions: *Use brainstorming to identify the sources of conflict on your team. List the issue or issues involved, the players involved, the likely reasons why the conflict exists, and the potential consequences for the team if the conflict is not resolved soon. Make additional copies of this exercise for use on other conflicts that exist.*

CONFLICT #1

• What is an issue producing the conflict?

• Who is involved in the issue?

• Why does this conflict exist? *What* (not *who*) is causing it?

• What is likely to happen if this conflict is not resolved soon?

CONFLICT #2

• What is an issue producing the conflict?

• Who is involved in the issue?

• Why does this conflict exist? *What* (not *who*) is causing it?

• What is likely to happen if this conflict is not resolved soon?

CONFLICT #3

• What is an issue producing the conflict?

• Who is involved in the issue?

• Why does this conflict exist? *What* (not *who*) is causing it?

• What is likely to happen if this conflict is not resolved soon?

Identifying and Clarifying Perceptions of Conflict Strategies

Directions: *Have each team member answer the following questions.*

1. Have you ever seen a conflict situation handled in a constructive manner? What happened in that situation?

2. What was the most destructive conflict situation you have seen in your work career?

3. What are the advantages of having some conflict in organizations? What are the disadvantages?

4. What are common causes of conflict between people in organizations?

5. What are common causes of conflict between groups in organizations?

6. How do you let go of the past in order to deal with current conflicts?

7. What are the many ways of dealing with conflict? What are the options when conflict arises?

8. What do you usually do when you are faced with a situation that is ripe for conflict? How would you describe your conflict resolution style?

9. Who in your organization is particularly skilled at dealing with conflict?

10. What is your greatest strength in dealing with conflict?

11. What would you have to or want to work on to become more skilled
    at dealing with conflict?

Avoiding

If the issue is minor and the need for harmonious relations is high, try
using the *avoiding* approach (e.g., ignoring, withdrawing, separating,
repressing). It might help if you just occasionally ignore comments
made by the offending party and encourage others to do likewise.
Behavior that is not reinforced in any way tends to diminish. Would the
parties be willing to forgive and forget? Is it possible to adjust the team's
procedures so that the parties in conflict rarely have to interact with
each other? These are all methods of using the avoiding approach. Be
careful, this strategy could actually make things worse. Some small
issues should be nipped in the bud instead of ignored. However, if the
issue is not very important and the parties don't need to really work
things out, this may be a successful strategy.

Accommodating

If the issue is important to one party and not the other, but the need for
harmonious relations is high, the *accommodating* approach (e.g., yield-
ing, defusing, delaying) should be considered. In this approach you
either accommodate the person or accommodate the situation. You can
say something like, "This is obviously much more important to you
than it is to me. Why don't we just do it your way this time?" Or you can
find a way to defuse the explosive situation by cracking a joke at the
right time or saying something like, "Come on now. We have been

teammates for some time now. Let's not let this issue create hard feelings between us."

Have you ever found yourself in a conflict situation where you feel that if it goes on any longer, you might say something you will regret later or the other party may be about to say something that you really don't want to hear? Accommodate the situation by asking for a time out. Don't try to settle it now. Just ask that you and the parties involved get back together at a specified time when cooler heads can prevail. If you try this, make sure you get the parties back together. If you let it slide, you may lose some credibility. In fact, keep in mind that whenever you use the accommodating approach, it can backfire on you. People might see you as being unable to stand up for your point of view, or fearful of conflict and thus unwilling to let people really express their feelings. It can come across as condescending. Thus, consider using the accommodating approach, but don't overuse it. As is the case for all these approaches, the key is matching the approach to the people and situation involved.

Competing

If both parties feel very strongly about an issue and the relationship is not as important as doing the task correctly, the *competing* approach (e.g., convincing, debating, voting, exerting power, etc.) should be considered. This is an approach to use with people who are not easily threatened by conflict. The key to using it well is to make sure there is an open and fair debate on the issues. The facts must be determined and emphasized. You need to be clear about when you are expressing opinions and when you are making factual statements. By the way, if the difference between the conflicting parties is more a manner of values and opinions than it is facts, do not use the competing approach. Adults don't change their values through logical debate.

The competing approach begins with the parties' efforts to convince each other who is right and who is wrong. If this fails, then the arguments are presented in a forum that includes people who have the power to make the decision. For example, the parties present their views in a respectful manner before the other team members, who vote on which path of action to take. Or the perspectives could simply be presented to the appropriate manager or leader, and that person decides what is to be done. The good news is that the issue gets decided and, if the discussion is handled respectfully, both parties can feel they were treated fairly. However, this approach sets up winners and losers, and losers tend to try to get even. As was discussed earlier in this chapter, when competition is at the heart of a conflict, often the person who does not get his way responds in a passive-aggressive manner. If you use the competing approach, make sure you reach out to that person and help him save face in a manner that keeps him involved.

Overuse of the competing approach tends to encourage the use of political behaviors. While politics naturally occurs in every organization, you don't want to encourage it—especially if it leads to divisiveness. People try to line up their votes and find out who is on their side. The competing approach has a place in any democratic institution, but your job as leader is to try to ensure that it is handled in a fair and civil manner.

Compromising

If the issue is somewhat important to both parties and developing good relations is also somewhat important, the *compromising* approach (e.g., splitting the difference, meeting halfway) should be considered. Ask the other party, "Is there a middle ground we can move to?" or, "What is the halfway point between your position and mine?" A compromise helps both parties feel that they have gained something. It also promotes a feeling that they can work together to come up with a satisfactory solution. It gets the issue settled and often produces some feelings of fairness.

However, a compromise might not be possible. The biblical story about King Solomon comes to mind. Two women present a baby to Solomon, each claiming that the baby is hers. The king suggests a compromise: cut the baby in half. Of course this is not a workable solution. If I need you to produce twelve units an hour and you say you can only produce six, what good does it do for us to compromise and agree to nine units an hour. If I need twelve, nine is not sufficient. If you can only produce six, why commit to nine? In fact, frequent use of the compromise approach tends to encourage the political strategy of "highball/lowball." We ask for more than we need and we offer less than we can deliver, knowing that in the end we will be compromising. This produces a settlement but tends to reduce trust because we are engaging in gamesmanship. The compromise approach is best used when the issue just needs to get settled between two parties that have made genuine offers and it is not crucial that they maximize the solution to the problem.

Collaborating

Finally, if the issue is very important and the development of good relations is also very important, the *collaborating* approach (e.g., "win-win" creative problem solving, principled interest-based negotiating) should be considered. This differs from compromising in that the solution reached is something neither party could have thought of on her own. Each party offers perceptions, and that creates new perspectives for both. It is neither "my way," "your way," nor "let's meet halfway." It is an attempt to produce a new way. The parties gain insights instead of merely being convinced. This creative, often exhilarating and exciting process creates the most innovative high-quality solutions to complex problems. When a win-win solution emerges, the parties feel that together they can do great things. Thus, the collaborating approach addresses both the task and relationship side of team problem solving. Members of the Harvard Negotiation Project examined the keys to producing win-win solutions. The principles they discovered were published in the book *Getting to Yes* by Roger Fisher and William Ury (1981), as outlined in table 16.

If you are a leader attempting to help teams achieve win-win solutions, you first need to remind them to focus on the issues rather than who is presenting the issues. As stated earlier, the key is to turn the

---

TABLE 16

The Four Principles of "Win-Win" Bargaining

1. **Focus on the issues, not on the people/personalities**
   - Identify what we need to discuss, not who is presenting it
   - Be willing to bend for people but be hard on the issues
   - Listen to their words, not to your interpretation
   - Don't blame; help them save face
   - Don't merely present a solution, involve them in planning

2. **Focus on interests, not on positions**
   - Look for a sense of direction, not a way to keep score
   - Identify which interests are shared, which are opposing, and which are merely differing
   - Focus on shared interests, goals, and objectives

3. **Satisfy mutual interests**
   - Invent options for mutual gain
   - Suspend judgment; brainstorm options
   - Find ways to capitalize on differences
   - Look for "apples for oranges" trades

4. **Use standards to judge options**
   - Apply objective, not subjective, criteria to decide
   - Find external standards for comparisons

Source: Adapted from Roger Fisher and William Ury, *Getting to Yes* (Boston: Houghton-Mifflin, 1981).

blame game into systematic problem solving. It is also important that people not state their solutions at the beginning of the discussion. The members must identify the issues and what they would like to accomplish through the resolution of those issues, not their bottom line. For example, the parties should not begin the discussion by demanding how many or how few units they can produce per hour. Instead the discussion could begin with a statement of interests like, "We want to be able to produce at the level we are capable of and at the level our customers demand."

All parties may share this desire to be realistic and keep customers satisfied. The interests of both parties are examined to determine which interests they share, which merely differ without being in conflict with each other, and which directly compete with each other. These competing interests cannot produce win-win solutions unless they can be framed in another way. As for common versus differing interests, the parties must be willing to brainstorm options and packages of options creatively and then identify those that satisfy mutual interests. Once those options are identified, plans must be made to determine the steps for taking action. Ideally, the value of those options should be evaluated by an external, objective source. I had one client where the union and management members of the team came up with a creative formula for rewarding teams of workers for producing quality units. Instead of relying on either party to determine whether production lived up to quality standards, they agreed that if any of their products were selected by the J. D. Power firm as being one of the top five in its class, the bonus formula would be activated.

As you attempt to help your teams reach more collaborative solutions to their conflicts, you will need to encourage the use of certain skills including diplomacy (see chapter 9), good communication (see chapter 5), and systematic problem solving (see chapter 6). State the principles of win-win negotiations at the beginning and develop a set of ground rules for the discussions consistent with the principles. When people insist on stating their bottom-line position, ask questions and listen for the interests that may underlie their position. Encourage the spirit of inquiry and discovery rather than advocacy. When a solution is reached, make sure the group still spends the time necessary to develop an implementation plan. Conclude the meeting with reflection on what was learned during the session.

For an exercise in finding a win-win solution, see "The Exotic Orchid Role Play Exercise" located in appendix A. In the scenario presented, if the parties engage in accommodating, competing, or compromising, lives will be lost. If they respectfully initiate the discussion, share their information clearly, and effectively listen to each other, they can find a solution that addresses the needs of both parties.

The Behavioral Negotiations Alternative for Resolving Conflicts

I have frequently been asked to intervene when two members seem to be locked into some conflict and it is holding the rest of the team back. I find it helpful to first gain agreement on what role people want me to play in such an intervention. Table 17 outlines various roles one could assume to try to help. I actually never agree to serve as an arbitrator between parties. I have frequently been accused of being a "marriage counselor" when I have taken on these assignments. You should carefully negotiate your role and the ground rules that are to be used during the session.

I prefer to meet first with each party separately and try to gauge their commitment to trying to work things out. I suggest to each that the sessions will be used to trade agreements regarding behaviors. Outlining this approach is table 18, which I sometimes give to the "combatants." We don't use the sessions to figure out who was right and who was wrong. We ultimately identify what each will do to make the situation better. We have follow-up sessions to verify whether the parties are following through on their commitments. Sometimes I have them sign a behavioral contract clarifying their commitments. Form 1 provides a sample contract you may want to use as you attempt to be the X-factor in the resolution of conflicts in these stalemates.

Dealing with Difficult People

While the alternatives listed above should cover 90 percent of all conflicts that arise, there are always people who are particularly difficult to deal with. In *Tools for Team Excellence* (pp. 155–158) I included an approach for dealing with difficult people that was developed by Piaget and Binkley. Since the publication of that book, I have refined the approach based on my own experience.

Before I describe my seven-step method, try to identify who it is you find most difficult to deal with. Is it the know-it-all? The person who

TABLE 17

Roles and Responsibilities in Disputes

FACILITATOR

- Clarify purpose and procedures for discussion

- Moderate discussion so that only one person speaks at a time and no one dominates

- Ask questions for clarification

- Help the group use techniques such as brainstorming to generate options separately from passing judgment on the options

- Summarize discussion points and check whether parties agree with the summary

- Work with each party to think through issues separately and confidentially

- Serve as a messenger between parties

- Check to see whether parties agree without making decisions for them

MEDIATOR

- Assume all responsibilities of the facilitator, above

- Offer options on content for possible solutions to disputes, still without making decisions for the parties

ARBITRATOR

- Assume all responsibilities of facilitator and mediator, above

- Make decisions for parties in accordance with arbitration agreements

TABLE 17 CONT'D

CONSULTANT

- Help parties take an honest look at themselves and their situation
- Gather data through interviews, surveys, etc.
- Bring the parties together to examine their situation and facilitate planning for what to do about it
- Offer change strategies as options that may help the situation
- Help parties understand the pros/cons of various change strategies
- Facilitate session(s) where parties try to choose a change strategy
- Facilitate teambuilding and other interventions aimed at improving relations between the parties
- Provide training to enhance the knowledge or skills of clients and their constituencies
- Facilitate meetings designed to roll out the change strategy
- Gather data to help evaluate impact of change strategy efforts
- Examine systems to help ensure sustained, successful change efforts

TRAINER

- Gather data to identify training needs
- Work with parties to establish objectives of the training sessions
- Develop materials to be used in the training sessions
- Design training session activities (e.g., exercises, cases, role plays, etc.)
- Facilitate training sessions
- Present information and materials when appropriate
- Help evaluate impact of the training
- Help parties plan how to utilize knowledge/skills gained

TABLE 18

Suggestions for Our Meeting

What is the purpose of this meeting?

To establish an effective and satisfying professional relationship between this pair of team members.

How should we proceed?

1. The following ground rules are to be followed in our sessions:

   • No blaming or judging
   • Clear statements of what we want from each other, but no long explanations of why
   • Separation of idea generating (brainstorming) from critiquing and deciding
   • No sharing of ideas generated at these sessions outside the meeting without permission of the other party

2. The key to success in these sessions is that all agreements of behavioral changes be made on a quid pro quo basis. Thus you will be asked to specify what behaviors you want the other person to

   • Continue to keep doing
   • Do more often
   • Do less often
   • Do differently

   The other person will do the same. The sessions will result in an exchange of these behavioral requests.

3. I am here to facilitate this discussion, not to evaluate or decide anything. You agree that in this role I should

   • Interrupt at any time to help focus the discussion
   • Interrupt when I see a violation of ground rules
   • Attempt to summarize/clarify points of discussion or decisions

> **TABLE 18 CONT'D**
>
> 4. If behavioral agreements are negotiated, the participants will develop an implementation plan so that both can monitor progress and reinforce any efforts made to fulfill agreements with each other.
>
> 5. We will conclude each meeting with a determination of what the next step should be.

holds a grudge? The person who doesn't communicate? The person who is easily angered? The guilt-tripper? The politician? The liar? The intimidator? A person you resent? The clown? The person who is unreliable? Notice how different the various "difficult people" can be. Someone who is difficult for me to deal with may not be that problematic to you. Actually the most difficult type of person to deal with is the person on whom your usual methods of dealing with conflict will not work. Did you catch that? Your usual methods just won't work on that person. You probably won't change that person, but if you attempt a breakthrough conversation with him or her, you will need to change how you react to what he or she does or says. If you are willing to give it at least one more try, here are some steps I would recommend.

1. **Decide whether it's worth it.** You first have to decide whether it is worth dealing with this person. I know that sounds harsh. However, it will probably take some hard work and could be emotionally risky for you to confront him. However, it may be worth it if you need to work closely with him to get the work done. You may also think it is worth taking a chance because there is something intriguing about being in a relationship with him. If you do not need to interact with him very much and if your work is not intricately interdependent with him, you might consider minimizing your interactions. If that is the case, use the avoiding and accommodating strategies described previously instead of attempting a breakthrough conversation.

FORM 1

Behavioral Contract

1. I, _____, believe that we could work more
   effectively if you would

   • Do the following things more often:

   • Do the following things less often:

   • Do the following things differently (explain):

2. If you agree to make these changes, I would be willing to reciprocate
   by agreeing to

   • Do the following things more often:

   • Do the following things less often:

   • Do the following things differently (explain):

Signed,

2. **Observe and prepare.** Observe the person for about a week. Note her patterns, including what she does and especially what she tends to say. Try to ignore your preconceived notions about her. Treat her as a scientific experiment, as if you were trying to document an objective pattern rather than trying to catch her doing something wrong. Get clear in your own head why you want to work things out with this person. Prepare and practice your opening line.

3. **Initiate the confrontation and announce the issue's importance for you.** Pick a time and a place where the person will not have to save face. Do not attack, discount, or demean him. Do not begin by stating your position or what you want as a solution to the problem. Instead, your opening lines should simply state (1) that you believe that the two of you have not always worked well together and (2) that it is important to you that the two of you try to build a better working relationship. Then ask this person if he is willing to sit down with you and help brainstorm different ways the two of you could work better together. Be brief and then be quiet and wait for a response.

4. **Use your descriptive listening skills.** Whatever the person says after your opening comments, repeat back to her her own words in a non-mocking tone. Now is the time to practice your best descriptive listening skills. This allows her to hear herself and perhaps take back some of what she has been saying (thus opening the door for negotiating a better relationship). At the very least, it gives her some respect and attention, and that is just what some difficult people want. Take the high ground and be sure you demonstrate respect. Hear what she has to say so that the two of you can verify and set a tone for the need to clarify assumptions. If she makes a broad, general accusation of you, merely repeat the accusation and express the implications that it holds for you. Do not attack or defend at this point.

5. **Ask clarifying questions and repeat your request to jointly identify no fewer than three options to improve the way the two of you work together.** Emphasize that you are not interested in identifying who is to blame for anything. You just want to discover better ways

to work together. Do not argue about value differences. Adults do not change their values through debates. Be patient. Every problem is caused by many things, and there are many solutions to every problem. Perhaps the toughest mental discipline you need to work out a difficult conflict is using creativity in finding a solution. If the other person agrees to work with you to generate options to improve relations, don't fall into the trap of generating all the options yourself. It just lets him pick out the flaws in whatever you come up with. Difficult problems do not have perfect solutions. The only way you and this difficult person are going to resolve your conflict is if you agree to an imperfect solution together.

The two of you need to generate no fewer than three ways to improve the way you work together. If only one solution is being discussed, the two of you may compete over whether it is right or wrong. If you each proffer only one solution, the two of you will probably argue about whose solution is better or you may be tempted to split the difference and call it a compromise. Try to come up with many more than three options between you. You may have to postpone the discussion until you both have had time to think of some options. Make sure that it is clear when the two of you will get back together to discuss the options and that there is agreement that both of you will develop several options. After you generate options, you still have to choose which one(s) you will try. Both of you must specify what you will do to implement your chosen actions. If the two of you get to this step and then follow through, you have accomplished a breakthrough conversation.

6. **Do not chase or badger.** If the person refuses to discuss the nature of the problem and what the options could be, or if she just walks away, say in a loud but not a mean voice: "I want to work this problem out. It is important to me. I will see you at __ o'clock tomorrow [pick some alternative time] to see if you want to talk about it then." Then make sure you go see the person at whatever time you stated. First ask the person if it is a good time to discuss the matter. Show a

willingness to negotiate the time the two of you will meet but make it clear that it is still important to you. If she agrees, return to step 5. If she still refuses to generate options with you, go to step 7.

7. **If all else fails, state your goals and your willingness to negotiate how they will be attained.** Be very clear on what you want as an outcome. If you need a certain report or piece of information to do your job, state *what* you need but be willing to negotiate *how* the person is to provide you that information. Ask the person if he needs any further explanation of what your goals are. At this stage, repeat back to him virtually anything he says and then repeat your goals and your willingness to negotiate how to achieve these goals. Be assertive rather than aggressive. If this does not work, state the consequences of failing to achieve the goals. Try to not make it sound like a threat but be very clear. Make sure you follow through on anything you say. Do not bluff a consequence. If the person does change his behavior, make sure you praise any improvements (probably in private). If the person interferes with the goals being reached, apply the consequence and recognize that this is likely to end the relationship or at least generate retribution. You may have to repeat any agreements made, and this may rekindle an argument. Just be clear on the goals, your willingness to negotiate how the goals are to be met, and any consequences that will occur if the changes do not occur. Follow through very consistently but don't be a nag. Consistency is the key to rebuilding trust between any two people—even enemies.

Summary

There are many reasons why conflict exists on teams and in organizations. Conflict is natural and even has some potential positive side effects. However, conflict can also tear a team apart. The purpose of this chapter was to prepare you to help teams help themselves through times of conflict to accomplish the following outcomes:

- Higher-quality, more realistic solutions to complex problems
- Higher-quality, more realistic relationships
- Reduced stress levels
- Enhanced belief in the team approach

Guidelines were provided to produce more constructive resolution of conflicts through the following actions:

- Recognizing that conflict is inevitable and noticing when it occurs
- Assessing the relative importance of the issue and the relationships involved
- Using the approach that matches the assessment
- If the issue is to be confronted, doing so in a manner that reduces the need for defensiveness
- Being sure all parties agree on what the issue is
- Separating value differences from the tangible effects of the conflict
- Separating opinions from facts
- Using active listening skills
- Treating the conflict as a problem and applying a systematic approach to solving the problem
- Focusing on the issues, not the personalities; that is, on what the issue is, not who is right or wrong
- Avoiding stating a position regarding the outcome—focusing instead on the interests of the parties
- As interests may be shared, opposed, or just different, attempting to focus on the shared interests
- Summarizing agreed-upon solutions to verify the conclusion of the discussion
- Discussing what was learned about the subject matter and the team after the conclusion

Your role as team leader should probably not include being the judge who settles conflicts between team members. Your role is to serve as a facilitator, mediator, consultant, or trainer. Your responsibilities might include

- Recognizing conflict when it occurs
- Modeling constructive conflict resolution behaviors, especially listening skills
- Summarizing the resolution once it is achieved
- Helping the group learn from the conflict

Finally, you need some strategies to help people deal with conflict. Determine which of the following you are now prepared to use:

- Avoiding
- Accommodating
- Competing
- Compromising
- Collaborating
- Negotiating a behavioral contract
- Using the seven-step approach to dealing with difficult people

AFTER-CHAPTER REVIEW

Now that you have completed reading this chapter, it is time for you to challenge yourself to see what you remember, establish what it is you learned, and decide where and how you are going to apply what you learned. The outline provided below can help you get started. The relevancy of this chapter may necessitate that you expand on your thoughts elsewhere. Make sure you benefit from your reading by capturing your thoughts and turning them into actions.

1. Describe at least five things you remember from the material in this chapter.

   -
   -
   -
   -
   -

2. Identify the insights you gained from reading the material in this chapter. These insights may have come directly from the points raised or by stimulating recollections of your own experiences.

   -
   -
   -

3. Identify at least one situational opportunity for applying what you learned and describe the steps to be taken (including who will do what with whom, where, and when).

   Situational opportunity:

   Steps to be taken:

   -
   -
   -
   -

CHAPTER 8

MOTIVATING AND COACHING TEAMS TO SUCCESS

Reinforcing Team-Oriented Behaviors

•

Many people have suggested that under a team concept we need managers and leaders to act more like coaches. But what is really meant by that? Think about the coaches you may have had as a youth or the college and pro coaches you may have seen on television. Weren't many of them overly intense and seemingly unhappy? Haven't you seen some of these coaches yelling and screaming at their players? Is that what you want to become? I don't think so. I remember a couple of coaches who pushed me until I felt I couldn't go any further. When I survived and felt my body become stronger, I quit resenting these coaches and felt the pride of becoming a stronger young man. Yet, while authoritarian, iron-fisted coaches may help young men get through the angst of adolescence, only a few of them succeed at the professional level of sports.

•

As a manager or leader of teams in an organizational setting, you must act like a professional coach. You don't have the limited schedule that high school and college teams play. You don't have the luxury of coaching people who see work as a boot camp and are looking forward to earning a badge of courage or a varsity letter in a year or two. Your people may potentially "play" together for twenty or thirty years. Yes, those coaches from your youth may have elicited something good from you, especially if they showed they believed in you in addition to pushing you to the limit. However, you will need another model of coaching to succeed with adults in organizational settings. In this chapter we examine what research and practice have found to be better pathways for motivating team members. This will give you a better understanding of motivation and coaching and some tools to successfully help you help the members of your team perform at a championship level.

P = f(A x M x O)

The performance of a team member (or of a whole team for that matter) is a function of three things: *abilities, motivation,* and *opportunity*. It is the fundamental formula that explains human performance in the workplace. What can you do as coach to enhance the abilities, motivation, and/or opportunities of your players? Abilities include a person's natural talents as well as the knowledge and skills he or she gains through training and experience. Unless people have the talent, knowledge, and skills to get the job done, things won't get accomplished. In chapter 2 you were encouraged, as leader, to assess the talent of team members and help develop a plan to enhance the knowledge and skills needed. If there is a deficiency, then providing or arranging for training may be called for. However, don't assume training is the answer to all your performance problems. Coaching can help reinforce natural talents as well as the knowledge and skills learned during training. A coach can be a terrific advocate for planning personal development and helping identify options to consider when addressing organizational issues.

However, coaching is more than developing talents. The abilities that exist on your team represent only one-third of the performance equation. Sometimes team members know what to do but don't put their full energy behind doing it. Training won't help with this problem. This is a problem of motivation. Basically there are two key things you need to understand about motivation. One is that expectations must be made clear. The other is that fulfillment of the expectations—or lack thereof—must be reinforced.

People must know what they are expected to do and believe that these expectations are appropriate. They must also expect that if they do accomplish the task, someone will notice. Haven't you had work experiences where you did what you were asked to do but then received no feedback whatsoever? Maybe you wondered if you could have gotten away with not putting out the effort. Maybe you resented being taken for granted. Maybe you were expected to feel good just because you weren't yelled at. Maybe you were just curious whether you did the job well. In many organizations you find out if you screw up but receive no feedback if you do the job well. How clear are the standards regarding the tasks that your team members are performing? To what extent are you helping team members receive feedback regarding the fulfillment of expectations?

Motivation requires that reinforcement be provided to people who show the effort and accomplish tasks. The "reinforcers"—rewards, punishments, or threats—you use must have real meaning to your team members. If they don't, they will not have an impact on behavior and thus performance. People differ widely on what is important to them. Some workers will go all out for you provided they obtain some recognition. Others seem to require more tangible rewards and punishments. Some people you can just look at and they will change their level of input. Others require lengthy and repeated discussions to adopt the behaviors you want to encourage or to eliminate or reduce the behaviors you wish to discourage. This means you had better get to know your people. Motivating people, just like dealing with conflict, is more an art than a science. It contains a major emotional component, and thus mere logic is insufficient. The most important thing you can do is to be consistent. Consistently clarify expectations and consistently provide reinforcement for jobs well done.

The third element of the performance formula, opportunity, must also be addressed. Hollywood is full of actors who have talent and motivation but aren't performing in great movies at your local theater complex. Unless people (in our case, your team members) are given the opportunity to utilize their talents and channel their motivation toward the accomplishment of team goals, performance will not occur. As a leader/coach, you can help by adjusting roles and responsibilities to gain the opportunities for your members. You may need to negotiate with other levels of management to gain these opportunities. This is a major way you can help others help themselves.

So there you have it, coach. The formula for getting your teams to perform well spells out what you need to do. Identify and develop the abilities of your players. Clarify the expectations for each player, hold them accountable, and provide reinforcement for fulfillment of the expectations. Make sure they have the opportunity to use their talent. Sounds simple and straightforward, but we all know it is not that easy. In chapter 3 we had the "Ten Commandments of Teambuilding." Let's venture up that mountain again but now come down with the "Ten Commandments of Coaching" (see table 19).

In addition to these general dictates, however, you need some practical tools for activating the formula. Let's look at some tools to help you succeed as a coach in the workplace.

Tools for Coaching Talent

Research by the Gallup organization and others has discovered a basic difference between highly successful managers and leaders and their more common counterparts. The best managers and leaders spend far more time focusing on people's strengths than working on their weaknesses. The typical leader notices mistakes and tries to

TABLE 19

The Ten Commandments of Coaching

  I. Thou shalt realize that team members make the coach, not the other way around. They know more about themselves than you ever will. Remember, you are there to help team members help themselves.

 II. Thou shalt listen more than talk. Members need to hear themselves. Keep your comments to a meaningful few.

III. Thou shalt not rely on self-reports alone. Be sure you observe members in action—not merely accept what they say they do. If you are coaching another leader, see if he or she would like to engage in 360-degree feedback.

 IV. Thou shalt not solve team members' problems. Reflect, listen, and provide options, but have members choose the solutions. Turn problem solving into action learning.

  V. Thou shalt keep team members connected to the system. They cannot develop in a vacuum. The system provides the context for what will actually make a difference.

 VI. Thou shalt spend more time discussing strengths than weaknesses. Identify opportunities where members can use their natural talents more often and more effectively. They will probably never become great in their areas of current weakness. Just help them avoid the catastrophes their weaknesses could cause.

VII. Thou shalt encourage both a task and a relationship orientation. Team members need to produce business results, and they must have constructive interpersonal relationships with many people inside and outside the system.

VIII. Thou shalt keep every coaching session focused. Keep the purpose and goals of your contact with members in the forefront of your mind.

 IX. Thou shalt encourage follow-through without nagging. Keep the sessions connected: there is no such thing as a one-shot miracle. Provide members with gentle reminders, but don't assign penance if they fail to follow through. It is their responsibility.

  X. Thou shalt ask for feedback on your efforts to coach. Learn from each coaching attempt. Be a model for how to seek feedback.

get people to manage their deficiencies. What Buckingham and Coffman (1999) have discovered is that it is more important to discover what talents exist on your team and make plans to capitalize on them.

Certain talents are "hard-wired." Some people purposely try to nurture and deliver these talents while others either take them for granted or dilute their use by trying to become good at everything. Excellent performers are not really well rounded. They are good at certain things and they find ways to contribute these strengths. They don't ignore their weaknesses but they spend the majority of their time using their strengths. They use training to develop the knowledge and skills associated with their weaknesses not with the thought that they will become great at those things. They just want to make sure they can do those things adequately so they can avoid catastrophes—essentially a damage control strategy. They find others to partner with who can handle the things they don't naturally do well.

Coach yourself to excellence in addition to coaching your teams. You took the first step back in chapter 2 when you assessed your own talents (see exercise 5, pp. 33–34). What do you do consistently in a near-perfect way without hardly thinking about it? What comes naturally to you? You have been given some gifts, and it is your responsibility to nurture and deliver those gifts. Start with yourself and then help team members discover their talents, too. It is important for the team to be aware of the talents it has to work with. You and your teammates can dedicate a session to discovering your strengths on your own using exercise 27, the "Designated Bragger Exercise." It is designed to spare individuals from having to state their own strengths. Pairs of teammates interview each other, and then each partner in turn announces to the team what talents the other partner brings to the team. The inventory of talents resulting from this exercise provides a starting point for negotiating team roles and responsibilities. It can also help uncover what talents needed for task accomplishment are missing from the team. Once talents have been identified, you need to encourage their use.

EXERCISE 27

The Designated Bragger Exercise

Directions: *Have each team member pair up with another member and follow steps 1 and 2 below. Then, as a team, complete steps 3–5.*

PAIRS

1. Choose which partner will be the "designated bragger" first. This person (partner A) will

   - Interview the other partner (partner B) to help identify which key skills, knowledge, and personal qualities partner B brings to the team that are directly related to the performance of his or her job assignments, as well as which things partner B does that help the group of individuals function as a team.

   - Add to partner B's responses any perceptions partner A has of the talents partner B brings to this team that partner B might not have thought of.

   - Prepare an attention-getting "reintroduction" of partner B to the rest of the team. It will be partner A's job to brag to the team on behalf of partner B. However, the bragging must be genuine and clearly point out the job- and teambuilding-related talents partner B brings to the team.

2. Switch roles (partner B is now the designated bragger for partner A) and repeat step 1.

TEAM

3. Each member in turn as designated bragger is to deliver a great "introduction" of his or her partner to the rest of the team.

4. Someone should volunteer to record on a flip chart a running inventory to capture the collective talents of the team members.

5. After all the introductions have been made, the team discusses the inventory, focusing on these questions:

   - What does the inventory tell us about this team?

   - To what extent is the talent of this team being utilized? What is our plan for using this talent?

   - What talents—knowledge, skills, and personal qualities—are missing from the team?

Tools for Motivating Team Members

Understanding motivation is simple but not easy. Remember, motivation is basically a function of two things: expectations and reinforcements. The team charter described in chapter 4 contains a section on clarifying expectations regarding member roles and responsibilities. Some responsibilities are shared by all team members, but if everyone is responsible for everything, many things will fall between the cracks.

To help make members' roles and responsibilities clear, you should consider helping your team create a "Team Roles and Responsibilities Matrix" like the sample shown in table 20 for a work team in an engine manufacturing plant. It has proven to be a great tool to help clarify expectations. Dedicate a team meeting for members to systematically identify every activity and task the team must execute during a typical work period (a week, month, etc.). These items form the rows of the matrix. Names of team members along with titles of resource personnel assigned to assist can be listed across the top, forming the columns of the matrix. Letter symbols are to be placed in the appropriate squares. Your team will want to establish its own set of symbols, but consider using some or all of the following used in table 20:

P = **Primary responsibility.** This team member is being relied on to accomplish this activity or task for the team.

R = **Rotate.** The primary responsibility to accomplish this task is rotated among the team members designated with this symbol.

A = **Advisory responsibility.** This team member should be consulted before this activity is completed.

S = **Support.** This team member should help out on this activity if time permits or if there is a particular problem associated with the performance of the activity on a particular day.

V = **Veto.** This team member has veto power over decisions associated with the activity. Other members may be involved, but this member can decide whether the activity will go forward or not.

TF = **Task force.** This team member is to evaluate whether the activity is being performed effectively and efficiently.

TABLE 20

Team Roles and Responsibilities Matrix (Sample)

Activities and Tasks	Team Members	Elected Team Leader	Management Representative	Union Representative	Maintenance Contact	Engineering Contact
Production to build schedule		P	S			
Day work schedule	R	S				
Job assignments/rotation	S	P				
Overtime scheduling			P	A/V		
Absenteeism/tardiness records		P	S			
Identification of safety concerns	R			S		S
Documentation of corrective actions	TF				S	S
Documentation of costs	TF		S			
Documentation of quality (scrap, rework)	TF		S		S	
Housekeeping	R					
Documentation of production counts	R		S			
Scheduling/facilitation of team meetings		P	S			
Documentation of problem-solving efforts	TF		S			
Machine maintenance scheduling		S	A/V		P	
Tools, supplier, stock requisitions	R				S	
Disciplinary records		P	P	S		
Vacation scheduling		P	A/V			
Training certificates and scheduling		S	P			

P= Primary responsibility; R = Rotate; A = Advisory responsibility; S = Support; V = Veto; TF = Task force

Be sure that time is dedicated for clarifying expectations regarding your role as well. As a team leader who is also a peer to other members of the team, what special duties are you expected to perform? Will you represent the team at meetings within the organization? Are you the person the team expects to meet with management to set productivity goals? Are you expected to be the point person to interface with the team's "customers" and "suppliers"? If you are an area manager associated with several other teams, how often are you expected to interact with each team? Should you attend every team meeting? Do you need to check in with each team at shift start-up and closing time? Who is expected to enforce team rules? Are you in charge of discipline when team rules are violated? The bottom line is that every person on the team needs to have a clear understanding of what is expected of them. Motivation is as much a function of expectations as it is reinforcements.

Tools for Reinforcing Effort and Performance

Now let's focus on strategies to reinforce efforts to fulfill expectations. Reinforcement means holding people accountable. When people meet or exceed expectations, they must be recognized and/or rewarded. When they fail to fulfill expectations, they must be given feedback so that they have the opportunity to learn. There are four principal methods for providing reinforcement, or reinforcers—*positive reinforcement, punishment, negative reinforcement,* and *extinction*—and many ways to activate each category.

Positive Reinforcement

This reinforcer involves providing members with something desirable after they demonstrate a team-oriented behavior. This should include plain old recognition (e.g., a thank-you, an announcement at a meeting, a handshake of gratitude, feedback on what helped and why, etc.), some kind of symbolic reward (e.g., a jacket, a hat, a title, food, etc.), or some reward of greater monetary value (e.g., bonus money, a pay raise, a promotion, greater access to new equipment, the opportunity to attend a training event out of town, etc.). Beware of providing a "Most Valuable Player" award as a means of positive reinforcement. While the recipient of the award may feel particularly good, teammates may feel jealous and resentful. MVP awards can create a sense of competition, and as was noted in the previous chapter, competition is a main source of conflict.

Punishment

This reinforcer involves providing something undesirable after the person fails to fulfill expectations (e.g., being confronted at a team meeting for failing to follow through on a job assignment, having to pay money into a pool for showing up late for a team meeting or otherwise violating team rules, etc.). It might feel unpleasant to apply punishments, but motivation also requires negative consequences to hold people accountable if they fail. It has been my experience that people on teams do the right thing at least 80 percent of the time. Thus, I would expect that team leaders are providing four times as many positive reinforcers as they are punishments. While the ratio should be much higher, the absence of any application of punishment may send the message that anything goes. The key reinforcement principle is to provide a consistent system that helps people learn from their mistakes and feel good about doing what is desired.

Negative Reinforcement and Extinction

These two reinforcers are a little trickier to apply. Negative reinforcement involves providing the opportunity to avoid receiving something undesirable (e.g., an opportunity to avoid being embarrassed for failing to follow through or to avoid being yelled at or scorned by team members, etc.). This is more commonly referred to as peer pressure. It can help keep team members in line, but it can also add stress to their lives.

Extinction involves completely ignoring the behavior you want to see go away (e.g., no one laughing at excessive clowning during team meetings, not proceeding with the agenda until everyone gives their full attention to the current item of discussion, etc.). Sometimes this can be used subtly, but more typically someone needs to point out that the response is purposeful and aimed at the elimination of an undesirable behavior. At this point you are actually making it clear that you are using silence as a form of punishment.

Planned Spontaneous Reinforcement

On your next commute to work, identify one or two specific behaviors you hope to see members of your team exhibiting that day (e.g., lending a hand to a teammate to get a job done better, providing encouragement to a peer, suggesting an item to add to the agenda of the next team meeting, etc.). If you see the behavior displayed during that workday, it is time to provide some constructive feedback, as we discussed in chapter 5. Make sure you start by describing the behavior you saw performed. Use language in your first sentence that is descriptive and nonjudgmental. Be a mirror that helps people look at themselves objectively. In order for your efforts to have a developmental impact, you need to get their attention. Attention is a prerequisite to learning. Feedback provides the focus for the learning. If you, as leader, can turn work into an ongoing learning experience, you will be enhancing the quality of the work lives of the people on your team.

On the following commute to work, identify some behaviors you hope you will not see teammates performing that day (e.g., returning late from breaks or lunch, ridiculing a fellow team member's ideas, etc.). If you do see any of these behaviors demonstrated, be sure the first words out of your mouth are again descriptive and nonjudgmental. Since feedback that is solicited is more powerful than feedback that is imposed, first check to see if feedback is desired. Start your attempt to provide feedback with a statement like, "I have noticed some things about your behavior on the team. Would you like to hear my observations?" If the person says yes, turn it back around. By that I mean, ask her to state what she has noticed about her behavior on the team that day. She may bring up the very issue you want to bring up, and this may take the sting out of having it pointed out by someone else. If there is additional feedback you want to provide, stick to the facts and then check to see if she agrees with your description. Be specific rather than general. If there is agreement as to what is happening, ask her what she thinks the facts mean. Ask whether she thinks the behavior has any consequences—good or bad. If you do end up making a judgment statement, criticize the behavior or idea, not the person. Don't say things like, "You must have been nuts to try to. . . . " Don't say things that imply the person is inadequate. Focus on the actual behavior and the potential consequences to performance. But if the person says no to your offer of observations, then you have to make a judgment call. If the incident is not too serious, you might let it slide and then if it happens again, impose the feedback on the individual. Or you might feel you need to impose the feedback on the individual right then and there.

Direct the feedback toward things that the receiver can do something about. If the issue boils down to a matter of differences in values, emphasize the tangible effects of the differences. Do not try to convince the person he should think or feel differently. Make sure the discussion does not center on who is at fault but rather what can be done behaviorally to make a difference in performance. Allow the receiver to suggest changes in behavior before offering options yourself. If the feedback leads to agreements, summarize who will do what with whom by when at the end of the conversation.

Remember, feedback does not mean criticisms only. You need to provide feedback regarding behaviors that are truly strengths as well. You need to reinforce talent and not take it for granted. You need to get team members to identify strategies to make even better use of their talents in addition to attempting to correct deficiencies. Your ability to provide feedback effectively completes the reinforcement cycle needed to motivate people to deliver their talent for the sake of the team.

Motivating the Whole Team

Thus far, we have focused on the dynamics of motivating individual team members for the sake of the team's performance. However, in a team concept organization, you will have opportunities to motivate the whole team as well. In sports this commonly boils down to focusing the team to defeat a common enemy. However, with work teams you need to be on the lookout for when your system of reinforcement causes your whole team to compete with other teams in the organization. I have seen teams come in early and move supplies to their location within a plant so they can earn a bonus and some other team, who also needs the same supplies, cannot. Your system of reinforcement must be good for the overall organization and not just for the team you are motivating.

Rather than defeat the "common enemy," you want your work team to reach its established performance goal. The basic tactic of identifying expectations and then providing reinforcement still applies. The expectations include not only the performance goals but also the roles the players must play to pull together to accomplish those goals. The reinforcers you use need to encourage further bonding among team members. It is hard to find tangible rewards that are appealing to all members. You will probably have to rely primarily on recognition and symbolic reinforcers.

Team pictures, hats, and shirts display unity. Special events such as team picnics, banquets, and group attendance at sporting events not only reinforce accomplishments, but also can provide opportunities for people to get to know each other as people. However, they tend to cut into personal and family time and should therefore be used sparingly. Just make sure you are not imposing these events on people or using guilt to motivate people to attend. Also, these events should be planned by a task force of members, not you alone. Make it clear to this task force that they are to accommodate as many schedules as possible. Some members will not be able to attend events that occur outside of work time. This may set up an unintended "in crowd" versus "out crowd" dynamic, which is quite opposite from the desired result.

When attempting to motivate a team, you must also decide when you primarily want to reinforce effort and when you want to reserve rewards for results. As a rule of thumb, when a group is newly formed, you want to reward effort and not wait until you get the results. This is to motivate the team to keep trying. As the team matures and the members become veterans, you primarily want to reward results and behaviors that produce learning.

What can be done to punish teams when they collectively fail to meet expectations? In the real world, teams don't typically get punished, individuals do. In fact it is usually the leader who pays the price of team failures. If this occurs, I would not keep it secret. Try not to guilt-trip the team, but instead try to rally some loyalty and support. Instances when a whole team is punished typically involve situations where the whole team needs to put in undesired overtime or where the whole team loses out on some opportunity. If this occurs, be on the lookout for members playing the blame game. Try to keep the team focused on learning what can be done to avoid these punishments in the future, not who is at fault for this particular incident.

Tools for Gaining Opportunities for Team Members

If your team members have the abilities and the motivation to perform but don't really have the opportunity to use their skills and energy, you will have a frustrated team instead of a high-performance one. Perhaps you should facilitate a team meeting and get the input of the members regarding what additional opportunities they would like to take on. Members may be counting on you as a leader to initiate efforts to negotiate with higher levels of management to adjust goals, roles, and responsibilities to match the talents on the team. If that is the case, you need to hold a session with your boss to gain the needed clarity and negotiate the additional opportunities. Perhaps you should first practice for such a meeting. Exercise 28 can help you prepare. You should

EXERCISE 28

Practice Meeting with Your Boss

Directions:

1. Try to find two people in your organization who also have group leadership responsibilities and who are also considering meeting with their boss. In this threesome, arbitrarily designate leader A, leader B, and leader C to participate in a practice session for a meeting with the boss, following the scenario below.

2. Leader A will be the initiator of the practice session. He or she should explain to leader B how to act like leader A's boss as required. Leader C will act as an observer and later be asked to provide detailed feedback on what the initiator did that helped in the practice session. Leader C should also propose other strategies or words for the initiator to consider using in the meeting with his or her boss to make it more effective.

3. Rotate the roles to ensure that each member gets a chance to receive constructive feedback on his or her approach.

Scenario: You are being asked to meet with your boss in the next couple of weeks to negotiate a plan for introducing changes to make even better use of the talents on your team. Begin preparing for this meeting by answering the following questions:

• What do you hope to accomplish by meeting with your boss?

• What could be done to make this meeting "real," that is, really make a difference?

• How could you best present the information you have regarding the talent and motivation on the team?

• Is there a compelling need for change?

• What changes are you proposing for you and your team?

• How can you best ask for your boss's input on this plan?

• What do you want from your boss to help you fulfill this plan?

conduct this exercise with two fellow team leaders to practice the skills needed to maximize the effectiveness of the session and to receive feedback.

Team Training Sessions As a Means of Improving Performance

Training can be used to enhance knowledge and skills. For some people—especially those who have a relatively high need to learn and grow on the job—training sessions can thus also be a source of inspiration and motivation. Training certainly provides an opportunity for teams and their members to work things out. Thus, a key way that organizations can support efforts to use a team concept as a business strategy and structure is to provide training that is relevant to team performance. However, I have seen too many organizations just throw training at problems without much analysis to determine if it is an effective solution. It may be relatively easier to arrange for training than to address organizational issues such as compensation, staffing, and roles and responsibilities. Leadership must devise a plan regarding what kind of training is useful, how to provide it, and how to ensure that people can use what they learn during the training. All too often, training sessions are fun and inspiring but are not integrated into a plan to transfer the learning from the session to on-the-job performance. This ends up frustrating team members rather than enhancing their efforts.

In my first consulting work over twenty-five years ago, I naïvely thought that my role as team trainer was to excite people about the benefits of working together. I found my audiences receptive and usually very enthusiastic. However, I did not find many of them following through with efforts that made a difference for their organization and the people within it. I learned through experience that good ideas do not produce behavioral or organizational changes. I relearned the obvious: Adults are active, not passive, learners. They had hired me as an expert to teach them about teams. However, I found I could help my clients more by getting them to sit down together, analyze their current situations, speculate on plans, and systematically apply the procedures and frameworks I could provide them. So over the last couple of decades, I have developed some rules for myself as a team trainer. I would urge you to adopt these rules for yourself and add others that you have learned from your own experiences.

- Never talk for more than fifteen minutes without getting people to do something with what you are talking about.

- Don't present anything about teams until you get near unanimous agreement from members that their current situation needs to change.

- Don't sell the team concept, but rather pose questions and provide options and get the participants to think about which options might fit their situation.

- If the workshop includes union leaders and managers, remember that they got where they are today by being willing to be the focus of attention. Don't set up a workshop where you are the center of attention. Make sure your audience participants are the stars, not you.

- Most adults—especially "old school" leader types—are lousy listeners. However, when reminded or even challenged to listen, they can listen effectively. Remind your audience to listen to each other, not just you. Get everyone involved and work effectively and efficiently together through the use of small group exercises/discussions.

- Be aware that insights are seductive. While it can feel so good to help participants understand things from a different perspective, insights don't produce change. You need to diplomatically push people to spell out the implications of their insights. In particular, push them to spell out who would have to do what with whom for the insight to result in actions that would make a difference. If they are not ready for this level of planning, at least have them commit to a timeline for developing the process.

- Start workshops with small group exercises and discussions, especially when members do not know each other very well. By the end of your workshop, make sure participants are placed in small groups with people they will have to work with back at the workplace. Make sure that instructions to the later exercises include an emphasis on making verbal or written commitments regarding how they intend to make use of what they have learned and/or relearned. It seems to help to have witnesses to these commitments whom one will have to face later.

- Team training sessions should never be one-shot efforts. Start each session with a review of what members learned from the previous session, what commitments were made, and what actions actually took place. At a minimum, make sure you include a review activity on the agenda at the next team meeting.

Summary

Leaders are expected to motivate and coach their teams to greater performance. Motivation is simply a function of expectations and reinforcement. Coaching requires recognizing and encouraging natural talents and occasionally providing training to reduce deficiencies in knowledge and skills. Leaders also need to find motivational opportunities for the team and its members within the greater organization. Teams provide a structure for employee involvement. Your coaching can be the X-factor that turns involvement into commitment. What do you understand about motivation, and how will you use that to coach your team members to excellence?

AFTER-CHAPTER REVIEW

Now that you have completed reading this chapter, it is time for you to challenge yourself to see what you remember, establish what it is you learned, and decide where and how you are going to apply what you learned. The outline provided below can help you get started. The relevancy of this chapter may necessitate that you expand on your thoughts elsewhere. Make sure you benefit from your reading by capturing your thoughts and turning them into actions.

1. Describe at least five things you remember from the material in this chapter.

   -
   -
   -
   -
   -

2. Identify the insights you gained from reading the material in this chapter. These insights may have come directly from the points raised or by stimulating recollections of your own experiences.

   -
   -
   -

3. Identify at least one situational opportunity for applying what you learned and describe the steps to be taken (including who will do what with whom, where, and when).

   Situational opportunity:

   Steps to be taken:

   -
   -
   -
   -

CHAPTER 9

LEADERS AS AMBASSADORS OF TEAM-BASED CHANGE EFFORTS

Building Diplomatic Ties in the Organization

•

Nick was an area manager of a large component parts factory producing fuel tanks and bumpers for the auto industry. He understood the need for change. Although manufacturers want components delivered "just in time" to reduce inventory costs, they never want parts delivered late. Nick's plant had jeopardized production runs at other facilities before. He understood his plant manager's vehement command to never let that happen again. Nick also believed in the people who worked in his section of the facility. His people knew how to make the components and overcome obstacles to get the job done.

Believing that a team concept would empower people to make the business successful, Nick was willing to find ways to get them to attend meetings to be part of the development of solutions and not merely recipients of new orders. He co-chaired committees that got people involved, gained the support and trust of key union leaders to ensure a joint process, and dedicated part of his budget to provide team training to people in his three-shift operation. Nick would sometimes show up in the middle of the night to make sure even the night shift knew he was serious about the use of teams as a strategy and a structure for getting the work done.

Nick was also willing to stand up to his managers when they expressed doubt. He helped supervisors understand the new role for them in the team-based culture he was championing. Nick was an ambassador for teams (some called him St. Nick), but he made it clear that his support was based on good business sense. He helped transform the plant's culture—he made a difference.

•

Are you ready to be an ambassador? You can be the person who educates key people throughout your organization about the assets and issues associated with your teams. You are also in a position to educate your teams about the issues your organization is facing. As a leader, you are key in getting others to understand the need for change.

Being an Ambassador for Teams

Leadership at the top of the organization promotes and campaigns for the effective use of teams. Coaches and resource professionals connect team leaders to key departments and power players. Peer team leaders are often expected to represent their teams at meetings. The other members are usually not even invited to these meetings. It is crucial that the image of your team be a positive one—and that the organization views your team as an asset. It is also crucial that the members of your team understand that they are not empowered to do whatever they want. They are empowered to make their part of the business success-ful to fulfill the needs of the larger organization. Change may be uncomfortable for most people but it is inevitable in today's world. Without change you don't need leaders; you just need administrators. Diplomacy is a tool you will need to use to give your teams the chance to succeed. When you accept the fact that you are a leader, you take on the responsibility of being an ambassador.

You should be aware of the temptations you are likely to face. You will know about the "dirty laundry" of your team. Someday, when your boss is grilling you about the less-than-stellar performance of your team, you may be tempted to complain about the members. Conversely, someday you may find yourself tempted to become popular with your team members by bad-mouthing upper management, declaring them to be out of touch or failing to provide adequate support. Team leaders are the connectors in an organization dedicated to utilizing the team concept. You need to put a genuine positive spin on imperfect efforts aimed in the right direction. You also need to confront broken promises and inadequate efforts in order to be credible. You are the per-son in the middle. This will feel awkward. This may be uncomfortable. But if you do not step up to this task, the use of teams will not trans-form the organization.

In addition to being the messenger—remember what happened to the messenger in the famous Greek myth?—you need to find innovative ways to play matchmaker. You need to identify opportunities to connect members of the teams you are helping to the rest of the organization. An organizing tool that might help you with this is commonly referred to as the "star" system. Encourage five of the members of your team to serve as "points" of your star team. Figure 1 provides an example.

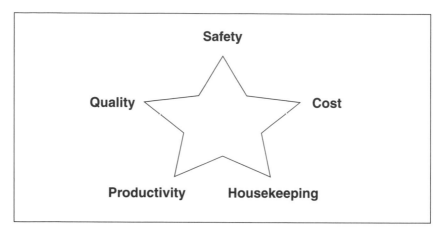

Figure 1: The "Star" System (Sample)

One team member helps track the team's safety record; you connect him with Plant Engineering to coordinate efforts to ensure a safe and healthy work environment. Another member monitors quality issues (scrap rates, tolerances, internal customer satisfaction, etc.)—you connect her with resource people providing training in Six Sigma, Quality Assurance, and other tools and techniques. Another member systematically charts cost data as materials flow through your team's department. You connect him with key professionals in the accounting and purchasing departments. Another team member keeps his peers informed about the production schedule and whether the team is keeping up with it. Still another member champions efforts to keep the workplace clean and have all tools and materials returned to their proper location.

You help these five point people meet the internal authority and resource people for your team's benefit. This may get your teammates invited to represent the team at meetings and to play an important role at your own team meetings on their subject matter expertise. You let them know that they are the "go-to" guys on the team for their area. Such a system not only ensures that the team concept doesn't rest solely on the shoulders of one team leader, it also makes sure that the team does not become insulated. The star system keeps people involved in meaningful ways.

One of the dangers in using a team concept is that members start to focus only on their own corner of the operation and fall prey to tendencies to compete with other teams. Your team's purpose is not only to build relations between members and find productive ways to complete its task; it also is to interconnect teams as part of a strategy to get the overall organization to succeed. As mentioned in chapter 7, members may unconsciously associate the use of teams with competition between teams. Sports teams are not expected to find ways to collaborate with other teams in their league, but work teams are. What is the mental model of teams among the members in your organization? Exercise 29 should prove useful for trying to get your members discussing this point, and it's fun. You need to help team members feel good about themselves and feel good about being part of the overall organization. You need to promote a mental model of teams as the vehicle for achieving a better organization. Jobs are secured by the success of the organization. Teams and collaboration between teams are key forces in creating a productive and satisfying work life.

Being the Ambassador for the Organization to Your Team

On the other side of the coin, your organization is probably looking to you to promote a positive image of itself to your team. In particular, you are in a prime position to help the team recognize the need for change and the plans the organization has for the future. People tend to resist change. What can you do to help overcome this resistance? Richard Beckhard (Beckhard and Harris 1987) developed this famous formula: $C>R$ when dVf. That is, *change* will overcome *resistance* to change when three factors occur simultaneously: (1) there is *dissatisfaction* with the status quo; (2) there is a *vision* of what could be or should be; and

EXERCISE 29

Mental Models: The Arm-Wrestling Exercise

Directions: At a team meeting or training session, have each member pair up with another member and assume the arm-wrestling position. Instruct each pair that they will be given fifteen seconds to see how many victories they can score in that time.

Within most pairs, members will compete and the number of victories will be few or even none. But perhaps some pairs will collaborate. The partners will alternate moving one partner's hand down for a victory and then the other's. Together they may score fifteen, twenty, twenty-five victories in the time allowed. If no pair thinks of doing this, demonstrate the collaborative strategy for them. Point out that the instructions merely called for achieving as many victories as possible.

The participants' mental model of arm wrestling led them to compete. Those with a different model probably scored much higher. Direct the discussion to how your team's mental model may lead it to compete with other teams within the organization when it really should be exploring a collaborative strategy. Identify what actions could be taken to explore a more collaborative mental model of the use of teams in an organizational setting.

(3) *first steps* are being taken that clearly move the organization away from the status quo and toward the vision.

This formula has some very important implications for how you can serve as your organization's ambassador for change to your team. Don't introduce change ideas to your team by trying to sell the vision. There must first be a compelling case made for the need for change. Start by sharing information about the need for change and listening for reasons why the members of your team may be dissatisfied with the status quo. When enough people recognize that they can no longer operate the way they have and still be able to compete in the marketplace, there will be enough energy available for a change effort. Complacency is the enemy of excellence. Be the leader who helps the team feel good about its progress yet stay hungry for getting even better.

Being dissatisfied with the status quo produces energy, but that energy has to be channeled or else it will be burned up with complaining, anger, and/or depression. Leadership must articulate a vision. Mohandas Gandhi once said, "We must become the change we want to see." The vision statement must paint word images so that organizational members can "see" what they want to become. It must answer questions such as, What do we mean by teams? How will teams make a difference? How will they help us address the compelling need for change? and, What will be different about our team-based organization from what we were? The vision does not have to spell out every detail, but it must be clear enough for all to see where they are headed. It cannot be just a "motherhood and apple pie" notion that teams are good and therefore we should all just get along with each other. The vision must help members see the use of teams as a business strategy and structure.

What is your vision of team excellence? Exercise 30 challenges you to articulate your vision. After you have captured your thoughts on teams, see if it is consistent with the "elevator speech" about your team you developed in exercise 14 (p. 94).

EXERCISE 30

Your Vision of Team Excellence

Directions: *Have each team member answer the questions below about the team's vision. Then, in a whole-team effort, develop a collective response to each question.*

- Why is the organization interested in establishing a team concept?

- What constitutes a team in this kind of work setting?

- What does it take to achieve team excellence?

Even if you have people dissatisfied with how things are currently being handled, and even if they are excited about the vision of team excellence, you still need to draw attention to the steps being taken to make the vision a reality. Many organizations have rallied the troops around some slogan, put up banners in the cafeteria, and given people hats, shirts, or jackets, declaring it now has a team concept, without successfully changing. Actions must be consistent with words. The organization must take visible first steps to demonstrate its commitment. Any inconsistencies and missteps will provide fuel to those members who would rather resist change. While a small percentage of employees may be willing to jump on any innovative bandwagon, the majority will wait to see whether management is serious. The devil is in the details.

Working together on teams may sound appealing but it still involves change, and many people are uncomfortable with change. Leadership may have to do away with work systems and procedures that have been around for years but which now are inconsistent with the vision of a team-based organization. The temptation to regress to the old ways will be strong. People may fall back to these comfortable methods instead of taking the risks necessary to activate the plan for the team approach. As leader, you need to model the new behaviors and encourage people to follow you.

Thus, in order to overcome resistance to moving toward a team concept, it will help if you can develop three strategies based on Beckhard's formula:

- Stir up dissatisfaction with the current situation
- Establish a compelling vision of what could or should be
- Develop and activate a concrete plan and take the steps toward the vision

Peter Senge says that "People don't resist change. They resist being changed." If you are encountering resistance, see what you can do about involving people in these three matters rather than trying to impose change on them. Use exercise 31 to identify three sets of strategies you can use with your people to overcome resistance to the change toward a team-based organization.

EXERCISE 31

Strategies for Overcoming Resistance to Change

Directions: *Brainstorm three sets of strategies you might be able to use to help overcome people's resistance to the team-based change effort being considered in your organization. In each category, devise approaches that involve people in brainstorming and planning.*

1. Strategies to overcome resistance by encouraging people to identify their dissatisfactions with the status quo (and thus identifying the need for change):

•

•

•

•

2. Strategies to overcome resistance to change through encouraging people to verbalize a vision of what a team-based change effort might be able to do for them and for the organization:

•

•

•

•

•

3. Strategies to overcome resistance to change through encouraging people to identify actions that are moving them from the status quo toward their vision of team-based change:

•

•

•

•

•

Tipping Points

Although Beckhard's formula provides a useful model for overcoming the resistance to change, do not expect change to occur in a logical, linear fashion. Change spreads more like a social movement than a step-by-step march—once it catches on, it produces a momentum of its own. There is also a tipping point after which much can happen in a hurry. As a leader, you not only have to be the ambassador that introduces and solicits ideas for change, you have to recognize the flow and encourage it to take hold. In Malcolm Gladwell's excellent book *The Tipping Point* (2000), he describes the three laws of change movements, as outlined in table 21 and described below. These laws provide you with additional tools to use as an ambassador of a team-based organizational change effort.

The Law of the Few

The first law states that initially you don't need to have the majority of the people in favor of becoming a team-based organization, but you do need a few special allies. Gladwell identifies "connectors," "mavens," and "salesmen." You may be one of these types of people and you may also benefit from recruiting a couple of these characters.

True to their name, connectors provide connections between groups and individuals. They don't hang out with the same people every day, but rather interact with several different groups and types of people. They aren't necessarily friends with all these people, but they have no qualms about talking with them even if they are not part of their circle. You might see them talking with union leaders one day, with upper management or with people from different departments the next. They may be freer to talk across racial, gender, and age lines. You need these people to hear about the elements of your organization's team concept early on. If you only present things to your supporters, or you try to rigidly adhere to the chain of command, the word might not spread fast enough to produce momentum. Connectors are your key to word-of-

TABLE 21

The Tipping Point Laws

1. **The Law of the Few**
   - Some people matter more than others do
   - The 80/20 rule (crime and disease spread by the activities of a few; social epidemics the same way)
   - A few exceptional people are more sociable, energetic, knowledgeable, or influential among peers

   Who should be communicating your change plans and ideas? Who are the connectors, mavens, and salespersons in your organization?

2. **The Stickiness Factor**
   - Epidemics tip when something happens to transform the epidemic agent itself
   - *Stickiness* means that a message stays with you; catchy phrases are strong influences
   - Unless you remember what someone tells you, it is unlikely it will change your behavior
   - Messages can become stickier through small changes in the presentation and structuring of information
   - The magic number 7: People don't remember lists of more than seven things

   What needs to be communicated, and how? How do you make the messages "sticky," and what distractions need to be removed?

3. **The Power of Context**
   - Circumstances, conditions, and particulars of the environment influence people's behavior
   - The weather, the number people around, and other contexual factors diffuse the sense of responsibility
   - The rule of 150: When an organization exceeds 150 people, informal means of influence no longer work well

   What are the contexts/conditions for this change effort, and what do they communicate? What can you do to establish an environment that will send the right message?

Source: Adapted from Malcolm Gladwell, *The Tipping Point* (New York: Little, Brown and Co., 2000).

mouth advertising for the need for change and the benefits of a team concept. Who are the natural connectors in your organization?

Mavens love to learn and to use what they learn to solve problems. They are not know-it-alls; they just like to figure things out. If you were going to buy a new stereo system or computer next week, isn't there someone you would call and ask their opinion about which brand to buy and where to shop? Mavens keep up on things. They enjoy knowing the details. It helps them solve their own problems, but they also welcome requests from others for help. Who are the mavens on your team? If members had questions about how a team concept is supposed to work, whom would they go to? Who do they believe will have examined the fine print and would help them understand the features of the company's team-based approach to change? Make sure your mavens have access to accurate information about your organization's change effort. You don't even have to know it all yourself. You need credible allies that people can go to for answers.

Salesmen—and saleswomen—are the closers. They push people past understanding. They get people to decide to buy. Organizational change efforts, especially those that are team based, are bound to have pros and cons associated with their strategies and steps. No change effort is risk free. Even after you get people to agree that there is a need for change and that the overall vision is a good one for their future, you will still have people debating the merits of the effort. Have you been in meetings where people end a discussion with "Let's agree to disagree"? While that is a respectful way to avoid further conflict during that meeting, it doesn't get anybody anywhere. At some point decisions have to be made and actions have to be taken to implement the decisions. Yes, teams are a way of democratizing organizations and encouraging free speech, but that does not mean members vote on every issue or that everyone's vote is equal. Teams within the organization can't be making decisions that contradict each other. They can solicit ideas, as well as discuss and debate them, but at some point they have to close the deal. You need an ally or two who are persuasive. They charm and convince people to take the plunge.

The Stickiness Factor

You and a small group of people can make a big difference in a change effort. However, it is not just a matter of who promotes the change. It's also a matter of what the change effort is about. The message communicated by you and your connectors, mavens, and salespersons must be what Gladwell describes as "sticky." That is, much of the details of a change effort will be forgotten—or never really listened to—but some core element must capture people's attention and stick in their mind. Yes, your organization's change effort may be complex, and it might take a day or three to explain it all, but guess what? People are going to leave those long sessions and remember just a few things—up to seven things on average, according to George A. Miller (1956). Carefully choose what messages you want to stick in team members' mind.

Politicians have learned that consistent, repetitive "sound bites" gain more votes than detailed explanations of their stances on issues. While we may not like this, we must learn from it. If you provide detailed handouts during team training sessions, they probably won't get read by the majority. If you provide bullet points highlighting the key elements, you will probably get more people to pay attention. If the majority can grasp the core principles of the change effort and know whom they can go to (e.g., you or a maven) for advice or more details, you have a better shot of helping the change stick. Remember the old adage concerning training presented earlier: "Tell people what you are going to tell them. Then tell them. And then close by telling them what you told them." Keep it simple, catchy, and consistent.

The Power of Context

According to the third law of tipping points, the environment in which a change effort is introduced has an impact on whether it catches on. People consciously or subconsciously pick up on signs that indicate whether a change effort is for real. If your organization claims to be advocating a team approach to getting work done, there had better be space available for teams to meet and interact. If the change effort emphasizes the need for an orderly and systematic approach to things, the facility ought to be kept clean and orderly.

If your organization has more than 150 people, you need clear rules and policies regarding the use of teams and the conduct of people on those teams. Informal agreements on how members are supposed to behave won't work in larger organizations. If your company is large enough that people don't know each other's names, informal procedures won't be enough. While peer pressure may influence behavior on a team of ten to twelve people, you need more formal mechanisms to ensure consistent behaviors across teams.

Some messages regarding your organization's change effort should be presented to everyone at roughly the same time to help ensure consistency. Perhaps an off-site or an all-employee meeting should be held to announce it. However, if it is a team-based change effort, most of the elements should be presented and discussed in small group settings. If the change is being made to get people involved, don't hold a session that asks people to be passive recipients of information. Break the large group into small groups and have them contribute input on why change is necessary and how teams can help address the need. Upper management (and union leadership in a joint setting) will have to sit in on many small group sessions repeating the message to all. While that may seem inefficient, it shows commitment and provides the context that matches a team-based change effort. By the way, these meetings between upper management and teams cannot be one-time events. Ongoing interactions are needed to sustain the change effort. All channels of communication should be explored. What can be done at your facility to establish communication boards or to establish computer links for easy transmittal of team documentation? Do you have the context to help tip the movement toward a team-based change in your organization?

Team-based change efforts are social movements in an organizational setting. Remember, the three laws described in *The Tipping Point* can help you become a more effective ambassador for helping your organization spread the change until it becomes a natural way of doing business. Exercise 32 provides a worksheet for you to apply these three laws to serve your organization and team.

Teams, Change, and Stress

Being a leader is certainly no easy task. While international ambassadors receive immunity and invitations to dinners and balls, you probably won't receive the equivalent at your organization. Remember that you are there to help others help themselves. Your team cannot succeed or fail based strictly on what you do. If that were the case, you wouldn't really have a team concept. You can make a big difference by doing some small things, as has been suggested throughout this book. However, success is still up to the team and many other key people throughout the organization.

While the use of a team concept can improve productivity and provide the opportunity for camaraderie and a sense of satisfaction, teams also create stress. People don't want to let their peers down. Team members may have felt the need for change because they wanted more say about decisions that affect their work life. I have heard many workers tell me that "management is too important to leave to management." However, this puts pressure on people to now make those decisions instead of just complaining. While it can be exciting to get to know people who are different from yourself, it can also be frustrating. While change may be needed for the organization to move forward, it can feel uncomfortable and thus stressful for most people. Change creates chaos, at least at first.

Are the stresses of change and the responsibilities of leadership all bad? Of course not. Up to a point, stress is a motivator. It energizes us to do something about what's causing it. Common sources of stress that you and members of your team may have to face at work include the following:

- Job setting (e.g., noise, danger, etc.)
- Job responsibilities (e.g., impacting lives and work of others)

EXERCISE 32

Applying the Three Laws to
Tip a Change Movement

Directions:

1. Brainstorm a list of people in the organization you think you may be able to influence. Then, commit to explaining the team-based change effort to at least three of these people. Be sure you recruit at least one connector, one maven, and one salesperson.

-
-
-
-
-
-

2. Identify the "sticky" messages underlying the changes you are trying to promote.

-
-
-
-
-
-

3. Develop a plan for when and where you will communicate your change efforts to the people you are committed to trying to influence. Be sure you have a context conducive to the content you are trying to deliver.

- Role in the organization (e.g., responsibility without much authority)
- Career issues (e.g., being underemployed, in over one's head)
- Relationships at work (e.g., jealousies, resentments)
- Recent events on the job (e.g., accidents, economic downturns)
- Culture of the organization (e.g., autocratic, competitive)
- Recent events away from work (e.g., divorce, traffic disruptions)

If the stress continues without resolution, it can be exhausting. The general adaptation syndrome describes the process this way: (1) people (as well as animals) are first alarmed by a source of stress; (2) stressors activate our adaptive responses of "fight or flight"—we either do something about the situation or get the heck out of there; and (3) if the source of stress continues, we become exhausted.

Burnout

Dealing with people, promoting good ideas, and even fighting change is hard work. In addition, sometimes we feel the angst of just doing our job day in and day out. Teams, individual members, and even team leaders (yes, even you) tend to suffer from burnout from time to time. There are many reasons for this, but the good news is that it is a curable condition. Let's face it: Things get old; the excitement and enthusiasm you probably felt when you first took on the task of helping teams in your organization wears off. What once was unique and adventuresome may later feel like a routine. Taking a disciplined approach to teams takes energy. Even the most gifted athletes have to drag themselves into the gym after a while. Even when you systematically go about the business of helping teams help themselves, things don't quite turn out the way you want them to. Reality in the workplace is different from textbook and playbook descriptions. Disappointments add up. Nothing comes out perfectly. Being a leader is stressful. Of course there will be some feelings of burnout.

Moderators of Stress

Certain situational and individual difference factors will help determine whether the change effort at your facility will be particularly stressful and lead to burnout. If you have plenty of time, money, equipment, supplies, and support, you are likely to be able to handle more sources of stress. Keep in mind that certain individuals will be greatly affected by the stress and others may not even notice it. The personality trait known as "hardiness" moderates the degree of reaction to stressors. Don't assume it is good to be hardy. Some people are thick-headed in addition to be thick-skinned when it comes to potentially stressful situations. They don't even realize that they *should* be nervous about the situation. It should also be mentioned that those people without supportive friends and co-workers—and those who value self-sufficiency so much that they won't turn to others in stressful situations—are more likely to suffer from stressful situations.

Consequences of Stress and Ways to Manage It

Up to a point, stress is motivating and may even create a push for short-term productivity. However, after that point, it can have serious consequences on the organization as well as on the individual, including sometimes costly problems:

- Organizational problems—absenteeism, turnover, lower productivity, more mistakes and accidents, lower morale
- Medical problems—heart, digestive tract, and respiratory illnesses; headaches; lowered immune system
- Behavioral problems—alcohol and drug abuse, violence
- Psychological problems—depression, anxiety, sleep disturbances

Stress, while it is a natural consequence of work life and life in general, can be a dangerous force. However, it can be managed. Table 22

TABLE 22

Three Main Strategies for Managing Stress

1. **Change the situation**
   - Reduce the causes of the stress
   - Apply systematic problem solving
   - Develop a plan
   - Negotiate demands
   - Assert your needs
   - Manage time

2. **Change your perception of the situation**
   - Reframe
   - Let go, accept
   - Stop the thought
   - Get counseling

3. **Activate your relaxation response**
   - Use Jacobson's Progressive Relaxation technique (see pp. 231–232)
   - Practice meditation, deep breathing, visualization
   - Increase exercise, improve nutrition
   - Seek support
   - Use biofeedback
   - Take a break
   - Use affirmations

---

outlines the three main strategies, which are then described in more detail.

Strategy 1: Change the Situation

One set of strategies involves addressing the sources of stress. Use your problem-solving skills to help reduce or eliminate the root causes of the stress. Develop a plan for turning things around. Team members can handle a lot more stress if they believe they have a plan that will deliver them from their current chaotic situation. If the source is coming from work overload or from the lack of role clarity, can you and others negotiate with management to establish more appropriate expectations? Working in a team can feel overwhelming, especially during times of change. Individuals and teams may benefit from a more systematic approach to time management. Is meeting time being used efficiently? Are members dedicating more time to tasks that are of higher priority rather than on tasks they may be more comfortable with? Peter Drucker suggests that truly effective managers do not add time-consuming efforts to all the work they are already doing, but rather figure out how to drop one activity for each one they add. What are you and your team doing to figure out your priorities to produce a more effective organization? Is the added work truly a short-term burden that will get smaller over time? When should you feel the shift in that burden?

Strategy 2: Change Your Perception of the Situation

When you find yourself overreacting to a situation, maybe you just need a different perspective. Have you noticed that you now deal with situations in a calm manner and yet know that you would have been very anxious in the same situations when you were less experienced? Norman Vincent Peale said, "Change your thoughts and you change your world." Experience seems to help. Perhaps at one point in your life, work was everything. Now you have kids to think about or maybe you have had a loved one die or maybe you have gotten involved in some community projects. Now you still care about doing great work but you know there is more to life than work. You have a new way to frame what is going on in the situation. You may be more able to accept imperfection without giving up on the goals of significant improvement. You no longer obsess or worry excessively. You are able to stop the thoughts that used to freeze you up.

Strategy 3: Activate Your Relaxation Response

Sometimes you can't do much about the situation and you and your teammates are looking at it realistically. The third strategy for dealing with stress entails activating your relaxation response. You can build up your relaxation response as you would a muscle. The more you exercise that muscle, the more capable you are of using it. Under stress, your heart rate increases and your breathing becomes more shallow. Inhaling deeply and exhaling slowly actually makes you more capable of relaxing under pressure. Meditation and visualization techniques help further this practice. If you exercise regularly and vigorously, your body is better prepared to activate its relaxation response. A diet of coffee, candy, and cola does not constitute good nutrition. Eating a balanced diet will make you more capable of relaxing.

Another terrific relaxation response technique is the "Progressive Relaxation" technique developed by Edmund Jacobson (1974). It is called "progressive" because with it you systematically progress the relaxation response from muscle group to muscle group throughout your body. Jacobson found that the sensations of relaxation are enhanced by contrasting tension with relaxation in each muscle group. Following a simple six-week program, you can train your body to bring about deep levels of relaxation at will. Activating your relaxation response is something you should be able to do for yourself. If you don't take care of yourself, you will not be as effective in your efforts to help others.

In the first two weeks of the Jacobson technique, you isolate your efforts to contrast tension and relaxation in small muscles groups. You start by tensing your fists and forearms for ten to fifteen seconds. You concentrate all your energy by focusing on the sensations of tension. Then you relax your fists and forearms for twenty to thirty seconds, focusing on the contrast between tension and relaxation and letting relaxation take over where the tension was. You work up your arms, one small muscle group at a time, and proceed to progress through all the muscle groups, from the top of your head to the tips of your toes. In all cases, you tense each muscle group for ten to fifteen seconds and then release it for twenty to thirty seconds.

You may want to make your own relaxation tape using this tool. However, it is actually best if you just do the exercise with your eyes closed all by yourself. In the first two weeks it will take you about twenty minutes a day. You need to do the long form of the exercise to build responses throughout your body. During the last four weeks, you do the short form, which takes only ten minutes a day. Aren't you worth it? I strongly advise that you find the time during the next six weeks and train your body to achieve this very deep level of relaxation. Detailed instructions are provided in appendix B.

Summary

As team leader, you have the opportunity to enlighten team members as well as the people above you in the organization's hierarchy. Your ability to be an advocate for the fulfillment of the needs of your team is important. You also have the chance to lead by example by demonstrating diplomatic methods of influencing people in powerful positions. Your willingness to share power with team members—perhaps using a system similar to the "star" system—actually increases the amount of power available to your team. It is easy to say that any organizational change effort must be viewed from an open systems perspective. Your efforts to connect your team to key players and to other teams operationalizes this open systems approach. Team leaders are the ambassadors for the team approach and they must be the organization's agents for change as well. This chapter provided you with strategies and tools to tip the momentum toward change. It also provided you with the help you may need to cope with the stress associated with these responsibilities.

AFTER-CHAPTER REVIEW

Now that you have completed reading this chapter, it is time for you to challenge yourself to see what you remember, establish what it is you learned, and decide where and how you are going to apply what you learned. The outline provided below can help you get started. The relevancy of this chapter may necessitate that you expand on your thoughts elsewhere. Make sure you benefit from your reading by capturing your thoughts and turning them into actions.

1. Describe at least five things you remember from the material in this chapter.

-
-
-
-
-

2. Identify the insights you gained from reading the material in this chapter. These insights may have come directly from the points raised or by stimulating recollections of your own experiences.

-
-
-

3. Identify at least one situational opportunity for applying what you learned and describe the steps to be taken (including who will do what with whom, where, and when).

Situational opportunity:

Steps to be taken:

-
-
-
-

MONITORING AND REVIVING TEAMS

Helping Your Team Get Unstuck

•

Is your team winning? Is that the only statistic you are monitoring for your team? Baseball teams have traditionally posted box scores listing runs, hits, and errors. Bill James (2003), author of the best-selling book series *Baseball Abstracts*, has changed how teams are managed by compiling and analyzing all kinds of baseball statistics. General managers (most notably Billy Beane of the Oakland Athletics, as documented in Michael Lewis's best-selling book *Moneyball*, 2003) have changed how they select players to build their teams, and field managers have changed how the teams play the game as a result of James's analysis. He calls his approach "sabermetrics" (after Society of American Baseball Research) and emphasizes the search for objective knowledge about baseball.

Instead of using hunches and "conventional wisdom," James has gathered data to either verify or debunk common team strategies. For example, many managers order their batters to make a sacrifice bunt (making an out in order to advance a runner from one base to another). James's research, however, shows that outs should steadfastly be avoided because more good things can happen if you have the batter hit away.

James has also shown that a statistic known as "on-base percentage" is a better measure of how valuable a player is than the traditional statistic of batting average. Batters who carefully pick which pitches to hit greatly add value to the offensive power of a baseball team. Billy Beane used this undervalued statistic to put together championship teams while reducing payroll costs considerably compared to other teams.

James suggests that managers should not believe clichés when they could be gathering measurements and applying logical analysis. He still admits that baseball is as much an art as a science but believes metrics help weed out misplaced beliefs. His dedication to eliminating biases has made a difference.

•

The seven key components of team excellence identified in this book separate the good teams from the excellent teams. They were compiled by gathering data on hundreds of teams in work organizations. Who is the Bill James in your organization? Who is gathering data to test the assumptions underlying your organization's approach to teams? Do you believe that team meetings should never be held on Mondays or

Fridays? How do you know that? Do you believe that the responsibility for team leadership should be rotated among all members of the team? What evidence have you gathered to test the impact of this strategy? This chapter will challenge you to work with your team to identify what statistics you should be gathering on a regular basis and how you should do it.

Data Gathering and Strategic Planning for Your Team

As team leader, you need to remind team members what the score is—and how they are doing this season—to motivate increases in team effort and performance. If the team is doing well, you need to help prevent complacency. If the team is in a slump, you need to work with the team to identify some useful adjustments. This chapter will provide you with some tools to keep score and to use the data to help your team get unstuck.

What kind of data does your organization gather to know if it is "winning"? Retail stores keep track of gross sales and returns. Factories monitor measures of productivity, scrap rates, and overtime hours. Law firms chart billable hours. Restaurants record the number of meals served, the percentage of tabletops filled, and gross receipts. What are the results your team should be monitoring to know if it is contributing to the organization's overall results? You need to develop a system that breaks down the broader metrics to capture the value added by each department, function, and team. Your team's scorecard needs to indicate whether things are getting better or getting worse, and why. Every successful coach knows the final score of the game and which statistics to look at to plan adjustments for the rest of this season and beyond.

Table 23 outlines the five steps of a strategic planning process. Teams should go through such a process at least once a "season"—however a season is defined in your kind of business (e.g., quarterly, car model

---

TABLE 23

The Five Steps of Strategic Planning

1. **Reviewing the team's past: What day is it in the life of this team?**
   - Study your vision/mission statement (to review why this team exists)
   - Identify key milestones (highlights and lowlights)
   - Describe what has happened and what has been decided over the last one to five years

2. **Assessing the current state of the team**
   - Recognize the need for multiple bottom lines
   - Assess your product (outcomes)
   - Assess your processes for achieving those outcomes
   - Assess your people (morale, growth)
   - Summarize with a "SWOT" statement

3. **Identifying and resolving current problems**
   - Awareness: Which weaknesses deserve attention?
   - Analysis: What are the chief causes of the problems?
   - Alternatives: What could be done differently?
   - Action: Who should do what with whom by when and how?
   - Assessment: Did it reduce/eliminate the root cause?
   - Appreciation: Were the persons responsible reinforced?

4. **Envisioning the team's future direction**
   - Identify likely future demands
   - Picture your ideal/preferred future
   - Brainstorm new features/directions for your team
   - Envision the milestones you would achieve

5. **Planning steps for implementation**
   - Identify the forces for and against a new and improved team
   - Identify the strategies to capitalize on the forces for
   - Identify the strategies to reduce the forces against
   - Identify the steps that must be taken for implementation
   - Identify who is responsible for which elements of the plan
   - Create a timeline for achieving the elements of the plan

year, semester, tourist season, Christmas season, etc.). The steps of your team's strategic planning process should occur regularly on a formal and an informal basis.

Step 1: Reviewing the Team's Past

At least once a year, teams should meet to identify the lessons they have learned during that period. This is especially important when new members have been added to the team. Unless you have a common understanding of your existence, how can you expect to unite for a better future? Begin the session with a reading of the team's purpose or mission statement. This could be done by a representative of upper management. Does the statement still define what the organization hopes to gain from the team's existence? Is this why the team exists in the eyes of its members? Should it be modified? The rest of the review, assessment, and planning should be done in light of the team's reason for existence.

How long has this team existed? What have been its highlights? What were the low moments? Exercise 33 can help you to outline your team's history. What would your team be worth in the stock market? What lessons can be learned from a review of the peaks and valleys of your team's lifeline? Are there any common causes of upswings? What was happening that led to downward trends? Each lesson can be valuable, but the identification of trends is even more important.

Step 2: Assessing the Current State of the Team

Where do you stand as a team today? What does your organization use to measure your team's effectiveness? Does your team track any other indicators to know what the score is? It is tempting to look for a singular bottom line to determine the effectiveness of your team. People want to know if you are successful or not. But organizational life is not really that simple. A single metric of productivity provides important

EXERCISE 33

Our Team's "Stock Price" and Analysis

Directions: *Modify the form below to match the time period of your team's review. It is currently set up for an annual review taking place at the end of the calendar year. If your team has existed for more than a year, develop a chart that shows every year (and perhaps every quarter in every year) of your team's existence. First have each team member answer questions 1–3 privately and then facilitate a discussion of those questions and produce a chart that represents the team's overall self-assessment. Then facilitate a discussion of questions 4 and 5.*

1. Compared to the typical team (whose "stock price" we'll say averages around 50), what was our "stock price" when we first formed as a team? When estimating stock price, include your combined assessment of how productive the team was, how satisfying it was to be a member of this team, and how well we used team processes to work together.

2. At what times was our stock price highest? Why? What was happening during those times?

3. At what times was our stock price lowest? Why? What was happening during those times?

4. What does our collective assessment of the worth of our team teach us?

5. Where is our stock price headed? What can we do to enhance the value of our team?

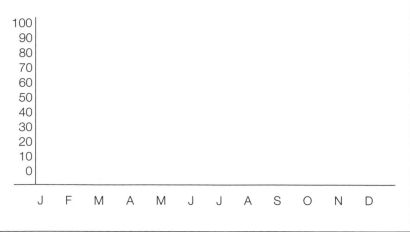

information but could orient decision making toward short-term solutions. It may mask safety risks, quality shortcuts, and worker dissatisfaction issues that may cause a monumental collapse down the road. As a team leader, you need to work with management to determine the key metrics. In addition, the metrics must be aligned at each level. You need to help your team members pay attention to the right data points to track several bottom lines and help them understand why. Ideally, there should be no more than seven key figures to track.

Tracking the Three Ps (PPP). Even seven things is a lot to expect people to pay attention to systematically. Let's make it simpler. Let's track the three Ps: product, process, and people (PPP).

1. **Product: Our outcome metrics.** What does your team make? Does it produce goods, reports, services, sales? How much did it produce? How well did it produce these things? How much did it cost for your team to produce at this level? To what extent did the team achieve the goals listed in its charter? You need someone or some system to gather and monitor productivity (units produced per person hour, number of customers served, etc.), quality metrics (scrap rates, customer complaints, etc.), costs (for supplies, inventory, labor, etc.), and other measures of goal accomplishments. If your team set "SMART" goals (see chapter 4), you will have already identified the metrics that will serve as the basis of your team's assessment. Which data points indicate that the team has matched or exceeded what is expected of it? Which data points show that it is on target to achieve its goals within the time frames previously identified? These last two sets of data points indicate strengths—don't take them for granted. The team needs to analyze why these positive results were achieved. This will aid later planning efforts by identifying things the team should continue doing and maybe even accelerate or accentuate these positive actions. The team also needs to identify its weaknesses. Data points that are only slightly below expectations indicate the need for some problem solving. Data points that indicate that

the team is way behind may call for a more drastic rethinking of the team's strategies and procedures.

2. **Process: Our throughput metrics.** In addition to measuring the results, a team needs to know whether it is getting better or worse as a team. What is it doing that helps team members work well together, and what is it doing that is hindering them? The Team Diagnostic Questionnaire (TDQ, exercise 34) is an instrument I've developed over the years to assess the seven key components of team excellence and to answer those questions. Following the exercise is a table of norms you can use to compare your team's TDQ results against those of other teams.

    Team members should complete a copy of the TDQ individually and anonymously. When members have completed the questionnaire, the team leader or a designate should then collect the copies and average the scores for each item. All team members should be provided with a copy of the team's results. You should have your team complete this exercise approximately once every three months. In addition to the TDQ results, members should identify other aspects of how they work together as a team. What do they think the team does well? What doesn't it do so well? What isn't it doing that it should be doing? What is it currently doing that maybe it should quit doing?

3. **People: Team member satisfaction metrics.** How satisfying is it to be a member of this team? Do members feel their work provides them with a fulfilling experience? There are a number of ways to attempt to measure team morale. The final question on the Team Diagnostic Questionnaire simply asks members to estimate on a scale of 0–100 how satisfying it is to be a member of the team. An alternative approach is provided in exercise 35. It breaks down the concept of team satisfaction to component parts paralleling Maslow's hierarchy of needs. Results can be used to measure the level of satisfaction for the current time period and then be compared to previous results to determine if morale is getting better or worse.

EXERCISE 34

Team Diagnostic Questionnaire

Make copies of this exercise so that each member can participate individually.

Name of team: _____

Directions to team members: *To help identify your team's strengths and weaknesses, please provide honest and independent responses. Your responses are confidential and will be collected in a manner that protects your anonymity. The average responses for each item will be calculated and fed back to each team member.*

Using a scale of 0–4 (0 = not at all; 4 = very much), rate each of the following statements (1a–7c) as they relate to your team now.

1a. The goals of our team are appropriate and clearly   0 1 2 3 4
stated.

1b. The members of our team are committed to the   0 1 2 3 4
accomplishment of our shared team goals.

1c. Our team accomplishes its goals.   0 1 2 3 4

2a. Our team collectively contains the full range of talents   0 1 2 3 4
we need to be an effective unit.

2b. The talents of the members of our team are fully utilized.   0 1 2 3 4

3a. The role of leadership is competently fulfilled by one or   0 1 2 3 4
more people on this team.

3b. Each member of our team clearly understands the role   0 1 2 3 4
he or she needs to play for us to be an effective unit.

3c. Each member of our team clearly fulfills the role he or   0 1 2 3 4
she is expected to play.

4a. Our team uses effective and efficient procedures to   0 1 2 3 4
work together to complete our tasks.

4b. Our team uses effective and efficient procedures to   0 1 2 3 4
identify and resolve problems as they occur.

4c. Our team holds effective and efficient meetings.   0 1 2 3 4

EXERCISE 34 CONT'D

4d. Our team uses effective and efficient procedures to
ensure that information is shared and received.   0 1 2 3 4

4e. Our team uses effective and efficient planning procedures.   0 1 2 3 4

4f. Our team effectively monitors its progress.   0 1 2 3 4

5a. Team members deal with conflict in a constructive manner.   0 1 2 3 4

5b. Team members provide enough support to each other
to encourage a sense of belonging to the team.   0 1 2 3 4

5c. Team members provide enough positive challenge to
each other to encourage high levels of performance.   0 1 2 3 4

5d. Team members get along with each other well.   0 1 2 3 4

6a. Team members provide each other with enough
recognition for working together as a team.   0 1 2 3 4

6b. Our team receives enough recognition from outside
sources for our working together as a team.   0 1 2 3 4

7a. Our team recognizes and actively pursues opportunities
available in its external environment.   0 1 2 3 4

7b. Our team recognizes and actively addresses the threats
it is facing in its external environment.   0 1 2 3 4

7c. Our team has constructive relations with other teams
and individuals it interacts with.   0 1 2 3 4

Then answer the following two questions:

1. Overall (on a scale of 0–100), how would you rate our team's effectiveness ?

    _____

2. Overall (on a scale of 0–100), how satisfied are you to be a member of
this team?

    _____

Scoring the Exercise

Record the averaged Team Diagnostic Questionnaire results of your team members in the "Team Average" column below. Create a composite average for each component by adding the individual item results for each component and dividing by the number of items (e.g., for "Goals," there are three items). Upon its completion, distribute the form to the team members.

(Database = 98 teams seeking team development help; items scored on a scale of 0–4: 0 = not at all; 4 = very much)

Questionnaire Item	Team Average	Database Average	Component
1a. Clear and appropriate goals	___	2.14	
1b. Commitment to goals	___	2.35	Goals
1c. Accomplished goals	___	2.20	
Composite average	___	2.23	
2a. Full range of talents	___	2.66	
2b. Full use of talents	___	2.02	Talents
Composite average	___	2.34	
3a. Leadership role fulfilled	___	2.41	
3b. Clear understanding of roles	___	2.06	Roles
3c. Each role fulfilled	___	2.08	
Composite average	___	2.18	
4a. Work procedures	___	2.07	
4b. Problem-solving procedures	___	2.01	

EXERCISE 34 CONT'D

Questionnaire Item	Team Average	Database Average	Component
4d. Communication procedures	___	1.86	
4e. Planning procedures	___	1.78	Procedures
4f. Progress-monitoring procedures	___	1.76	
Composite average	___	1.86	
5a. Conflict handled constructively	___	1.92	
5b. Support provided to each other	___	2.03	
5c. Challenge provided to each other	___	1.94	Interpersonal Relations
5d. Getting along well	___	2.54	
Composite average	___	2.11	
6a. Peer recognition provided for team	___	2.11	
6b. External recognition for team	___	1.34	Recognition
Composite average	___	1.72	
7a. External opportunities pursued	___	1.64	
7b. External threats addressed	___	1.82	External Relations
7c. Constructive external relations	___	1.95	
Composite average	___	1.80	
1. Overall effectiveness rating (0–100)	___	66	
2. Overall satisfaction rating (0–100)	___	71	

EXERCISE 35

Team Morale Survey

Directions for team leader: *Periodically have each team member complete this survey anonymously. Use the collective results to determine whether morale has improved or gotten worse.*

Directions for team members: *Rate each of the following statements on a scale of -2 to +2 (-2 = strongly disagree; -1 = disagree; 0 = neutral; +1 = agree; +2 = strongly agree) by circling the appropriate number to the right of each statement.*

Circle one

1. I am paid fairly for the work that I do on this team.   -2 -1 0 +1 +2

2. I feel safe and secure while performing the work   -2 -1 0 +1 +2
   I do on this team.

3. I have satisfying work relations with my teammates.   -2 -1 0 +1 +2

4. I have the opportunity to responsibly achieve things   -2 -1 0 +1 +2
   for this team.

5. I have the opportunity to learn, grow, and fulfill   -2 -1 0 +1 +2
   myself through my work on this team.

This component parts approach to measurement also provides an opportunity to identify which specific elements need to be addressed to improve satisfaction levels.

Both methods described so far involve self-reporting metrics. One might argue that this is appropriate for measuring something as subjective as satisfaction/morale. However, some teams use surrogate objective metrics instead. Rates of absenteeism, grievances, tardiness, and accidents can be recorded objectively, and they have been found to be highly correlated with estimates of team morale. The team concept should be good for the organization and for the people on the teams. Which metrics should your team use to monitor satisfaction/morale?

The team concept provides many learning and developmental opportunities for employees. Members of your team may have learned each other's jobs. Team training sessions may have provided the opportunity to develop skills in conflict resolution, scheduling, budgeting, planning, problem solving, and other areas. Your team's PPP scorecard ought to be able to capture how much more knowledgeable and skilled members have become—either by using self-estimates or tracking successful completion of training programs. Some companies have gone to certifying knowledge and skill levels through testing. This may be a good idea especially when people will be paid for knowledge and skills.

Summarizing the Data. Data must be fresh to have an impact on performance. Ideally, data gathering is performed on a daily basis. Some data are more amenable to this than others. Some data should be reviewed before every shift or at every team meeting (e.g., product data). However, the rest of the PPP balanced scorecard is best utilized in team problem-solving and strategic planning sessions. A "SWOT" (Strengths, Weaknesses, Opportunities, and Threats) analysis is a common method of summarizing multiple data points and the resulting assessment discussions. Use exercise 36 to summarize your team's SWOT assessment discussion.

Step 3: Identifying and Resolving Current Problems

Step 3 of strategic planning involves systematic problem solving. The list of weaknesses identified in your SWOT analysis can serve as the *awareness* stage of your problem-solving efforts. The team prioritizes the weaknesses and then conducts an analysis of the causes of those it chooses to address in this planning/problem-solving session. *Alternatives* are identified, and the team comes to a consensus decision regarding which alternative it is committed to activate to eliminate or at least greatly reduce the weakness. *Action* plans to implement the solu-

EXERCISE 36

A SWOT Assessment

Directions for team members: *Use the form below to capture the main findings from your examination of the data gathered for your team's scorecard this season. What is your assessment of our team? Categorize the findings by identifying our current strengths and weaknesses as well as the future opportunities and threats that lie in our team's near future.*

Strengths (what we currently do well):

•

•

•

Weaknesses (what we currently don't do well):

•

•

•

Opportunities (what might come up in the near future, or forces outside our team that we should try to capitalize on):

•

•

•

Threats (what might come up in the near future, or forces outside our team that we should try to guard against):

•

•

•

tions the team develops must be established. Follow-up actions including *assessment* and *appreciation* verify whether the intended impact was achieved and reinforces the team's efforts. The systematic problem-solving model discussed at length in chapter 6 and the tools provided can help serve your team's strategic planning process.

Step 4: Envisioning the Team's Future Direction

In step 4, the team brainstorms ideas for new directions to consider adding to its charter. It should scan the external environment and examine the opportunities and threats listed in the SWOT analysis. What new strategies, procedures, or roles should you develop to address them? What might your "customers and suppliers" demand from you in the future? Will your current procedures be sufficient to address these demands? Do you have reason to believe that your "competitors" will be doing things better or differently in the near future? Will there be new sources of competition for you to address? What is your vision for your team for the coming season? What new features and directions should your team adopt? How will you know if you are succeeding with these new elements? What milestones are you committed to achieving? What is your preferred future?

Step 5: Planning Steps for Implementation

Step 5 requires action planning for the new team directions identified in step 4. What forces might push your team to truly adopt the new features? Perhaps more important, what forces might get in the way? What obstacles, sources of resistance, and pitfalls can you anticipate if you do make the changes identified in step 4? Plans must be made to capitalize on the forces for change and to minimize the forces against it. These plans must be detailed enough so that each team member understands the steps to be taken and who is responsible for activating each step. A time frame and plans to obtain the necessary resources must be established.

Heisenberg's Uncertainty Principle

You are being urged to help your team develop a system of metrics so that they know the score. You want to be able to present evidence to others in the organization that the team-based change effort you are assisting is working. A word of caution: You cannot truly prove that things are objectively working or not working. Teams and organizations obviously do not live in scientific laboratories. Many factors are influencing every outcome you desire. In addition, all measurements are to some degree subjective, even so-called scientific measurements. Werner Heisenberg, the scientist who founded quantum mechanics, showed that when we try to measure things, we change them. The old Newtonian version of physics assumed that the "real world" existed independently of our observations. Heisenberg discovered that each concept has a meaning only in terms of the experiments used to measure it. So no measurement is truly objective.

Your team's efforts to measure productivity, quality, team process effectiveness, morale, and so on will all have subjective elements associated with them. Your team should have discussions on what determines "quality" and how it should be measured. Such discussions help focus a team's energy and inspire a group to pull together. However, measurements drive behaviors; anything the group pays attention to causes changes. As a result of paying attention to scrap rates, will the team pay less attention to the costs of tooling? As a result of measuring satisfaction, will the team be less disciplined at team meetings and allow members to express themselves on any topic regardless of the current agenda topic? So be sure your team considers the implications of the metrics it chooses to record on its scorecard.

Perfection is impossible—there will be a downside to every good measurement strategy chosen. Just try to anticipate the implications and make decisions. There are trade-offs for every choice made. Yes, some measurements will have a more obvious subjective element, but just make sure the data on that element are gathered systematically. The point is to help the team determine if it is getting better or worse, not to determine if it doing good or bad in absolute terms.

Summary

Teams need to know where they stand. In this chapter a balanced scorecard was presented for incorporating metrics to assess the three Ps (product, process, and people). The primary tool provided was a strategic planning process. Teams should engage in strategic planning at least once a season. However, waiting to address problems once a year would be foolish. Data must be gathered on a daily basis to help a team know whether it is getting better or getting worse. Data should be analyzed to determine if preconceived notions of how to operate as a team have their desired impact.

Teams go through slumps. When scores on your PPP scorecard indicate the team is plateauing or even regressing, it is time to engage in systematic problem solving and strategic planning processes. You need to help teams continually assess outcomes and clarify goals, talents, roles, procedures, interpersonal relations, reinforcement, and external relations. As leader, you need to make sure that teams are performing consciously. Unless they are aware of the data and aware of what they need to succeed, they cannot reach and sustain excellence. Are your teams on track? Is it time for you to facilitate a strategic planning process for your teams?

AFTER-CHAPTER REVIEW

Now that you have completed reading this chapter, it is time for you to challenge yourself to see what you remember, establish what it is you learned, and decide where and how you are going to apply what you learned. The outline provided below can help you get started. The relevancy of this chapter may necessitate that you expand on your thoughts elsewhere. Make sure you benefit from your reading by capturing your thoughts and turning them into actions.

1. Describe at least five things you remember from the material in this chapter.

   •

   •

   •

   •

   •

2. Identify the insights you gained from reading the material in this chapter. These insights may have come directly from the points raised or by stimulating recollections of your own experiences.

   •

   •

   •

3. Identify at least one situational opportunity for applying what you learned and describe the steps to be taken (including who will do what with whom, where, and when).

   Situational opportunity:

   Steps to be taken:

   •

   •

   •

   •

CHAPTER 11

HELPING A WHOLE TEAM OF LEADERS

Leading Leadership Teams

•

I have been honored to help hundreds of teams over the last twenty-five years or so. My biggest challenges have been in trying to help a couple dozen teams made up of leaders from across organizational functions. I have tried to help teams of executives, plant managers and their operating committees, boards of directors of nonprofits, and executive boards/bargaining committees of local unions. Let me share an example.

I worked with a plant manager relatively new to his position named Jim. He had been area manager years before and now was being brought back to resurrect a plant that had fallen behind in productivity and quality. He was an African American as were his newly appointed human resources director and controller. He formed a relatively large operating committee (fourteen

members) that included current area managers—
all of whom had been passed over for promotion
in their twenty-plus-year careers—and all major
support function heads. He recognized that the
"team" was not pulling together. He suspected
underlying resentments and knew he had only a
year or so to turn plant operations around.

Jim originally asked me to provide a bonding
experience for the group of leaders he was
depending on. I convinced him to allow me to
conduct a series of confidential one-on-one interviews with each member, to observe his team
meetings, and to have the members complete my
Team Diagnostic Questionnaire. He allowed me to
present the data at a special session of his operating committee; we used it to collaboratively
design a series of off-site teambuilding sessions
to improve members' ability to hold constructive
meetings, use a disciplined approach to systematic problem solving, build more open and
respectful interpersonal relations, and ultimately
establish a comprehensive strategic plan. As a
result of these sessions, it was decided to
reduce the operating committee from fourteen
members to eight—the other six did not lose
their job but rather attended committee meetings
only upon request to provide their subject matter
expertise. The strategic planning process helped
them to identify and resolve issues that significantly boosted productivity and quality. The committee members reduced operating costs,
improved morale, and became an example of a

diverse set of individuals learning and working together. When I saw them last, they were working on a plan to "market" their plant within the corporation, which was also their major "customer."

•

The committee still had problems, but members were capable of functioning as a team when required rather than as a group that was merely obliged to meet every Monday morning. These individuals became a team that understood the function and purpose of leadership teams as well as some of the unique difficulties of building teams at the top. This chapter will help you to do the same for your leadership team.

What Constitutes a Leadership Team

A team can be defined as a small group of people who need to work interdependently to produce something. Leadership teams are made up of people who are used to being responsible for their own units within a larger organization. The group of leaders at the top of an organization's hierarchy may or may not be a true team. The members usually want to be seen as part of a leadership team to be able to influence the overall organization. I have seen groups who declared themselves a team just because they meet once a week to inform each other about what they are working on. I have seen groups of leaders brought together to be chastised on a regular basis by the head leader for any less than perfect performance. And I have been lucky to see some leadership teams that have truly benefited from the collective wisdom of the group and who developed innovative strategies to address the complexities of their organization in an effort to cope with ever-changing environments and business conditions.

Organizational life becomes more complex every year. Can your company really count on a single individual to provide overall leadership? If we know that teams that make things outperform groups of individuals, shouldn't a team of leaders do a better job of providing strategic direction than a single president or CEO? More and more companies are using executive leadership teams in these complex times. Collectively the members may have the wisdom to help identify current realities and develop strategic initiatives to realize the team's vision for the future.

Determining What the Team Really Wants

Success of any teambuilding intervention is directly dependent on how clear the organization is about what the team is to accomplish. My first question when asked to work with any leadership group is, "What is the purpose of this team?" If the group exists to produce an actual product (e.g., a mission statement, a strategic plan, a community service event, a launch of a new organizationwide system, a strategy to address or avoid a current or potential crisis, etc.), I treat it as a team and ask to conduct some diagnostic activities. One activity is to interview members for the purpose of identifying general impressions of the team and what could be done to improve it, using questions such as those listed in table 24. In such an interview, all responses must be kept confidential and anonymous. The themes that emerge should be reported later at a special session, where all members must be present and make decisions regarding what to do about the results.

If members are committed to collectively producing something and are willing to share decision-making power in some manner and establish a system of mutual accountability, then I suggest turning the group into a functioning team. Subsequent steps for developing a true leadership team are discussed later in this chapter. But first let's look at some other reasons underlying requests by leaders for teambuilding.

TABLE 24

Leadership Team Interview Questions

- What is it like to be a leader at this organization?

- What does this leadership team do well?

- What does this leadership team need to do better or differently? Is there a compelling need for this team to change and improve?

- What might be pushing this leadership team to improve? What might motivate this group of leaders to work more effectively as a team?

- What might get in the way of this leadership team's efforts to improve itself? What barriers, pitfalls, obstacles, or sources of resistance might interfere?

- If a session (or series of sessions) were scheduled to help this team work more effectively, what skills should be worked on? What issues should be on the agenda?

- As leaders, you have some independent responsibilities and some objectives that you must work on collectively. What is an opportunity/project/issue/activity that this group could attempt to work on as a team?

- What could you do to help this leadership team become more effective?

- What do you expect from me as a facilitator attempting to help this leadership team help itself?

Reasons for the Request for Teambuilding

Conflict between key leaders is a concern, and it prompts many requests for teambuilding. If some key leaders at the top of the organization are operating in an independent manner and complaining about other leaders, an intervention may be needed. Teamwork is not the same thing as functioning as an effective team, but it is still an important objective. Many of the tools provided in the previous chapters can be used to help develop teamwork even if the leadership team does not intend to work as a true team.

If the purpose of the intervention is to promote camaraderie and cooperation, many networking opportunities are possible, fun, and interesting and may fill the bill. The members may need to get to know each other (using exercises such as those described in chapter 2), improve their conflict resolution skills (see chapter 7), and/or work on their communication skills (see chapter 5) to ensure that the left hand knows what the right hand is doing. Confidential interviews with each of the top leaders and observations of their meetings provide valuable diagnostic insights regarding what kind of interventions to propose. The more you involve these powerful people in the design of the intervention, the more likely it will have a chance to make a difference. I have found that leaders at the top of their organization agree to attend all kinds of off-sites but don't always use the sessions to actually change their behaviors unless they feel it was their idea in the first place.

Another purpose underlying a request for teambuilding at the top is to get two or three key functions to work closely together to solve a problem that stretches across organizational boundaries. Instead of dragging the entire leadership team through some teambuilding activities, I usually suggest that a subgroup receive help in becoming a model problem-solving task force. The subgroup clarifies its purpose and verifies whether it has enough people with the knowledge and skills to investigate the matter. We then use the opportunity to impose the team discipline of systematic problem solving as the cornerstone of their procedures for meeting together. The 4-A Plus 2 problem-solving method (see chapter 6) pushes the group to determine what the issues are, rather than play political games to determine who is at fault. The method enhances the effectiveness and efficiency of the task force's effort and serves as a model for other problem-solving teams throughout the organization. It may also set a precedent that the larger leadership team holds regular meetings just to keep each other informed but uses task forces when there is truly something to produce, such as a solution to a specific problem.

I have also had leadership teams request my teambuilding services because they were launching a team-based approach to change at the shop-floor level and they felt they needed to set an example. The key question to ask is, "What is the group supposed to produce?" If it is not truly producing something, you don't want to point to it as a model of an effective team. Team members at the shop-floor level work with each other every day for their whole shift. Leadership teams may meet once a week and either produce no products or services or produce plans that may take months to develop. However, leadership teams do need to produce a vision statement and a plan for the organization's team concept and thus may need teambuilding to help them succeed as a steering committee. It is more important that this group of key leaders provide a sense of direction for the overall team-based change effort than to set itself up as a model of how teams are to function.

Leaders at the top of their organization must provide support for shop-floor teams that make things and for problem-solving committees and task forces that resolve issues to help the overall organization benefit from a team-oriented approach. Communication of this support comes in the form of a well-articulated plan for the use of teams and provision of the resources needed to activate the plan. The leaders need to make sure that the actions that occur are consistent with their words, and they must be experts on the team concept process. They need to be able to answer questions from members of self-directed work teams and task forces about the game plan for teams. Leaders must also show their genuine belief in teams—not merely go through the motions. They need to lead with their heart as well as their mind. The message has to be heard consistently from each and every leadership team member, and the message cannot be delivered at the launch of a team concept and never heard from again.

Leadership teams often feel that they should go through the same teambuilding sessions they are prescribing for others. While it may be helpful for them to go through many of the same exercises to gain greater empathy for the difficulty work teams and committees may face, if those "teambuilding" sessions emphasize only communication and cooperation, this may send the wrong message and be cascaded inappropriately. Leadership team members can share lessons from these training programs and their own efforts to work together to produce plans, principles, and events. Don't leave the impression that getting along is the only thing it takes to have a healthy, effective team.

Why Teambuilding for Leadership Teams Is Difficult

Leaders are very busy people. They don't have much time to spare, and many assignments can be handled individually. Real team efforts at the top are in direct conflict with the strong single-leader approach that exists in most organizations. It is very difficult to break that pattern of behavior. Executives have been conditioned to follow another set of rules that helped them get to their current position, and unfortunately most of those rules did not require the discipline needed to work as a true team. Jon Katzenbach's marvelous book *Teams at the Top* (1998) provides a list of contrasts between traditional single-leadership approaches and a true team approach.

Katzenbach points out that leaders at the top direct the actions of large numbers of people. Team leaders mold the talent and motivations of small numbers of people. Executives are supposed to exercise personal judgment to assess risks and options, whereas teams are supposed to make collective judgments by being open with each other and working through the conflict. Executives take on or pass on assignments according to individuals' formal position in the hierarchy. True teams make assignments according to who has the knowledge and skills to do the specific task regardless of formal position. Leaders at the top primarily look at the big picture. They are responsible for broad strategy and policy decisions. Teams need to be focused on specific goals and performance results to function well. Leaders have so many things to do that they are always looking for quick and efficient approaches to perform their duties and move on to the next thing on their list. Teams take time to discuss and debate matters. They may make better decisions as a result, but their decision-making process rarely feels efficient at the time. Finally, Katzenbach points out that leaders are held accountable individually for whatever happens on their watch, whereas teams emphasize mutual accountability and collective action.

I have also found that the egos of the members of the typical leadership team may also create added difficulty in efforts to help them work as a team. In their defense, they need to have strong egos to handle the responsibilities of their position. They are used to being the center of attention in their domain. Each is seen as the person responsible for setting the direction for the team's function and taking the heat if the team doesn't succeed. We expect so much from them and are often quick to revel when they fail. We have a long tradition in America of knocking people off their pedestal. Leaders must lead. They are in a position to scan the external environment and assess the apparent opportunities and threats. They must establish the sense of urgency required for change to happen. They need to set the bar regarding work and ethical standards. They need to be strong and perhaps be held to a higher standard than others in the organization.

While most high-level leaders want to be seen as being part of the leadership team, others see it as a necessary evil: another meeting to go to and one where they are likely to end up with additional assignments. Some use the opportunity to impress the recognized head leader, while others see it as an obligation aimed at making the head leader look good. In addition, leaders at facilities that are part of a corporation have dual reporting relationships. For example, a plant controller reports directly to the plant manager but also reports to the corporate finance leadership group. The controller may actually face conflicting objectives if the manager is pushing a team approach requiring sacrifices across functional areas while corporate management pushes strictly for cost-saving measures.

Key to Helping a Leadership Team
Function As a True Team

Despite all the obstacles, perhaps the leader of your company still wants the leadership team to operate as a true team. Who can help such an auspicious group? Perhaps the highest-ranking member of the group can spearhead the effort. Lower members of the team could try if they have the nerve and the support of the top leader. Maybe the head of the human resources function or the coordinator of the team concept efforts could serve as the change agent. More commonly, an external consultant is used due to the political ramifications associated with attempting to unite powerful people as a collective team. If you volunteer or are asked to serve as consultant, how can you help them help themselves? The answer should not be a surprise to you at this point. If the group of individual leaders truly wants to produce effective team performance, it must develop the seven key components of team excellence required of any group that wishes to function as a team: clear goals and sense of direction, identification of talent, clear roles and responsibilities, agreed-upon procedures, constructive interpersonal relations, active reinforcement of team-oriented behaviors, and diplomatic external ties.

Above all, underlying the leadership team's performance goals must be a meaningful purpose. Why should this group be declared a team? What work is it expected to produce? The development of a team charter is again a great place to start. The group of leaders may be empowered to create its own charter. If the group reports to a board of directors or to other corporate entities, you should at least suggest that you be involved in the charter's development. Exercise 13 (see p. 91) can still serve you well as you attempt to help this leadership team. However, when you get to the point of the team attempting to identify its "SMART" goals, make sure that the goals of the team are not merely a restatement of the goals of the facility. Yes, the leadership team has overall responsibility to help the plant achieve productivity and profitability goals, but so does everyone else in the company. Push the group to identify what it specifically will produce by when. If the goal is to produce a strategic plan to achieve productivity targets, when should the plan be ready for presentation? If the goal is to change the operating system of the facility from its current method to one that embraces the principles of lean manufacturing, what will the leadership team produce and share with its stakeholders? If this group of individual leaders wants to truly work as a team, the goals of its collective efforts must be clear and will likely change as each plan and rollout is produced.

To operate as a leadership team, the right people need to be on the bus. There is no substitute for managerial competence—belief and confidence in the organization are based on it. The talent has to be there and it has to be put to use. If the egos of leadership team members get in the way of utilizing the knowledge and skills of these key people, the whole organization suffers. Who should be actual members of the leadership team, and who should serve as resource people brought in occasionally to provide assistance on specific elements of its work? The talent required depends on the product the team is expected to produce. If the product is a strategic plan to set direction for the whole organization, then the team needs to include members with the subject matter expertise of the functional areas involved. But if the team is too large, it will be difficult to demonstrate the discipline needed to function as a team. Events may be staged to get input from many constituencies, and membership of the leadership team making the final decisions may be limited to a core group of leaders.

Members need to understand their individual role on the leadership team. Individual responsibilities must be clearly defined in addition to any set of collective responsibilities. What task-related role is person X to deliver in order for the team to produce? What is expected of that person for the team to work together? What dysfunctional roles should be modified or eliminated for the group to actually function as a team? Who should be involved in the negotiation of these roles to provide leadership to this team? Typically the highest-ranking member has this responsibility, but others must step up as well.

Leadership teams that model how to run meetings, make decisions, solve problems, and produce plans can set the tone for teams throughout an organization. They need to follow a disciplined approach to these procedures to show others that this is the key to excellence. Constructive interpersonal relations must also be modeled. Leadership teams that don't have conflict and quickly agree on most issues are likely to be seen as a bunch of yes-men. Conflict and debate must take place, but they must not be conducted as personal attacks. People must see that the passion of conflicting points of view produces improved organizational strategies and plans.

Rarely do leadership teams receive collective bonuses for their collective success. Each member has a set of objectives that drives whether he or she receives a bonus. If those objectives motivate members to compete with each other rather than collaborate, the likelihood of working as a true leadership teams is low. Recognition for team-oriented behaviors can provide the reinforcement needed. Leadership team members must not personally or publicly criticize their colleagues. In fact they should be boosters, bragging about their teammates' wealth of knowledge and skills. No one can know everything needed to run a great company today. When employees see the pride and admiration leadership team members express to one another, these behaviors can be contagious.

Leadership team members cannot isolate themselves. They cannot be perceived as some secret committee that makes key decisions that greatly affect the work lives of all organization members. Members of true leadership teams understand that they are servant leaders, in a position to help several constituencies: employees, customers, shareholders, and the community at large. Leadership team members need to be credible individual leaders and responsible team players. No wonder it can be such a challenge to help leadership team members help themselves. Let me share with you another example.

A Leadership Team Story

I was working with the leadership team of a large manufacturing plant in the West that would be launching a whole new production system over a one-year period. They needed to designate sessions to work together as a team to establish a vision of the new way of doing business and design an implementation plan to move to the new system. This rollout required a team at the top. However, most of their time still needed to be dedicated to keeping the plant running. They worked as a group of individuals to keep their colleagues informed and sometimes sought input regarding current operational problems. They were the subject matter experts of their functions and areas. They united to transform the overall organization and keep their specialties successful yet aligned. Most members had dual reporting relationships. Each reported to the plant manager, but most also reported to a corporate vice president dedicated to their functional area. This need to please two bosses led to some tension. The plant manager tended to use a laissez-faire leadership style, and this produced a power vacuum on the team and competition between team members for more influence. As their shared sense of direction for the plant's new production system grew, cohesion of the leadership team members also grew somewhat. However, this lack of unity of purpose—and of style—proved to be the team's Achilles' heel from time to time.

About half the members of the team are New Englanders recently transferred to the plant by the corporation. Team members need to constantly fight the temptation to isolate themselves and work out the change plans on their own. They are learning the importance of gaining input from the long-term employees rather than trying to sell a plan to the workforce. They have come to be seen as very bright men and women. They come up with great ideas but sometimes lose credibility by failing to follow through on those ideas. They are now working on better ways to collaborate with the workforce to ensure that the elements of the new culture come from within rather than be seen as something imposed by the corporate heads back east.

Summary

One of the most difficult groups of people to help function as a true team is a group made up of leaders. Nevertheless, since today's business world is so complex and changes at such a rapid rate, the need for and use of leadership teams at the top has increased dramatically in the last decade. An effective team approach requires the application of team discipline. It is crucial to make clear which initiatives would most benefit from the time and effort required to use a team approach at the top.

It is important for leaders to remember that they do not need to function as a team all the time. In fact often they will be acting independently and as leaders of their respective function or area. Their knowledge of what the leadership team at the top is trying to accomplish for the overall organization should inform and guide their individual actions.

AFTER-CHAPTER REVIEW

Now that you have completed reading this chapter, it is time for you to challenge yourself to see what you remember, establish what it is you learned, and decide where and how you are going to apply what you learned. The outline provided below can help you get started. The relevancy of this chapter may necessitate that you expand on your thoughts elsewhere. Make sure you benefit from your reading by capturing your thoughts and turning them into actions.

1. Describe at least five things you remember from the material in this chapter.

   •

   •

   •

   •

   •

2. Identify the insights you gained from reading the material in this chapter. These insights may have come directly from the points raised or by stimulating recollections of your own experiences.

   •

   •

   •

3. Identify at least one situational opportunity for applying what you learned and describe the steps to be taken (including who will do what with whom, where, and when).

   Situational opportunity:

   Steps to be taken:

   •

   •

   •

   •

SUMMARY:
THE LEARNING LEADER
MAKES A DIFFERENCE

Reviewing What You've Learned

Congratulations! If you have read all the chapters and used some of the tools, you should have learned some things and improved some skills. If you have completed the after-chapter reviews, you have a running inven-tory of your knowledge and your plans to use that knowledge. If you took the steps needed to activate your plans, you have had addi-tional opportunities to learn through experience. To what extent are you now prepared to be a more valuable leader within a team concept organization? This final chapter provides chapter-by-chapter questions that will help you to review what you've learned.

1. **The Need for Team Leaders at All Levels**
   - What have you learned about leadership?
   - Do you appreciate the value of providing leadership by helping others help themselves?
   - What are you doing to raise the awareness of members of the team(s) you are associated with?
   - Can you help people take an honest look at themselves and their situations without being judgmental?
   - Are you helping your team look at both the task and relationship issues as they arise?

- Can you encourage people to think of alternative ways of dealing with their current challenges? Can you add options for them to consider?
- Have you gained the patience and appreciation for having people make decisions rather than telling them what to do? Have you seen the value of gaining their commitment rather than compliance?
- Knowing that team concept organizations need leaders at all levels, who are the general managers in your organization providing leadership at the top? Who are the key resource people providing coaching assistance to teams as they need it? Who are the team captains providing leadership by being willing to influence their peers?
- What are you doing to develop yourself to serve as one or more of these sources of leadership in your organization?
- How much credibility do you have as a leader? What are you doing to enhance your trustworthiness, competency, and enthusiasm?
- Are you taking a focused approach to your development as a leader rather than trying to be all things to all people?

2. **Your Natural Leadership Strengths**
   - Have you identified your natural strengths?
   - What do you do well without hardly having to think about it?
   - Do you have a plan for using your talents even more effectively?
   - Can you describe your personality and personal qualities?
   - Are you a Sensible Technician, a Sociable Facilitator, a Noble Funlover, or a Novel Transformer?
   - Are you now more aware of the tendencies associated with your natural preferences?
   - Have you used the *Myers-Briggs Type Indicator®* instrument to understand the personalities of your teammates and other leaders in your organization?
   - Have you attempted to use different strategies to communicate with others based on your understanding of their personality?

3. **Effective Teambuilding**
   - Has your company clarified which types of teams it wants to empower?
   - What is motivating your company to try to use teams as a business strategy and structure?
   - Are you attempting to help work teams, committees, task forces, and/or leadership teams?
   - Can you state the seven key components that separate excellent teams from the mediocre ones?
   - Are you willing to try to be the X-factor in your team's efforts to achieve excellence?
   - Are you adjusting your approach based on the developmental stage of your team?
   - Have you identified or designed any team training sessions to meet the needs of your team?
   - Do you understand that team development is an ongoing process? What are you doing with this understanding?
   - Are you pushing team members to identify and utilize what they learned from the teambuilding sessions?

4. **Knowing Why the Team Exists**
   - Do team members know why the team exists?
   - Do they understand the goals they are to accomplish? Do the goals as written satisfy "SMART" criteria?
   - Have you helped members develop a team charter defining what is expected? As times have changed, has the charter been revisited and modified in order to adapt and evolve?

5. **Communicate, Communicate, Communicate**
   - What are you doing to share information more effectively with your team(s)? Are you finding ways to keep it interesting? Are you sharing enough information without overwhelming your teammates?
   - Are you a better listener now than when you first started reading this book? What specific things are you doing to be a better listener? Are these things making a difference?

- Have you provided feedback to team members? Did you first describe what you noticed before you stated whether you thought the behaviors were "good" or "bad"?
- What have you learned about providing feedback to others?
- What have you learned from the feedback that you have received yourself?
- How are your team's meetings going? Have you helped make the meetings become more effective and efficient?
- Have you attempted any 1:1 communication sessions with team members? How about any dialogue sessions?

6. **Problem Solving and Decision Making**
   - Does your team take a disciplined approach to problem solving and decision making?
   - Do members take a wide range of issues into account as they reach decisions? Have they decided how they are going to decide? Are they attempting to reach consensus decisions?
   - Do you help team members recognize when they need to broaden their thinking with brainstorming techniques, and when they need to critique options and come to conclusions?
   - Are team members aware of the problems that may be interfering with their performance and their ability to work together as a team? Do they focus on one particular problem at a time?
   - Have you helped team members become more skilled at analyzing the causes of the problems they have identified? Do they concentrate on root causes that are within their own sphere of influence?
   - Do you help team members unleash their creative abilities and think of alternatives even if these options represent "outside-the-box" thinking?
   - Have you encouraged team members to choose options that are practical and within the parameters defined by the team charter?
   - Do you help team members help themselves by facilitating action planning sessions that clearly define who needs to do what with whom by when in order to implement the chosen alternative?
   - Have you encouraged team members to conduct an assessment of the actual impact of their problem-solving efforts? Is apprecia-

tion being expressed to those persons who helped the efforts succeed?

7. Resolving Conflict

- Do you now better appreciate the advantages of having some conflict on your team(s)?
- What is causing the conflict that team members are experiencing? Are they handling it constructively or dysfunctionally? Are they playing the blame game? Have you had some success turning the blame game into systematic problem solving?
- Can you use all five basic approaches to conflict resolution? Which approach do you overuse?
- What have you done to enhance your conflict resolution skills? Are you capable of facilitating a win-win approach?
- Have you helped team members negotiate exchanges of behaviors so that their relationships do not interfere with the team's efforts to achieve excellence?
- Have you been a behind-the-scenes X-factor resulting in constructive interpersonal relations?
- Do you have any "difficult" people to deal with in your organization? Have you attempted to have a breakthrough conversation with them?

8. Motivating and Coaching Teams to Success

- Do you understand that your team's performance is a function of its abilities, motivation, and opportunities?
- Do the members of your team(s) clearly understand what is expected of them? Are they being held accountable?
- Are you spending much time positively reinforcing actions consistent with expectations?
- What are you like as a coach? You aren't a yeller or a nag, are you?
- What are you doing now that makes you an even better coach?
- Have you attempted to negotiate opportunities for individual members or for whole teams to capitalize on their talents?
- Are you providing recognition and rewards in a manner that encourages collaboration rather than competition?

9. Leaders As Ambassadors of Team-Based Change Efforts

- Have you told others about the progress of your team(s)? Do you emphasize the positive elements and keep team members' complaints private?
- Have you been confident enough to encourage leadership to emerge within your team?
- Have you found ways to connect team members with managers, union officials, and professional resource people in key positions in your organization?
- Have you helped your team realize the importance of considering the impact of its actions on other teams and on the broader operations of your organization?
- Have you been willing to serve as an ambassador for the change efforts advocated by top leadership in your organization?
- What have you done when you have encountered people resisting change? Have you helped them see why they can't continue doing things the way they have been doing them?
- Have you been able to help channel dissatisfaction with the status quo into actions that help make things better?
- Have you taken efforts to ensure that members of the team and the organization have a vision of where they are headed? Are you doing what you can to ensure that actions taken are consistent with the move toward that vision?
- Are you helping tip the momentum toward needed changes?
- Have you identified connectors, mavens, and salespersons to serve as allies in your efforts to be an ambassador for teams and change?
- Have you thought through your messages so that they stick in people's mind?
- Are your team's discussions about change ideas conducted in a context conducive to the principles underlying the change?
- How are you dealing with the stress associated with attempting to be a leader in a team-based environment?
- Are you helping yourself and your team attempt to change the elements causing stress? Are you helping people gain a perspective on potentially stressful situations?

- Have you learned how to better activate your relaxation response?

10. Monitoring and Reviving Teams

- Does your team know the score? How is it doing this season?
- Have you helped your team(s) create a PPP scorecard that clarifies the extent to which they have been productive and to use effective team processes? Have you helped them to be satisfied and growing people?
- Have you conducted sessions to help team members learn the lessons of their past?
- Do they know what day it is in the life of their team?
- Are members able to identify the team's current strengths, weaknesses, opportunities, and threats? Have you helped them use systematic problem solving to address their weaknesses?
- Have team members spent time anticipating what demands they may have to face in the future? Have they developed plans to deal with those new demands?
- Are team members thinking strategically? What are you doing to help a team that is "stuck" or complacent?

11. Helping a Whole Team of Leaders

- Have you been asked to help a team of leaders help themselves?
- Did you get them to clarify whether they really want to think of themselves as a team? Have you offered them options depending on whether they simply want to get along together more effectively and have better meetings or to truly work as a team and produce something collectively?
- Do you better understand why it is difficult for a group of leaders at the top of an organization to function as a team?
- If your group wants to function as a leadership team, are their goals clear? Do they have the right people on the team? Do members understand their individual role on the leadership team?
- Are members willing to use disciplined approaches to function as a team? Are they committed to generating constructive relation-

ships among all members? Will there be any recognition for being team oriented?

- How will the team avoid isolating itself and build key relationships with people and groups outside its domain?
- Will the team be setting a good example within an organization claiming to be a team concept company?

Make a Difference

In closing, I hope that you continue to make a difference. I interviewed nearly two hundred team leaders for a study and found that they all had stories about how they made a difference. Some made a difference in small ways (e.g., smiling, being approachable, treating team members to food at meetings, etc.), and some in big ways (e.g., helping clarify goals, helping a team find solutions to production problems, helping a teammate believe in herself, helping a team find ways to significantly improve the way it works together, etc.). Their stories were quite touching. While each of them had some way of describing how he or she has made a difference, nearly all of them also added that it was more a matter of "we as a team" that made the real difference. The theme throughout this book has been to help others help themselves. That is the essence of effective leadership in the team approach. You aren't better than the collective power of your team. You are just willing to put yourself out there to make a difference. I wish you the best.

Your Summary and Conclusions

Reexamine the after-chapter reviews you completed. Think as well about your answers to the questions listed in this chapter and identify the key learnings you gained through reading this book. You devoted time and energy to reading it; now make sure you and your organization benefit from your work. How would you summarize what you have learned, and what you are going to do with it? You can use the after-book review on the following page to help you summarize. I would love to learn from what you learned. Please share your summary and conclusions with me. You can reach me at greg.huszczo@emich.edu or send a copy of your summary to me at my office: MSHROD Program, College of Business, Eastern Michigan University, Ypsilanti, MI 48197.

AFTER-BOOK REVIEW

Hopefully you answered many of the questions provided in this chapter as a way of reviewing the key points raised in each of the other chapters. It is time for you to challenge yourself to see what you remember, figure out what you learned, and decide where and how you are going to apply what you learned. The outline provided below can help you get started. The relevancy of this book to you and your circumstances may necessitate that you expand on your thoughts elsewhere. Make sure you gain from your reading. Capture your thoughts and turn them into actions.

1. What did you get out of reading this book? How would you describe it to a colleague? What do you remember most about it?

2. Identify the lessons you learned or relearned from the material in this book. Your insights may have come directly from the points raised or they may be insights you obtained by combining what you read and your own experiences.

   •

   •

   •

   •

   •

3. What is your plan for using what you learned?

4. Steps to be taken (what will you do with whom, where and when):

   •

   •

   •

   •

   •

THE EXOTIC ORCHID ROLE PLAY EXERCISE

This exercise is designed for use by four participants (two teams of two).

Setup:

A new exotic orchid has captured people's interest. It is a particularly beautiful flower and it is thought to have powerful chemical qualities. Approximately five thousand of these orchids were grown this year. One commercial florist, Mr. Greenthumb, has set up a nursery in Florida and has produced nearly four thousand of these plants. The other one thousand orchids are grown by amateur botanists worldwide. They typically grow just one plant each.

These exotic orchids flower only at this time of year. Recent magazine articles have brought further attention to the orchid and its growers. It is rumored that two pharmaceutical research firms—Company A and Company B—are very interested in the plants, but much secrecy surrounds the reasons why. To add further intrigue, in addition to being business rivals, these two pharmaceutical companies have filed a series of lawsuits against one another, with each company claiming the other has been guilty of industrial espionage.

Directions:

1. Pick a partner. You and your partner will either be assigned the roles of Dr. Heart and Dr. Diamond (chief representatives of Company A) or Dr. Club and Dr. Spade (chief representatives of Company B).

2. You have fifteen minutes to read additional information about your company's needs and to prepare for a meeting with your rivals. Only Dr. Heart and Dr. Diamond are to read the material provided about

Company A's needs. Only Dr. Club and Dr. Spade are to read the material about Company B's needs. Do not read the information provided for the use of your rivals. Develop a strategy for how you will work with your partner in this meeting. Prepare your opening statement and how you will use your conflict resolution skills.

3. When the facilitator gives you the signal, you and your partner will have a discussion with the two representatives from the rival organization. This meeting with your rivals is to last for only twenty minutes. Use your best conflict resolution skills. Try to reach an agreement with them. If you do reach an agreement, be sure you have an action plan to implement it. At least make sure you have a plan for any offers that would be presented later to Mr. Greenthumb.

4. The purpose of this exercise is for you to practice your conflict resolution skills. After this exercise, you will be asked to describe which conflict resolution styles you and your rivals used. Identify what worked and what did not. Discover what skills you need to work on to become better in conflict situations. What did you learn?

Additional Information for Company A's Representatives Only

(Dr. Heart and Dr. Diamond)

You are biological research scientists employed by a pharmaceutical firm, Company A. You've recently developed a synthetic serum useful in curing and preventing a newly discovered disease known as X12Y. This disease strikes African American females exposed to certain nerve gases, eventually causing internal bleeding and serious gastronomical pain. It has also been recently discovered that women who have had this disease and later become pregnant deliver babies with serious birth defects, unless they are treated within the first six weeks of their pregnancy. It turns out that all members of the U.S. Army are exposed to these nerve gases in training exercises. African American women who participate in these mandatory exercises are very likely to develop X12Y. You have found, with volunteer patients, that your recently developed synthetic serum cures X12Y in its early stages. The serum is made from the petals of the exotic orchid, of which only five thousand were produced worldwide this year. Additional plants will not be available until next season, which will be too late to cure this year's X12Y victims. (Review the setup on p. 281.)

(continued)

You've demonstrated that your synthetic serum is in no way harmful to pregnant women, and there are no side effects. The U.S government has quietly approved the production and distribution of the serum as a cure for X12Y. Unfortunately, the current number of African American women suffering from this disease is larger than expected and your firm will not be able to produce a large enough supply of the serum unless you acquire enough of the orchids soon. The health of these women and their children is at stake. Your firm holds the patent on the synthetic serum, and it is expected to be a highly profitable product when it is generally available to the public because it is thought to have other applications, too.

You are aware that Mr. Greenthumb, a commercial florist for the Everglades of Florida, is in possession of four thousand of the orchids in good condition. If you could obtain three thousand of them, you would be able to both cure present victims and provide sufficient inoculations for the remaining women at risk this year.

You have recently been informed that Dr. Club and Dr. Spade from Company B are also urgently seeking these exotic orchids and are also aware of Mr. Greenthumb's possession of the four thousand available. Dr. Club and Dr. Spade have also been working on biological research for the past several years, but you do not think the research is aimed at developing the same type of serum. There is a great deal of industrial espionage in the pharmaceutical industry. Over the past several years, their firm and yours have sued each other several times for infringement of patent rights and espionage law violations.

You've been authorized by your firm to approach Mr. Greenthumb to purchase three thousand orchids. You have been told he will sell them to the highest bidder. Your firm has authorized you to bid as high as $3,000,000 to obtain the orchids. Before approaching Mr. Greenthumb, you have decided to first talk with Dr. Club and Dr. Spade to influence them so that they will not prevent you from obtaining the orchids you need.

Note: Additional information for Company B's representatives only begins on the following page.

Additional Information for Company B's Representatives <u>Only</u>

(Dr. Club and Dr. Spade)

You work as research biologists for a pharmaceutical firm, Company B. You are trying to develop a cure for a particularly virulent form of Lyme's disease, now known as MGD40. The disease was first discovered after hunting season last year. It seems that Caucasian males who drink more than five alcohol-based drinks a day are particularly prone to catching this disease. The symptoms include extreme fatigue and severe blood and urinary tract infections. To make matters worse, carriers of MGD40 can transmit this disease through their bodily fluids. Thus a secondary outbreak has occurred among the wives and lovers of these men. It is important that the spread of this virus be stopped as soon as possible.

You've developed a synthetic serum that will stop the subsequent transmission of MGD40 from the original carriers to others. The federal government is working quietly to gain approval for the use of your cure. It should become official in the next two weeks. The injectable serum you have developed is made with a chemical taken from the stem of the exotic orchid, of which only five thousand were produced worldwide this year. (Review the setup on p. 281.) Your firm holds the patent on the synthetic serum, and it is expected to be a highly profitable product when it is generally available to the public because it is thought to have other applications, too.

You are aware that Mr. Greenthumb, a commercial florist for the Everglades of Florida, is in possession of four thousand of the orchids in good condition. The chemicals derived from thirty-five hundred orchids would be sufficient to slow and perhaps stop this fast-spreading epidemic.

You have also been made aware that Dr. Heart and Dr. Diamond from Company A are also urgently seeking to purchase these orchids from Mr. Greenthumb. Your firm is highly competitive with Company A. There is a great deal of industrial espionage in the pharmaceutical industry. Over the past several years, their firm and yours have sued each other several times for infringement of patent rights and espionage law violations.

You've been authorized by your firm to approach Mr. Greenthumb to purchase thirty-five hundred orchids. You have been told he will sell them to the highest bidder. Your firm has authorized you to bid as high as $3,500,000 to obtain the orchids. Before approaching Mr. Greenthumb, you have decided to first talk with Dr. Heart and Dr. Diamond to influence them so that they will not prevent you from obtaining the orchids you need.

JACOBSON'S PROGRESSIVE RELAXATION TECHNIQUE

Preliminary Instructions

- Isolate yourself if possible
- Remove contacts, eyeglasses, and distracting jewelry; wear comfortable clothing
- Sit in a comfortable position or lie down flat on your back if you prefer
- Keep your eyes closed throughout the exercise (as much as you can until you've internalized the instructions) but avoid falling asleep
- Tense each muscle group for 10–15 seconds (just guess...don't watch a clock)
- Relax each muscle group for 20–30 seconds (just guess...don't watch a clock)
- Allow yourself to relax (the key is for you to focus on the contrasting feelings of tension and relaxation)
- Progress the focus of your relaxation from muscle group to muscle group
- Do the long form (small muscle groupings) once a day for two weeks
- Do the short form (large muscle groupings) once a day for four weeks

Long Form Directions

Recite the instructions in the steps below to yourself in your own words. You do not have to say them exactly as written. They are not magical words. You will be breaking your body into small muscle groups and tensing and then relaxing each group. You start with your hands; work your way up your arms; and then work from the top of your head to the tips of your toes.

1. Relaxation of the arms (i.e., hands, fingers, wrists, forearms, biceps, triceps)

Settle back as comfortably as you can. Let yourself relax to the best of your ability. Breathe freely and gently; in and out. Now as you relax like that, clench your right fist and forearm. Clench your fist tight. Concentrate on what it feels like to tense your fist, fingers, and forearm. Hold it there for 10–15 seconds. *Now relax.* Let the fingers of your right hand straighten out and become loose. Feel the difference between tension and relaxation in your fist and forearm. Let yourself go and really relax all over.

Now let's do the same with your left fist. Clench your left fist while the rest of your body stays relaxed. Push the tension in your left fist, fingers, and forearm. Feel the tension there. Keep it there. *Now relax.* Feel the difference between tension and relaxation. Let the relaxation take over where the tension once was. Return your hands and arms to comfortable positions. Enjoy the difference. Let yourself relax.

Now bend your arms at the elbow. Put all the tension of your body in your biceps. Feel the hardness of the muscles in the upper part of your arms. Keep the tension there. *Now relax.* Straighten out your arms. Feel the relaxation take over where the tension was. Focus your attention on the contrast between tension and relaxation. Breathe freely and gently and continue to relax.

Now let's focus your tension in your triceps. Stretch your arms as far in front of you as you can. Feel the tension there. Feel it. *Now relax.* Return your arms and hands to a comfortable position. Focus your attention on the contrast between tension and relaxation. Relax your arms further and further. Even as relaxed as you feel, try to let yourself go that extra bit further. Relax deeper and deeper. Notice the comfortable heaviness that accompanies relaxation.

2. **Relaxation of the top of your body (i.e., shoulders, neck, upper back, face, forehead, and scalp)**

Let your whole body relax. Now let's focus on the top of your body. Wrinkle up your forehead and scalp. Feel tension by wrinkling up the muscles at the top of your head. Hold it there. *Now relax.* Feel the skin of your forehead and scalp become smoother and smoother as the relaxation takes over. Let those muscles relax. Feel the difference.

Now create tension by raising your eyebrows as high as you can without opening your eyes. Feel tension in your eyes and forehead. Feel it there. *Now relax.* Relax your eyes. Relax your eyebrows. Relax your forehead. Focus your mind on the contrast between tension and relaxation.

Now close your eyes tighter and tighter. Feel the tension. Don't hurt yourself but feel the tension around your eyes. Hold the tension there. *Now relax.* Feel how good it feels to relax your eyes. Keep your eyes closed but enjoy the sensations of relaxation.

Now create tension in the middle of your face by scrunching up your nose and pursing your lips. Push the muscles and create tension. Hold it there. *Now relax.* Relax your lips and nose. Let the relaxation spread over your face. Enjoy the feeling. Let yourself relax.

Now clench your jaw. Bite your teeth together. Feel the tension through your jaws and mouth. *Now relax.* Let your lips part slightly. Appreciate the relaxation.

Now press your tongue against the roof of your mouth. Create tension in your tongue and your throat. Feel the tension there. *Now relax.* Let your tongue return to a comfortable position. Breathe freely and gently, in and out. Let the relaxation proceed on its own.

Let's make sure we have worked all the muscles in your face. Make the most horrendous face you can. Tense every muscle in your face and head. Feel the tension throughout the top of your being. *Now relax.* Let every muscle relax. Relax your face. Feel your face smooth out as the muscles let go. Treat yourself to some relaxation. You are worth it. Let yourself relax. Continue breathing freely and gently, in and out, relaxing deeper and deeper still.

Now let's attend to your neck muscles. Press your head straight back. Feel the tension in your neck. Shift the tension by moving your head forward. Press your chin down toward your chest. Feel the tension in your neck. *Now relax.* Return your head to a comfortable position. Focus your mind on the contrast between tension and relaxation. Enjoy the difference.

Now press your head toward your right shoulder. Feel the tension on the side of your neck. Feel it there. Now shift your head to the other side. Press it toward your left shoulder. Feel the tension on the other side of your neck. *Now relax.* Again return your head to a comfortable position. Allow the relaxation to take over where the tension was. Let yourself relax.

Shrug your shoulders straight up. Feel tension in your shoulders, neck, and upper back by shrugging your shoulders up. Hold the tension there. *Now relax.* Relax your head and face and neck and shoulders and upper back. Breathe freely and gently as the relaxation progresses. Treat yourself to some relaxation.

Create tension by shrugging your shoulders straight back. Push as if your shoulder blades were trying to touch each other. Feel the tension in your chest and shoulders and upper back. Hold the tension there. Keep it there. *Now relax.* Let the tension go. Let the relaxation take over where the tension was. Relax deeper and deeper. Feel the difference.

Finally, create tension by shrugging your shoulders toward your chest. Feel the tension in your chest muscles. Feel the tension in the upper part of your arms, neck, and back. Push the tension. *Now relax.* Return to a comfortable position. Let the relaxation spread deep into your shoulders, your back, your neck, your head and face. Continue relaxing your arms and hands. Let the whole top of your body relax. Feel the difference between tension and relaxation. As relaxed as you have become, try to let yourself go even deeper into the sensations of relaxation. Let go and enjoy as the relaxation takes over.

3. **Relaxation of the middle section of your body (i.e., chest, stomach, lower back)**

Continue relaxing your body to the best of your ability. Feel the comfortable heaviness that accompanies relaxation. Breathe freely and gently, in and out. Notice how you become more relaxed with each exhalation. Now let's contrast tension and relaxation in the area of your chest muscles. Breathe in deeply. Fill your lungs with air. Hold your breath. Feel the tension throughout your chest. Study the tension. *Now relax.* Exhale and let the air out of your lungs. Don't force the air out. Just let it go. Then breathe freely and gently, relaxing deeper and deeper still. After relaxing for about 20–30 seconds, repeat this sequence. Fill your lungs again. Feel the tension in your chest for 10–15 seconds and then let it go. Relax your chest and lungs. Breathe normally now . . . freely and gently. Enjoy the relaxation.

Now let's attend to your stomach muscles. Tighten your stomach muscles as much as you can. Make your stomach hard. Feel it there. *Now relax!* Let your stomach go. Feel the muscles loosen and enjoy the relaxation. Concentrate on the contrast between tension and relaxation. Now pull your stomach muscles in as far as you can. Suck your tummy in. Pull it in. Feel the tension. *Now relax.* Let those muscles go. Feel how good it feels to relax your stomach. Continue breathing freely and gently. Allow yourself to sink into the feelings of relaxation. Now push your stomach muscles out. Push your tummy out. Feel tension in that region of your body by pushing your stomach muscles out. Hold it there. *Now relax.* Breathe freely and gently. Relax your chest and stomach more and more. Relax your whole body. Don't let tension creep in anywhere. Treat yourself to deeper and deeper feelings of relaxation.

Now let's attend to your lower back. Arch up your spine so that you feel tension along the lower region around your spine. Don't hurt yourself but create tension there. *Now relax.* Return to a comfortable position. Let the relaxation replace the feelings of tension. Feel the dif- ference in your body. Train yourself to notice tension vs. relaxation in the muscles. Relax the whole upper two-thirds of your body. Relax your lower back and your upper back. Relax your stomach and chest. Relax your shoulders and neck. Relax your face and head. Relax your arms and hands and fingers. Really let yourself go. Relax further and further, deeper and deeper. Treat your body to some deep relaxation.

4. Relaxation of the lower section of your body (i.e., hips, buttocks, thighs, calves, ankles, feet, toes)

Now let's attend to the remaining parts of your body. Flex your buttocks and thighs. Flex your thighs by pressing your heels to the floor as hard as you can. Feel the tension there. *Now relax.* Let the relaxation proceed on its own. Contrast the difference between tension and relaxation. Now create tension in your thighs by straightening your knees. Stretch your legs out in front of you. Feel the tension in the upper portion of your thighs. Hold the tension. *Now relax.* Relax your thighs and buttocks. Allow yourself to relax.

Now let's attend to your calf and feet muscles. Create tension by pulling your toes toward your head. Pull them up. Feel the tension in your calves and ankles and arches and toes. Hold it there. *Now relax.* Return to a comfortable position. Relax your legs. Relax your feet and calves. Once more create tension . . . this time by lifting your feet and pressing your toes down and away from your body. Feel the tension in your arches and toes and shins. Feel the tension there. *Now relax.* Return to a comfortable position and really let yourself go. Enjoy the experience of total body relaxation. Feel the relaxation all over. Relax your toes and ankles and feet. Relax your shins and calves and thighs. Relax the whole lower third of your body. Relax your back and stomach and chest. Relax your shoulders and neck and face. Relax your arms and hands and fingers. Keep relaxing more and more deeply. Make sure no tension has crept back into any muscle group. Keep relaxing like that for a while. Treat yourself to total body relaxation.

Cue Conditioning

As relaxed as you have become, you can become twice as relaxed by merely taking in a deep breath and slowly exhaling like a sigh. Do this and as you exhale say the word *calm* to yourself as you let the air go. Take a deep breath in and then let out that sigh very slowly but without using any tension to hold the air back . . . *calm*. Do this three times, each time taking air in and then slowly sighing out the word *calm* to yourself.

Feel how relaxed you have become. See how you can relax yourself. Enjoy the calm, relaxed, but alert feelings of relaxation. Enjoy the feelings as long as you want but, when you are done, count backward from four to one in your head. When you reach one, open your eyes and feel refreshed, alert, wide awake, and calm.

Short Form Directions

Use the short form after you have done the long form for two weeks. This will have allowed your body to consciously detect physiological cues in your muscles distinguishing tension from relaxation. The short form involves dividing your body into the four muscle group areas described above. You tense all the muscles in each group for 10 15 seconds and then relax them for a full 30 seconds. Repeat this twice for each muscle group. Finish the exercise by doing the deep sighs to your cue condition-ing word. Do this short form once a day for four weeks. You have now trained your body to relax very deeply. You should still conduct a "booster session" for yourself from time to time, especially after particularly stress-ful days. It is best to use the long form for these booster sessions.

BIBLIOGRAPHY

Baird, L., P. Holland, and S. Deacon. 1999. Learning from action: Imbedding more learning into performance fast enough to make a difference. *Organizational Dynamics* 27 (4): 19–32.

Beckhard, R., and R. T. Harris. 1987. *Organizational transitions: Managing complex change.* Reading, MA: Addison-Wesley.

Berra, Y. 1998. *The Yogi book: I really didn't say everything I said.* New York: Workman.

Block, P. 2000. *Flawless consulting: A guide to getting your expertise used.* 2d ed. San Francisco: Jossey-Bass/Pfeiffer.

Bridges, W. 1991. *Managing transitions: Making the most of change.* Reading, MA: Perseus Books.

Buckingham, M., and D. O. Clifton. 2001. *Now, discover your strengths.* New York: Simon & Schuster.

Buckingham, M., and C. Coffman. 1999. *First, break all the rules.* New York: Simon & Schuster.

Camp, R. R., P. N. Blanchard, and G. E. Huszczo. 1986. *Toward a more organizationally effective training strategy and practice.* Englewood Cliffs, NJ: Prentice-Hall.

Collins, J. 2001. *Good to great: Why some companies make the leap...and others don't.* New York: HarperCollins.

Covey, S. R. 1989. *The 7 habits of highly effective people: Powerful lessons in personal change.* New York: Simon & Schuster.

Csikszentmihalyi, M. 1990. *Flow: The psychology of optimal experience.* New York: HarperCollins.

Csikszentmihalyi, M. 2003. *Good business: Leadership, flow, and the making of meaning.* New York: Simon & Schuster.

Dannemiller Tyson Associates. 2000. *Whole-scale change: Unleashing the magic in organizations.* San Francisco: Berrett-Koehler.

Davis, M., E. R. Eshelman, and M. McKay. 1988. *The relaxation and stress reduction workbook.* 3d ed. Oakland, CA: New Harbinger Publications.

Doyle, M., and D. Strauss. 1976. *How to make meetings work.* New York: Jove Books.

Fisher, R., and W. Ury. 1981. *Getting to yes: Negotiating agreement without giving in.* Boston: Houghton-Mifflin.

Fleishman, E. A. 1998. Consideration and structure: another look at their role in leadership research. In *Leadership: The multi-level approaches,* ed. F. Dansereau and F. J. Yammarino, 51–60. Stamford, CT: JAI Press.

Gladwell, M. 2000. *The tipping point: How little things can make a big difference.* New York: Little, Brown.

Hersey, P., and K. H. Blanchard. 1996. Great ideas revisited. *Training and Development* (January): 42–47.

Hersey, P., and K. H. Blanchard. 2003. Situational leadership. In *Business leadership: A Jossey-Bass reader,* 111–116. San Francisco: Jossey-Bass.

Huszczo, G. E. 1996. *Tools for team excellence: Getting your team into high gear and keeping it there.* Mountain View, CA: Davies-Black Publishing.

Jacobson, E. [1938] 1974. *Progressive relaxation.* Chicago: University of Chicago Press.

James, B. 2003. *The new Bill James historical baseball abstract.* New York: Free Press.

Johnson, S. 1998. *Who moved my cheese? An amazing way to deal with change in your work and in your life.* New York: Putnam.

Jung, C. G. *Psychological types.* 1971. In *Collected works.* Vol. 6. Trans. R. F. C. Hull. Princeton, NJ: Princeton University Press.

Katzenbach, J. R. 1998. *Teams at the top: Unleashing the potential of both teams and the individual leaders.* Boston: Harvard Business School Press.

Kaufman, C., and D. Kaufman. 2002. *Adaptation: The shooting script.* New York: Newmarket Press.

Kirkpatrick, D. L. 1977. Evaluating training programs: Evidence vs. proof. *Training and Development* 31 (11): 9–12.

Kotter, John P. 1996. *Leading change.* Boston: Harvard Business School Press.

Kotter, John P. 1999. *John P. Kotter on what leaders really do.* Boston: Harvard Business School Press.

Kouzes, J. M., and B. Z. Posner. 1993. *Credibility: How leaders gain and lose it, why people demand it.* San Francisco: Jossey-Bass.

Kouzes, J. M., and B. Z. Posner. 2002. *The leadership challenge: How to get extraordinary things done in organizations.* New York: John Wiley and Sons.

Lewin, K. 1951. *Field theory in social science.* New York: Harper & Row.

Lewis, M. M. 2003. *Moneyball.* New York: W. W. Norton.

Locke, E. A., and G. P. Latham, 1990. *A theory of goal setting and task performance.* Englewood Cliffs, NJ: Prentice-Hall.

Management Research Group. 1998. *Leadership effectiveness analysis: LEA resource guide.* Portland, ME: Management Research Group.

Manz, C. C., and H. P. Sims. 1989. *Super-leadership.* New York: Berkley Books.

McGrath, B. 2003. The professor of baseball. *New Yorker,* July 14 and 21, 38–45.

Miller, George A. 1956. The magical number seven. *Psychological Review* 63 (2).

Nutt, Paul C. 1986. Decision style and strategic decisions of top executives. *Technological Forecasting and Social Change* 14: 77–93.

Orlean, S. 1998. *The orchid thief.* New York: Ballantine Books.

O'Toole, J. 1999. *Leadership A to Z: A guide for the appropriately ambitious.* San Francisco: Jossey-Bass.

Peters, T. J., and R. H. Waterman. 1982. *In search of excellence.* New York: HarperCollins.

Pirsig, R. M. 1974. *Zen and the art of motorcycle maintenance: An inquiry into values.* New York: William Morrow.

Redding, J.C. 2000. *The radical team handbook: Harnessing the power of team learning for breakthrough results.* San Francisco: Jossey-Bass.

Salas, E., J. A. Cannon-Bowers, and J. H. Johnson. 1997. How can you turn a team of experts into an expert team? Emerging training strategies. In *Naturalistic decision making,* ed. C. E. Zsambok and Klein, 359–370. Mahwah, NJ: Erlbaum.

Senge, P. M. 1990. *The fifth discipline.* New York: Doubleday.

Senge, P. M., A. Kleiner, C. Roberts, R. B. Ross, and B. J. Smith. 1998. *The fifth discipline fieldbook: Strategies and tools for building a learning organization.* New York: Doubleday.

Skinner, B. F. 1953. *Science and human behavior.* New York: Macmillan.

Thomas, K. W. 2003. *Introduction to conflict management.* Mountain View, CA: CPP, Inc.

Thomas, K. W., and R. H. Kilmann. 2002. *Thomas-Kilmann Conflict Mode Instrument.* Mountain View, CA: Xicom, Inc.

Tuckman, B. W., 1965. Developmental sequences in small groups. *Psychological Bulletin* 63: 384–399.

Tuckman, B. W., and M. A. C. Jensen. 1977. Stages of small group development revisited. *Group and Organization Studies* 2: 419–427.

Vroom, V. H. 1964. *Work and motivation.* New York: John Wiley and Sons.

Yates, J. F. 2003. *Decision management: How to assure better decisions in your company.* San Francisco: Jossey-Bass.

MBTI® Resources

Barger, N. J., and L. K. Kirby. 1995. *The challenge of change in organizations: Helping employees thrive in the new frontier.* Mountain View, CA: Davies-Black Publishing.

Bridges, W. 2000. *The character of organizations: Using personality type in organization development.* Mountain View, CA: Davies-Black Publishing.

Fitzgerald, C., and L. K. Kirby, eds. 1997. *Developing leaders: Research and applications in psychological type and leadership development.* Mountain View, CA: Davies-Black Publishing.

Haley, C. V., and R. Pini. 1994. Blazing international trails in strategic decision making research. In *Proceedings of the Myers-Briggs Type Indicator® and lead-*

ership: An international research conference. College Park, MD: National Leadership Institute.

Hammer, A. L., and G. E. Huszczo. 1996. Teams. In *MBTI applications: A decade of research on the Myers-Briggs Type Indicator*, ed. A. L. Hammer, 81–104. Mountain View, CA: CPP, Inc.

Hammer, A. L., ed. 1996. *MBTI applications: A decade of research on the Myers-Briggs Type Indicator*. Mountain View, CA: CPP, Inc.

Hirsh, E., K. W. Hirsh, and S. K. Hirsh. 2003. *Introduction to Type* and teams. 2d ed. Mountain View, CA: CPP, Inc.

Hirsh, S. K. 1992. *MBTI* team building program. Mountain View, CA: CPP, Inc.

Hirsh, S. K., and J. M. Kummerow. 1989. *LIFETypes.* New York: Warner Books.

Keirsey, D., and M. Bates. 1984. *Please understand me.* Del Mar, CA: Prometheus Nemesis Book Co.

Kroeger, O., and J. M. Thuesen. 1988. *Type talk: Or how to determine your personality type and change your life.* New York: Delacorte Press.

Kroeger, O., and J. M. Thuesen. 1992. *Type talk at work: How the 16 personality types determine your success on the job.* New York: Delacorte Press.

Kroeger, O., and J. M. Thuesen. 1994. *16 ways to love your lover: Understanding the 16 personality types so you can create a love that lasts forever.* New York: Delacorte Press.

Lawrence, G. 1979. *People types and tiger stripes: A practical guide to learning styles.* Gainesville, FL: Center for Applications of Psychological Type.

Myers, I. B., with P. B. Myers. 1995. *Gifts differing: Understanding personality type.* Mountain View, CA: CPP, Inc.

Myers, I. B., M. H. McCaulley, N. L. Quenk, and A. L. Hammer. 1998. *MBTI manual: A guide to the development and use of the Myers-Briggs Type Indicator*. 3d ed. Mountain View, CA: CPP, Inc.

Pearman, R. R. 1998. *Hardwired leadership: Unleashing the power of personality to become a new millennium leader.* Mountain View, CA: Davies-Black Publishing.

Tieger, P. D., and B. Barron-Tieger. 1992. *Do what you are.* New York and London: Little, Brown.

INDEX